By the Author

The Education of Chauncey Doolittle

Memory's Keep

Walking Toward Home

Child to the Waters

Poems from Scorched Earth

Our Father's Fields

The Classical Origin of Southern Literature

A Carolina Dutch Fork Calendar

Tiller

Faulkner the Southerner

Edited by the Author

Fireside Tales of Old Dutch Fork

Poetry and the Practical, by William Gilmore Simms

The Selected Poems of William Gilmore Simms

Selected Reviews on Literature and Civilization

Taking Root: The Nature Writings of William and Adam Summer

About the Author

Robin Lattimore, *On Ballylee: The Legacy of "Our Fathers' Fields"*

FAULKNER THE SOUTHERNER

Faulkner at the University of Virginia

FAULKNER THE SOUTHERNER
&
THE CONTINUITY OF SOUTHERN LETTERS

JAMES EVERETT KIBLER, JR.

Abbeville Institute Press

2023

IN MEMORY OF
SHELBY FOOTE,
GENTLEMAN, FRIEND AND MENTOR
(17 November 1916 - 27 June 2005)

I have always thought that a nice study could be made
out of the "ideals" in fiction and poetry represented by North and
South.

—Grace King (1903)

Faulkner is exceptional because he portrayed with an uncommon
poetic vision
the seemingly simple fact that our greatness as human beings is
found in our most
unpretentious acts and in our courage in defeat.

—Montserrat Ginés (2000)

CONTENTS

ILLUSTRATIONS

Frontispiece: Faulkner at the University of Virginia. Photo by Ralph Thompson.

Cover: Portrait of Faulkner by Marshall Bouldin, III housed at the Mississippi Department of Archives and History, Jackson Mississippi.

14. Hunt breakfast at Rowan Oak, 8 May 1938. Ned Barnett (center) wearing Col. W. C. Falkner's blue frock coat.

15. Ned and frock coat detail.

16. The University of Virginia Years.

17. Faulkner and Grover Vandevender at Farmington Hunt, 1960.

18. Faulkner with hunting horn at Farmington Hunt Club, 1960

19. "There is something about jumping a horse over a fence…."

20. Faulkner with his horse at his log stable at Rowan Oak.

21. Five-foot scroll signed in 1955 by Japanese scholars in appreciation of Faulkner's visit to Nagano in 1955.

RACCOON AND COLLARDS

> The taste and odor of the family victuals, which has the com-
> mon taste of a province or region, binds the solitary to the
> family and the family to a place.
> —Andrew Lytle, "The Long View,"
> *From Eden to Babylon*

There are now more words written on Faulkner than on Shakespeare. In addition to Michael Millgate's ground-breaking critical biography, *The Achievement of William Faulkner* (New York: Random House, 1966), there are eleven book-length biographies. These include Joseph Blotner's *Faulkner: A Biography* (New York: Random House, 1974), a two-volume work that weighs eight pounds and is 1,115 pages long. Other biographies are Ward L. Miner, *The World of William Faulkner* (New York: Grove Press, 1952); Frederick Hoffman, *William Faulkner* (New York: Twayne, 1961); David Minter, *William Faulkner: His Life and Work* (Baltimore, MD: Johns Hopkins Univ Press, 1980); Stephen Oates, *William Faulkner: The Man and the Artist* (New York: Harper, 1987); Frederick Karl, *William Faulkner: American Writer* (New York: Weidenfeld, 1989); Joel Williamson, *William Faulkner and Southern History* (London: Oxford Univ Press, 1993); Richard Gray, *The Life of William Faulkner* (Oxford,

UK: Blackwell, 1994); Jay Parini, *One Matchless Time: A Life of William Faulkner* (New York: Harper, 2004); Robert Hamblin, *Myself and the World: A Biography of William Faulkner* (Jackson, MS: Univ Press of Mississippi, 2016); and Carl Rollyson's two volume 1,168 page *The Life of William Faulkner* (Charlottesville, VA: Univ Press of Virginia, 2020). There are six particularly useful memoirs by family and friends, including his hunting companion, John Cullen, his two younger brothers John and Murry, his early friend and first literary agent Ben Wasson, his stepson Malcolm Franklin, and his beloved friend Meta Carpenter Wilde.

The academic industry that Faulkner has become is robust and growing. He is by far the most popular subject for literary critics worldwide—from France, Germany and England to Spain, Brazil, and Japan.

Five years before English scholar Millgate's *Achievement of William Faulkner,* he published *William Faulkner,* a little-known work of 120 pages, in Edinburgh, Scotland. He revised and reprinted it in 1966, before Capricorn Books of New York made it a part of its Writers and Critics Series in 1971. This little work is still not properly appreciated in Faulkner circles. My primary reason for discussing it here is Millgate's assertion that Faulkner is "the most deeply Southern of Southern writers" and Millgate did not hold this fact against him. At the same time that he acknowledged the Southernness of Faulkner, he realized Faulkner's universality (Millgate, 2). Still, despite Millgate's declaration about the importance of Faulkner's roots, few of his later biographers dealt with the topic in any great depth or at any length, and sometimes only in apology, the latter especially during the relentless media bashing of the South in the 1970s and 1980s and the anti-Southern bias of academia in the two decades after the turn of the twenty-first century, and at its height currently.

New Orleans author Grace King (1852-1932) was the grand dame of letters while Faulkner lived and wrote in the city in the mid-1920s. She kept a literary salon at her New Orleans home in the same years as Modernist Gertrude Stein did in Paris, and it was as important locally as Stein's. It was a popular gathering place for artists, writers, and historians, especially young aspiring ones who learned from Miss King's experience and benefited from her important associations in the Northern publishing and magazine world. She got her start by criticizing what she declared to be George Washington Cable's offensive and flawed treatments of New Orleans Creole culture and history. She was challenged by Northern magazine editors to write her own truer more accurate ones. This she attempted to do in stories for the Northern periodicals, which she then collected in *Tales of a Time and Place* (1892) and *Balcony Stories* (1893). The latter volume was thematically ordered in a manner similar to James Joyce's later work

Dubliners (1914). Joyce's work and Sherwood Anderson's thematically related story collections are now often referred to as prototypes for Faulkner's own collections (such as *The Unvanquished* and *Go Down, Moses*) that have thematic ties so strong and intricate as to create works approximating novels. King's works, however, are not mentioned by Faulkner scholars and are examples much closer to home.

As proof, Faulkner meant *Go Down, Moses* to be read as a novel rather than a collection of short stories, Professor James B. Meriwether told me that the one time Faulkner complained loudly to the editors at Random House was about the title of the first printing of the novel. It appeared as *Go Down, Moses, and Other Stories.* Faulkner successfully insisted that the "*and Other Stories*" be removed from later printings.[1]

Miss King's realistic novel *The Pleasant Ways of St. Medard*, a story of invasion and the war on civilians in New Orleans, was published in the decade before Faulkner arrived in New Orleans and was still the literary talk of the town. It is not known whether Faulkner ever went to King's salon or met Miss King, but she was the best-known writer of the area nationwide and had a large following. He would certainly have been aware of her, and especially that she was a professional writer who had made a living from her pen. In her chapter "The Little Convent Girl" in *Balcony Stories,* a poetically charged sentence runs over a page long and is very reminiscent of what has since become known as the Faulkner style. Her writing is characterized by subtlety and artistry and focuses on the intricate relationships of race, class, and culture and their influence.

Miss King's essays and her important *Memories of a Southern Woman of Letters* (1932) discuss the Southern attributes of Southern writers and the significance of the Southern way of seeing the world in such a way as to parallel many aspects of Faulkner's own world view. It is telling that not one of Faulkner's biographers, including the perceptive Mr. Millgate, has mentioned Miss King or her similarities to Faulkner.

Out of all this Mount Everest of pages devoted to Faulkner biography, there is still no volume that treats how he fits into the Southern literary tradition or adequately places him in the proper context of the culture that raised and nurtured him. The absence of Miss King in these works on Faulkner is symptomatic of the failure. The purpose of this volume is thus to look at Faulkner the Southerner in relation to the body of Southern writing and to the attributes that have marked that body over time. I wrote the first version of the text in 2010 and revised and expanded it in 2012, exactly fifty years after Faulkner's death. Here, in this present form of 2022, *Faulkner the Southerner* is now revised and expanded a final time.

This volume results from having studied Faulkner as undergraduate and graduate student for eight years in the

1960s, culminating in a doctoral dissertation at the University of South Carolina on *The Hamlet* in 1970, and then teaching his works to college students at the University of South Carolina and University of Georgia for over forty years. These classes ranged from freshman English courses and undergraduate Faulkner classes to graduate seminars devoted to Faulkner. My class rolls from 1970 to 2009 reveal that over 2,800 students studied Faulkner with me. In this span, I taught *Go Down, Moses, As I Lay Dying,* and *The Sound and the Fury* more than sixty times and never tired of them. I cannot imagine teaching any other fashionable American novels that often—say, classics like *The Scarlet Letter, Moby Dick,* or *A Farewell to Arms.*

The Sound and the Fury, *As I Lay Dying, The Hamlet, Absalom, Absalom!* and *Go Down, Moses* are works of the highest genius and impossible to exhaust. Reading *The Sound and the Fury* over again last year, I found it as fresh as when I first read it over fifty years ago. Many of my students were surprised that they liked it so well, as they often told me. They had hated the idea of Faulkner until they read him. *The Sound and the Fury* has been the cause of many a non-English major at the University of Georgia changing his or her major to literature.

Another classroom favorite was *Sanctuary* which I taught a dozen or more times in the early and mid-1970s. It may be the most underrated of Faulkner's early novels. The

6

fact that Faulkner called it a pot-boiler has not helped its reputation, but not enough critics know how carefully and extensively he rewrote the book in galleys at his own cost at a time when he had no money. He said that he did so, so as not to shame *The Sound and the Fury*, and, in my opinion, it most certainly does not. I think that if *Sanctuary* existed alone, Faulkner would still have a high place in American literature. I agree with Cleanth Brooks that it is a tragi-comic masterpiece resembling in many ways Shakespeare's *Measure for Measure*. In my opinion, it compares favorably with the best novels of Hemingway.

Other classroom successes were *Light in August* (another marvel), *The Wild Palms, The Hamlet* (still my favorite Faulkner novel), *The Unvanquished, The Reivers,* and *Sartoris.* The novel that disappointed them the most, perhaps owing to all the critical hype surrounding it in the 1980s, was *Absalom, Absalom!* Some critics still consider it Faulkner's masterpiece, but if forced to choose one work, I would propose *The Sound and the Fury* without hesitation. Luckily however we are not limited to one.

As Professor Millgate pointed out in 1961, it in no way diminishes Faulkner to consider him in terms of his Southern cultural background. I might go so far as to say that if one is to understand him fully, understanding his Southernness is actually essential. In the history of Faulkner criticism, a great many gaffs, goofs, and strange critical aberrations could have been prevented thereby. For example, when Lena Grove says in *Light in August* that she has walked a "fur piece," the Smith, or Vassar, or Radcliffe scholar at a famous early Faulkner conference would not have had to ask, why in the world in Mississippi in the middle of August in the blazing sun would Ms. Grove wear a fur piece? Understandably, this scholar wasn't on Lena's home turf (most literally) for the neatly manicured lawns of academe have little in common with the dusty red clay road upon which Lena Grove walked barefoot through clear-cut, despoiled woods—forests that Faulkner loved and whose destruction he lamented. The difference between those privileged lawns and a raped rural landscape perhaps goes a long way in explaining why academia has had such a hard time comprehending the true greatness of Faulkner.

Southern ways have to do with pressing *terra firma*. Barefoot is probably a good way to approach Faulkner, for more reasons than one. The first is to know the practical reason of going barefoot—to save precious shoe leather, one of the few things Southern farm folks could not make. My mother told me that in rural red-clay Upcountry South Carolina at the same time Lena walked her hill-country roads barefoot, she and my mother's sister, my Aunt Eula Mae, with the rest of the young women of their Depression era farm community did the same. In reading *Light in August,* I felt I was reading a little of my own family's story—minus the lurid racial violence. Lena Grove, as character, herself shares many of the traits that make Southern writing Southern, and her creator's fiction quintessentially so. Faulkner has the local color precisely correct in *Light in August*, but the concerns and implications of Lena Grove's character portrayal, the inner Lena Grove, run far deeper, and these become major thematic considerations of this present work.

As a South Carolinian growing up in the 1940s and '50s, I did not know then how close to Faulkner's world was my own. I did not quite comprehend the gravity of the common statement "Thank God for Mississippi" when South Carolina was saved from the last ranking of the nation's states by our fellow sufferer. South Carolina was still paying off its Reconstruction debts levied by legislators who robbed the people with bogus bonds bought with what little wealth an invading army had not burned or stolen in a miles long wagon train leaving the state in February 1865. For my people, Reconstruction was largely picking the carcass clean. The last Reconstruction debt was paid off when I was not yet quite a teen. No wonder the place I knew was "poor" and our people, both black and white, had to save shoe leather.

It was surviving, however, but certainly not flourishing, as I grew into my teens. The shadow of that dark era in which Faulkner grew up, still hung over my family in much the same way that it did Faulkner. Fifty years of history in South Carolina since Faulkner was born had not made much difference in my home state. I knew nothing of the man who wrote *The Sound and the Fury,* when I first read it in 1962. I only knew that his world looked, felt, and smelled a lot like mine. I read the novel under a spring wisteria vine in full bloom, as I recall. It must have been so, because a dried spray of wisteria is still in the cheap paperback book I read. Like Faulkner, already a gardener and lover of flowers, I used the wisteria as a bookmark.

In summer 1970, having just received my Ph. D., I traveled for the first time to England on a sort of literary tour to the Hardy Country of Dorset, to the Stoke Poges Church of "Elegy Written in a Country Church Yard" to the Canterbury of Chaucer's *Tales,* to Shakespeare's Stratford, Henry Fielding's Somerset, and T. E. Lawrence's Wells and Clouds Hill. It was not yet twenty-five years since the World War, and I still saw war's marks on the landscape and the people themselves. There were so many men with one leg or one arm. The reason why finally dawned on me. In an epiphany, I realized I was seeing the country that Faulkner was born into at the same length of time since the close of the great Southern war that had killed more by percentage of Southern soldiers than the English and had left an even greater impoverishment of wealth and the human spirit. I was twenty-five years old myself, so had a hard time comprehending time in the way it has stretched out before me today.

When I traveled to Germany a decade later, I saw even more maimed bodies, but the cities had been rebuilt and I understood that the Germans had had the Marshall Plan as the South had not (as Faulkner himself had pointed out to the Japanese on his trip to Nagano in 1955). Faulkner's South as he was growing up was a place of rotting mansions, real hardships, and poverty. In my South Carolina of the 1950s, I saw these same decaying great houses of a culture that had also been eclipsed.

The following chapters treat a dozen major Southern literary traits, themes, or habits of thought and seeing to be found in Faulkner's writing. Of course, there are more, but these are the ones I find to be most crucial and illuminating in delineating Faulkner the Southerner. I certainly trust I will not have the last word on the subject.

A special acknowledgment is needed here. I often site James Babcock Meriwether (1928-2007) in unpublished lectures, interviews, and conversations. Professor Meriwether, while earning his doctoral degree at Princeton in 1956, mounted the first exhibition of Faulkner's works—at the Princeton University Library from May to August 1957. In preparing the data that would become his dissertation, *The Literary Career of William Faulkner,* he worked part-time as

Faulkner's gardener and yard man at Rowan Oak in order to ask questions necessary for the work. At the time he was there, Meriwether told me that Faulkner was completing *The Town* and he often heard Faulkner's typewriter keys at work. He went on to edit Faulkner's last three novels. Meriwether, who became a close friend and fellow editor of several books with Michael Millgate, was the most knowledgeable and careful expert on Faulkner's texts. His sound critical understanding of the canon was also unsurpassed.

I feel confident in saying that Meriwether knew more about Faulkner than any scholar then or now, and it may be a knowledge perhaps never to be matched. Much of his expertise may be seen in the many footnotes citing him in Professor Millgate's *The Achievement of William Faulkner*. Unfortunately for us, Meriwether elected not to write the great critical work of which he was capable but was instead liberal in sharing his information with scholars and with his students in both classes and conversation. I have often wondered why he did not write on Faulkner the man but have since understood that to do so would be a violation of that bond of friendship of one gentleman to another. Reticence in personal matters such as this is a part of the old noble code. Meriwether shared it. As for not writing literary criticism, Meriwether in my opinion felt he was not quite adequate to treat such an exalted subject as the Faulkner canon. Such was his admiration of both the man and his work.

My association with Professor Meriwether began as an undergraduate student at the University of South Carolina in 1964, two years after Faulkner's death, and continued until Professor Meriwether's death in 2007. This volume owes no small debt to our forty-year teacher-student association. The Meriwethers hailed from red-clay Edgefield District, South Carolina. Dr. Meriwether, himself born and raised in Columbia, some thirty miles from my own place of birth, was also an alumnus of the University of South Carolina, and we both as fellow South Carolinians of the Upcountry felt a kind of kinship. I recollect my comment to him while a graduate student that he perhaps must be a bit torn in loyalties between the University of South Carolina and Princeton, having degrees from both colleges, to which he quickly answered that a person has, like one mother, only one alma mater. It was always clear to me which the *one* was. My reply was that by having all degrees from one institution, I didn't have to make a choice. In some sort of youthful bratty way, I was pulling rank in nativeness with my mentor, a gesture which did not go unappreciated, but which I have since regretted. For whatever Meriwether was (and he was at times a difficult character), he was a true son of Carolina, both the institution and the place.[2]

One of the deepest impressions Dr. Meriwether made upon me was his recounting of what his grandfather Babcock said that he saw as he stood and watched the sack and burning of Columbia in February 1865. Meriwether's narrative was all the more memorable owing to the catch in his throat and the mist in his eyes. After so long, for him, the tragedy was still real and raw as if it had but happened yesterday, and as fellow Southerner, he may have shared with Faulkner a bond that I shared with them both. At that moment in his office, the grandson was living there in time with his grandfather and suffered the trials of his people—our people—in their darkest hour. Our people had been through the fire, and still we were here. As I later learned from my scholarly delving, Faulkner's family had done so as well, and he was acutely aware of it. It was this courage in defeat that became a shared code of Southern honor recognized most recently by Montserrat Ginés, a scholar from Barcelona in his *The Southern Inheritors of Don Quixote* (2000).

If, as the nutritionists were fond of saying in the 1980s, you are what you eat, how could anyone doubt Faulkner's essential down-home Southernness when he reads John Cullen's account of Bill Faulkner, his life-long friend and hunting companion, at supper in the hunt camp. Cullen reports that Bill's favorite food was "coon and collards," so well-beloved in fact that Cullen says that Faulkner would want to eat it for breakfast.[3] Faulkner's hunting buddies, half serious, half in the tall-tale tradition of rural Southern folk humor, upon Faulkner's being honored with the Nobel Prize, wrote the King of Sweden inviting him to join them at the campfire in this particular rural repast. Faulkner's character in *The Hamlet*, V. K. Ratliff, would have richly enjoyed taking part in the scheme, and had the King of Sweden come to the hunt camp, V. K. may have served him the dish himself. The King's secretary's gracious letter to the hunters declining their invitation must remind the student of Southern literature of the contrast between dialect and elaborate elegant language so often practiced by the masters of Southern rustic humor from George Washington Harris and A. B. Longstreet to Mark Twain, Flannery O'Connor, Faulkner, Larry Brown, Harry Crews, Cormac McCarthy, and beyond. Faulkner was a master in this contrast, as in so many things literarily Southern. The following pages seek to explore these ways.

In 1988, Southern literary critic and founder of Algonquin Press, Louis D. Rubin, Jr., in his short essay "Changing, Enduring, Forever Still the South," listed six distinctive traits of Southern literature. All of these appear as chapters here, but Rubin made an essential point beyond his list—that by themselves these "hallmarks" are found here and there in various other literatures too, yet it is "their continuing mutual action upon each other" that signifies Southern literature. Professor

15

Rubin went on to say that not all these traits appear in each writer, but we might add that in Faulkner's case, they do. That is another reason why it is beneficial to view Faulkner in his Southern cultural context.[4]

My thanks are here due to the late Shelby Foote, who shared his understanding of Faulkner with me, particularly *The Hamlet*, which he felt to be Faulkner's masterpiece. My correspondence with Mr. Foote spanned more than thirty years and is now available at the South Caroliniana Library at the University of South Carolina. Particularly informative, for both Faulkner and Foote, is his letter on *The Hamlet*. I am also indebted to Jack Harbeck, Bob Mcgee, Claire Mcgee, Alex Moore, Henry Fulmer, Allen Stokes, Steven Vanderlip, Richard Hines, Clark Williams, Patrick Seay, and Donald Livingston. My thanks are also extended to my fellow Euphradian Society members at the University of South Carolina for sponsoring my campus address, "What Faulkner Thought—Faulkner and Honor," in 2013. The talk became an early version of Chapter Twelve. I am also grateful to the many students who have read and discussed Faulkner with me for over fifty years in two universities and, most recently, in the Abbeville Institute.

One final note: this volume was rejected by a famous university press after keeping it close to two years. The reader's report declared "there is nothing new here." The reader will have to decide upon the validity of that assertion.

ONE

OUTSIDE THE PALE

In 1957, Flannery O'Connor in "The Fiction Writer and His Country," took offense at a *Life Magazine* editorial that stated that the Southern writer is anguished because the South is isolated from the rest of the country. Displaying not a small amount of cross-grained contrariness, she declared, "The anguish that most of us have observed for some time now has been caused not by the fact that the South is alienated from the rest of the country, but by the fact that it is not alienated enough" (Collected Works, 802).

Contemporary North Carolina poet Fred Chappell in a lecture on Southern poetry in 1997 said a trait of modern Southern poets in contrast to national or international norms, is that they are "content to be contrary by nature." He spoke of what he called their "cross-grained contrariness."[1] Similarly, Dr. Meriwether said in an unpublished lecture in 1996 that Faulkner showed independence throughout his life, and concluded: "The Yankee world insists on conformity, and this increased Faulkner's nonconformity to the national norm, both in his writing and in his life."[2] Nearly a century before, New Orleans author, Grace King, wrote in 1903, "if Southern blood could be drawn away from the nation, it would drain away with

18

it such a mass of individuality that we would see only business corporations and associations left" (King, 386).

Southerners in general have usually questioned popular mass movements and fads, what Southern poet, John Crowe Ransom in 1930 called the American doctrine of perpetual newness.[3] Throughout the Southern experience, the traditional South's people have tended to resist homogenization and adherence to the "one-size-fits-all" mentality. That attempt at procrustean forcing is the way of radical extreme egalitarianism run truly amok.[4] In its political form, this way of thinking has led to totalitarianism, as Faulkner was to say in his Cold War essays to be treated in a later chapter. A few years ago, I heard a South Carolina writer on the subject of change so as to conform and to be in step with new popular attitudes nationwide, declare, "Here we don't embrace change, we *bear* it." Faulkner had a large degree of that same fundamental curmudgeonly attitude.

Faulkner was not concerned with being in fashion. He would have appreciated fellow nonconformist Oscar Wilde's definition: "Fashion is creating something so intolerable that it has to be changed every six months." But how quintessentially American it is to follow trends and embrace fads, even to the point of defining patriotism as throwing out the old and going out and buying the new deluxe model. One can see how fashion, relentlessly seeking the very latest in everything, would thus play into the American planned-obsolescent throw-away society. The throw-away mentality would be good for industry and for those who market its steady flow of products that have to be replaced before they are worn out. Of course, this is a very sweet deal for merchant and manufacturer alike, not to mention the advertisers, the product-pushers catering to the addicts they have helped to create. As we will see, Faulkner's essays show that he was aware of the scam of planned obsolescence and didn't succumb to hype.

It is clear from his writing and even the least discerning of his biographies, that Faulkner did not mind being out of step, especially when the regnant American way is to be lock-step in almost everything and especially when it comes to the latest fads and fashions. Faulkner rejected the mindless band-wagon herd mentality, and what he called "the universal will to regimentation."[5] What wonder that he put himself on record with the League of American Writers in 1938 "as being unalterably opposed to Franco and fascism."[6] Recent misguided attempts by a few historians and Faulkner's most recent biographer Carl Rollyson to link the South to fascism will have rough sledding here. There is a particularly good passage in *The Reivers* which speaks to this subject. Faulkner's wise Uncle Possum comments that there is a place where the law ends and just people begins. That is Faulkner's way, and that is the Southern way.

Faulkner was not one to embrace the flashy new. Instead, like most good Southerners, he took the long view. A classical training in the ancient writers formed for him, again like the traditional Southerner, the foundation of his education. Perhaps the best early summation of the Southern attitude toward the Classics is Charlestonian Hugh Swinton Legaré's "Classical Learning," (*Southern Review*, volume 1, February 1828, 1-39). Here he made the case for ancient literature as the staple for the education of the Southern gentleman. Faulkner taught himself to read Horace. He tried but failed to teach himself Greek. Instead, he would look at the English translation, and his Oxford Mississippi friend and mentor Phil Stone would read the Greek aloud as Faulkner followed.[7] Faulkner was serious about the Classics. The catalogue of his library underscores the fact (Blotner, *Catalogue of the Library of William Faulkner*). For a book-length treatment of the Southern writer's veneration of the classical tradition, see my own *The Classical Origins of Southern Literature.*

Donald Davidson's poem, "On a Replica of the Parthenon," treats the newly erected prefab concrete Parthenon in Nashville's Centennial Park. Its speaker asks,

> Why do they come? What do they seek
> Who build but never read their Greek?[8]

Here, Davidson calls modern progressives men "who slew their past" and now raising up this "bribe against their fate."

Faulkner, like the Fugitive-Agrarians, was not one of these past-slayers. Davidson's friend, Andrew Lytle, had a term for the fad worshippers, the materialistic *now* people who wanted only the gratification of the moment and were locked into the now, with regard for neither past nor future. He called them "momentary men" (Lytle, *From Eden to Babylon*). Faulkner, with his grounding in the ancient writers, had the opposing classical long view. That classical grounding was reinforced by his Southern understanding of history through family stories.

Traditional Southerners live with history, which becomes palpable, and Faulkner most particularly did. From *Sartoris* (originally *Flags in the Dust*) in 1929 onward, the impress of the past can be felt and seen in the powerful omnipresence of objects such as bricks worn by feet and thus cupped from use, thresholds worn from walking, and coin-silver spoon handles polished by use, so as to provide a world of linked continuities and an aura of timelessness. In a pertinent observation, critic Richard Weaver wrote that the South is the region that history has happened to (*Southern Essays*, 72). It is certainly more than Allen Tate's understatement in the English style of litotes, "the backward glance" (Tate, *Essays of Four Decades,* 545).

Faulkner's sense of that history is well-recognized. To be cognizant of history in an anti-historical, future-focused, progress-worshipping, machine-dominated, rootless, and planned-obsolescent America in itself makes one out of step and a nonconformist. To respect tradition in a supremely anti-traditional time like the twentieth century would make one even more so. In 2022, with the insistence on toppling statues and reinterpreting history through a cancel culture lens, America is reaching an extreme, and coupled with the insistent bullying to join the process or fear being canceled oneself. Faulkner would not be pleased. His hunting companion from youth put it best in 1961. Cullen wrote that Bill "always differs from the general public opinion. He is an individualist" (55).

M. E. Bradford perceptively wrote of William Gilmore Simms and Donald Davidson, that with them, "nothing is ever merely 'past'.... [Instead] the living word of the fable, in which each soul has a name" insures that "individual deeds count for everything" and the individual is sovereign and sacred.[9] As Bradford clearly understood, that is the view which has informed the celebrated great body of Southern literature.

Faulkner indeed celebrated the individual, but not an individual torn loose from family, community, and responsibility, as future chapters will reveal. He was not a fan of the individualism that becomes egocentrism, irresponsibility, narcissism, and loss of civic discipline. In the words of historian Eugene Genovese, Southern conservatism (like Faulkner's) counterposes an older notion of the God-given dignity of the person "to the bourgeois notion of the individual as center of the universe….[T]he very dignity of the personality requires roots in the community, and, above all, the family."[10] That civic responsibility was for Faulkner, more often than not, local, seeing that the nation at large had lost sight of these virtues. Genovese understood the Marxist mindset well, having been a fanatical one himself in his earliest writings.

Faulkner's "cross-grained contrariness" leads to a closely related trait. Chappell said in 1997 that the modern Southern poet, when it comes to national norms, "feels like an outsider." Faulkner, born in 1897, was a child of the post Reconstruction South. The shadow of invasion and destruction still fell on him and across his land with the ruins of the chimneys of burned homes still standing as reminders. He was always aware that as Southerner, he was an outsider in America. Nowhere was this clearer to him than at the obligatory New York City publicity parties thrown by Bennett Cerf and Faulkner's publisher, Random House. Professor Meriwether said that there he always stood on the periphery.

Faulkner's most recent biographer, while discerning that Faulkner felt "left out," like blacks and gays, attributes the problem to an inferiority complex. He was short, after all. Rollyson is far off the mark because he lacks the understanding of Faulkner's Southernness in being relegated to a secondary status in America. This is what Richard Weaver clearly understood in 1959 when he called the South America's step-child (73). Cleanth Brooks described the culture that produced Faulkner as "old-fashioned and provincial—quite out of the mainstream" in America, and for that reason always felt left out of the American narrative (Brooks, *Toward Yoknapataw-pha*, 328). Rollyson's psychoanalysis that most certainly puts Faulkner in a bad light appears all the more questionable when one considers the Southern cultural context. His attempt to explain this outsider's mentality as Faulkner's reason for sympathy with blacks becomes just another way of criticizing the South.

American historians have called the South of Faulkner's day "distinctly foreign" and "the forgotten region" (Gray, 16, 18). Professor Millgate got it right when he stated that Faulkner "was a member, nationally speaking, not merely of a minority culture but of a rejected culture, a culture that had in one sense been given shape and coherence by the very experience of military and political defeat and that continued to be sustained by its difference from, and opposition to, a dominant culture that was itself too secure in its dominance to concern itself with anxieties about its own identity" (Millgate, *Place*, 77). For Millgate, who has also been a perceptive scholar of Thomas Hardy's works, the difference between Faulkner and the mainstream involved Faulkner's critique of materialism, progressivism, industrialism, and empire, all topics which Thomas Hardy treated as well.

As proof of Faulkner's position outside the pale, contemporary reviewers of Faulkner's novels in the mainstream magazines and newspapers inside the pale usually relegated him to the *other*. When they took notice of him at all, he was considered an oddity. What wonder that he was not impressed by academics or literary critics. In a 1978 interview, Brooks noted that Faulkner "was afraid of academic people, dreaded them, didn't understand them, thought they were all trying to pick his brains to do things." He was "a little skeptical of the literary scholar as such, or the professor as such" (Brooks, Interview, 158-159).

He had good reason to be, judging from his treatment in the establishment press. When *As I Lay Dying* appeared in October 1930, the review in the *New York Times Book Review* was said to be "typical" (Parini, 157). It opened with the statement that the reviewer felt "intense annoyance" with the author for "spending his rich inventive faculty on such a witch's brew of a family as Anse, Vardaman, Jewel, Cash, Darl, and the dying mother, Addie Bundren." Faulkner could not be forgiven for wasting his time and talent, and the reader's patience, on such a subject and for the depths of existence he chose to plumb. Clearly the Eastern Establishment was still attacking George Washington Harris's Sut Lovingood without even knowing it. In *Patriotic Gore,* Edmund Wilson had called Sut "a peasant squatting in his own filth." He would find it fitting that nearly a century later, Faulkner had used Sut's "Well, Dad's Dead!" the luridly grotesquely comic story of the trip to bury a family member, as the framework for the plot of his novel.

Another excellent example of the unsympathetic Northern response is urbane New York professor Alfred Kazin's review of *The Unvanquished* in the *New York Herald Tribune* in 1938. Faulkner, he said, writes like the "willful, sullen child in some gaseous world of his own," where there are pages "which mean nothing" and he is "stringing truncated paragraphs together like dirty wash, howling, stumbling, losing himself in a verbal murk." Kazin declared that Faulkner had a "sullen attachment to cruel and silly folkways." Kazin described Faulkner's work as portraying a land that is dead and a people who insure "their defeat by their fear and violence."

Other learned critics, including Kazin, said that *The Unvanquished* was not a novel at all, just a haphazard collection of short stories. They and early Faulkner scholarship in general had a similar response to Faulkner's *Go Down, Moses,* a similarly structured novel in the manner of James Joyce's *Dubliners*. Even Faulkner's New York publisher failed to understand what Faulkner was attempting. When Random House released the novel in 1942, it appeared as *Go Down, Moses, and Other Stories.* Faulkner rarely concerned himself with his published works. He was too busy writing the next one. But this time he did. He was not pleased, and he saw to it that the novel's second printing had the *and Other Stories* removed from its title page. [11] *Go Down, Moses,* like *The Unvanquished,* was a novel, just not the usual straight-jacketed usual form.

These critics and publishers were not accustomed to the Southern looseness of oral telling. They only knew the controlled form of the book—rigidly controlled as if the book covers and margins were so many bars of containment in a loose flowing life that also must be kept under control. They didn't heed the statement by Faulkner's literary mentor Sherwood Anderson that novelists are betraying life by tying it up into neat little packages. "Life is a loose flowing thing," Anderson wrote. "There are no plot stories in life." Anderson himself said he was temperamentally a Southerner. He moved to New Orleans in the 1920s where he and Faulkner were drinking buddies, then to the mountains of Virginia where he died. His Celtic bloodline was obviously telling. Faulkner was having a little fun at Anderson's expense when he titled his early parody, *Sherwood Anderson and Other Famous Creoles.*

Those same critics who didn't understand the looser novel form have also said there is no such thing as the Irish novel because the works are not rigidly, chronologically plotted on the English novel system of a Jane Austen, Dickens, or Thackeray or American counterparts like Hemingway. Again we find Faulkner not conforming to accepted English-American templates. This was lost on most of his Northern reviewers. They just didn't get it.

I suppose the mass of critics wanted Faulkner to be Henry James of Boston, later expatriated to Rye, England, for James was the consummate anglophile. It is very telling that Faulkner did not receive a National Book Award until five years *after* the Nobel Prize; and then, I expect, it was the Nobel Prize that shamed them into bestowing it. Perhaps like their Cromwellian Puritan ancestors in Ireland, some Northern reviewers placed the *other* "outside the pale"—that is, outside the paling fort whose ramparts protected their hegemony by insuring control of everything messy and unruly (notably the dirty and irredeemably unwashed Irish natives). As an outsider from the regnant establishment culture, Faulkner was freed, as traditional Southerners are freed, to create from the centers of who they are. Adherents to lock-step cultures and Marxist ideologies of equality do not understand for the same reasons that they fail to produce the highest level of great art.

We might note that Faulkner's North Mississippi heritage of Scots, Irish, and Scoto-Irish Butlers, McAlpines, Murrys, and Faulkners—all four sides of his immediate family tree—made him acutely aware of his otherness from a New

England conformist Puritan dominated America. Faulkner himself added the Scots family Cameron to this list of four (Gray, 360). Joseph Blotner's monumental biography made much of Faulkner's sense of himself as a Highland Scot in America. Blotner wrote: "When a man asserts an ancestry as William Faulkner did the Scottish, you take proper notice" (Blotner, *Faulkner,* 3, 7). Faulkner gave a Highland Scot background to both his Compson and Sartoris families, as well as to his McCaslins, McCallums, and Stevenses. That explains his many references to the Battle of Culloden in *The Sound and the Fury* and other works.

Faulkner himself spoke on the issue of his Scots heritage. He wrote, "My ancestors came from Inverness, Scotland" (Blotner, 3) In titling his last novel *The Reivers,* he explained that he was using an old Scots word and, most particularly, "the old Scottish spelling" of it (*Selected Letters*, 456). As Richard Gray has perceptively pointed out, in using this word, "Faulkner was himself signaling his act of return and recovery, the feeling that he was looking back…to all those anonymous men and women who had preceded him by centuries—and who were still there, he believed, in his own blood" (360-361).

Faulkner attached firmly to Scots and Scoto-Irish tradition against the prevailing Northern English-oriented culture. One obvious good example is the naming of his home "Rowan Oak." The Scots legend of the Rowan (or ash) tree is that it wards off evil and is thus a symbol of peace and safety, in other words, sanctuary.[12] Edmund Spenser, Irish poet, also knew the Celtic tradition when he wrote in *The Faerie Queene*, "The ash for nothing ill" (Book I, Canto I, Stanza IX). Faulkner planted four rowan trees at the corners of his land, and thus gave his home linkage to the Gaelic legend. It was also appropriate that he did, for the home's original antebellum owner was born in Ireland. Blotner reported that Faulkner's own great-grandfather Murry in Mississippi lived to be a hundred and spoke only Gaelic (Blotner, *Faulkner,* 7). There were also pockets of Gaelic speaking Scots in rural Alabama in the nineteenth century. It is obvious that Faulkner was a product of the individualistic Celtic South, and consciously so. His Jeffersonianism did not stem from Jefferson's maternal Randolphs but from his father, Peter Jefferson a stalwart Celt of the upland pioneer South of his day in every way.

Faulkner's quotations from the nineteenth century Irish nationalist John Curran revealed that he was also aware of the long Irish struggle for freedom. Faulkner, like Southern writers from William Gilmore Simms to Margaret Mitchell and Cormac McCarthy, drew lines from these Irish and Scottish fights for local autonomy to the South's own bid for independence.[13] Cleanth Brooks noted that William Butler Yeats' "Ireland stands over against London much as Faulkner's South stands over against New York." Brooks continued that any

31

"Southerner who reads Yeats' Autobiographies is bound to be startled, over and over again, by the analogies between Yeats' 'literary situation' and that of the Southern author" (Brooks, *Yoknapatawpha Country*, 2-3).

Brooks' perceptive extended treatment of the similar "folk cultures of Ireland and the South in Faulkner and W. B. Yeats" concluded that a "vigorous folk culture implies… conservatism, old-fashioned customs and ideas, a paternalistic system centered in an aristocracy or at least a landowning squirearchy. In short, a folk society based on the land implies the Big House with landed proprietors and the ethos that goes with such a governing class" (Brooks, *Toward Yoknapatawpha*, 332.)

Brooks stated further, "Add to these elements certain historical conditions true to both Ireland and the South—defeat in war, economic stagnation, and a colonial economy—and one finds a consequence that history is very much alive in the minds of the people, for the dead lost causes are precisely those that live in memory" (338.) Millgate agreed with Brooks' premise that Faulkner's relation to his place had similarities to "Yeats's literary and personal relationship with his native Ireland" and that history was alive and not relegated to the past (Millgate, Place, 78).

Dr. Barbara Bellows, in her recent excellent comparison of the Southern Literary Renaissance with the Irish

Renaissance noted that the citizens of both cultures "experienced disenfranchisement" and "Contrariness and resistance to national conformity...was best summed up by the trenchant comment of the Anglo-Irish philosopher George Berkeley, 'We Irishmen think otherwise'" (Bellows, 65). Bellows elaborated that Padraig Colum while visiting Charleston "held forth until the wee hours about the Irish determination to reassert the Gaelic language and its folk tales and myths as part of their resistance to 'the conquest.'" Bellows continued, "Colum began to see similarities between Charleston and Dublin, two nibbled-away old cities brought to their knees by history. Yet they both still stood, unrepentant, unreconstructed, unforgiven, survivors shunned by progress, broken and bent" (Bellows, 64). In this particular way, Faulkner lived in a very similar Mississippi. His novel title *The Unvanquished* is a case in point. What Bellows says about the similarities between Ireland and the South applies remarkably closely to Faulkner.

Faulkner's resistance to Northern exclusivity was the same battle Poe and Simms had to fight in their day, when Poe called American writing hag-ridden—"ridden to death by New England."[14] By Faulkner's time, the Boston Frogpondians had only expanded their frog pond influence to the marshy fringes across America, but were still the in-group—just as small-minded, intolerant, and provincial as they had always been.[15] It is clear that Professor Kazin was making his bid for

Frogpondianship with his *New York Herald Tribune* drubbing of Faulkner. Faulkner when read carefully reveals that he made a subtle but concerted and extended effort to practice what Chappell calls the "strategy of subversion." His writing certainly often shows it on several fronts. Southerners had seen their world under siege since the 1830s and many of the South's greatest writers like Faulkner have been acutely aware of it. Future chapters will treat the subversion seen in the two ways one may read the novels, one for the native and one for the outsider.

In 1997, Alabama humorist Florence King observed of the South that "the three qualities she embodies that have made her the target of twentieth-century America's envious rage" are Identity, Eccentricity, and Complexity. Of Identity, she declared that the traditional Southerner has a "granite sense of self powered by a value-control center of pre-set codes guaranteed to threaten the kind of people who attend alienation conferences." Of Eccentricity, King declared, "The South cherishes her eccentrics as Italy cherishes her singers…. Big Brother and the Nanny State hate eccentrics. They're too hard to control and they identify with aristocrats." She quoted John Stuart Mill that eccentricity "has always abounded when and where strength of character has abounded," with the amount of eccentricity in a society being "proportional to the amount of genius, mental vigour, and moral courage." King defined

Complexity as "our tolerance for self-contradiction"—another way of saying one cannot be easily labeled or made to conform to a pattern. King's Identity, Eccentricity, and Complexity are helpful words to use with Faulkner in seeing him in his Southern cultural context.[16] Individual sovereignty is after all the Marxist's nightmare. As Red States and Blue States grow ever further apart, the cultural divide will become more noticeable. Faulkner is a very good way of gauging Red States' rejection of the Marxist ideal.

TWO

FAULKNER THE FARMER

To tend the soil, indeed, is to make one love it.
—W. G. Simms (1842)

Acrucial and fundamental Southern trait is Faulkner's valuing of a farming background. Like the great majority of Southerners, rich and poor, black and white, his family's roots were agricultural, and he was very much aware of it. The New England Puritan Winthrop-Mather concept of the "shining city on a hill" had no attraction for him. Unlike Hawthorne's Puritans in *The Scarlet Letter,* Faulkner and his society did not gather in villages around which they built stockades and paling forts to keep nature out. Nature was not inhabited by the devil and to be shunned and fought against. Hawthorne, to his credit, had agreed with the Southern way of thinking.

As seen in the previous chapter, Faulkner took the Greek and Roman Classics seriously. If the origins of Southern literature had to be summed up in one word, that word might be *Classicism*—specifically the Greek and Latin Classics, and Faulkner was in its line of succession. These works praised a life on the land. What wonder that the colonial libraries of Southern gentlemen included the Classics. By contrast, the New England libraries were theological, as were their early colleges, Harvard, Yale, and Princeton, colleges whose primary purpose was to educate Puritan preachers in orthodox theology.

Thomas Jefferson, in fact, with more than veiled scorn called them "the Northern seminaries" whose work infected the minds of Southern students with pernicious doctrines (Chinard, 511). The Puritan declared that belletristic, or "polite literature" as Southerners called it, was written in Satan's workshop. Puritan writers like Cotton Mather understood classical and belletristic literature's seductive power and therefore feared it all the more. It could not be allowed in the home lest it influence weak and vulnerable minds.

Jefferson's reading list for his nephew in 1785 is an excellent register of the importance of Greek and Latin literature for the Southerner. Jefferson himself was influenced by Homer, Cicero, Horace, Tully, Epictetus, Seneca, Vergil, and Euripides, to name only a few. His readings show that he sought to balance the Roman stoics with the epicureans to create a harmonious life. Jefferson was a most reasonable man from the Age of Reason, and, like most Southerners, eschewed anything that smelled of intellectual fanaticism.

The students at antebellum Southern colleges received a broad classical education designed to produce a gentleman who could excel in all walks of life. The object of education was to help a man to do many things well so that he would be proficient in his agricultural fields, his library, and his drawing room. John Gould Fletcher's chapter in *I'll Take My Stand* (1930) concluded that the purpose of education in the colonial and antebellum South was "to achieve character, personality, and gentlemanliness in order to make lives an art and to bring souls into relation with the whole scheme of things, which is the divine nature" ("Education, Past and Present," 120). After nearly a century, Fletcher's assessment is perhaps still the soundest and most insightful on its subject

As an example of the classical base of a Southern education, entering freshmen at South Carolina College in the 1830s were required to have a good knowledge of Latin and Greek grammar, to have already read the whole of Vergil, Cicero's orations, Xenophons' *Cyropædia*, and at least one book of Homer. At South Carolina College in 1835, there were a professor of Greek and Roman Literature, a professor of Belle Lettres and Logic, and a professor of Sacred Literature. Literature, most particularly *classical* literature, was thus a staple at the college and at all antebellum Southern institutions, including the college in Faulkner's Oxford, Mississippi.

Southern historian, Francis Butler Simkins, in his *A History of the South* (1963) wrote that from the earliest days, Southern colleges and universities stressed study of the Greek and Latin Classics and that the "devotion of Southern students to the Classics and their participation in recitations and debates of the literary societies accounts to a large degree for the grace of manner, classical allusions, and flowing melody of the Old South's numerous orators" (Simkins, 168-169).

This was not the case in the North, however. The Northern colleges from the beginning abandoned the Classics in favor of theological and scientific works. With thorough secularization after colonial times, the Classics were still rejected. For example, Noah Webster of New England (1758-1843), a professor at Yale, stated that the study of the Classics is retrogressive for a Democratic people. For us today, this sounds strange. Although many Southern young men had been trained at Yale in the early years, it sounded strange for them as well, particularly since their tutoring back home had been at the hands of classically trained teachers, many from England. Contradicting Webster were many strongly-worded Southern defenses of Classicism. This fact shows in high relief the great difference between the regions. Faulker again shows himself to be a product of Southern thought.

Most notably among these defenders of Classicism, Charleston scholar, editor, and essayist Hugh Swinton Legaré (1797-1843) challenged Webster specifically on the importance of Classics to a Democratic people. He called the Greek and Latin Classics essential in teaching liberty. Jefferson said the same and was a case in point. English historian Michael O'Brien has called Legaré the most learned American of his day who struggled to synthesize classical thought with American culture. O'Brien concluded that Legaré's "mind is of permanent interest" in the field of intellectual history (O'Brien, *Legaré*, xii).

Legaré was educated in the classical tradition at South Carolina College, where his participation in the Clariosophic Debating Society augmented the school's classical curriculum. He was valedictorian there in 1814. Two of his key and masterful essays on the necessity of the Classics as basis for learning were "Classical Learning" (*Southern Quarterly Review*, 1 [February 1828], 1-49); and "Roman Literature," (*Southern Quarterly Review*, 1 [May 1828], 358-410.) These brilliant treatise-length works go to the heart of the matter. Professor Dr. Hooper of South Carolina College had cards printed for members of the senior class in 1844 with a quotation from Legaré's essay extolling Cicero's works as "impossible to imagine anything more sublime or consoling" (James Henry Carlisle/ S. M. Reynolds S. C. College text of *De Senectute*, JEKL).

Poet and essayist William John Grayson (1788-1863), like Legaré, classically trained at South Carolina College in the 1810s, in the same decade as Legaré, clearly understood the connection between the South and the Greeks and Romans of antiquity, and particularly their agrarian culture. Cicero's lessons on the republic were not lost on him. Grayson also denounced Noah Webster's anti-traditionalism. His autobiography reported attending a commencement at Yale around 1817 and found the busy scene at least lively and good for business and most useful for providing husbands for the local young women (Grayson, 103-104). Other than on the utility of that, he made no comment.

Charleston author, William Gilmore Simms, born in 1806, called Noah Webster that "notorious offender of the tongue who hath through equal ignorance and conceit, entirely overthrown the better English orthography, and who hath corrupted half of this goodly nation." His corruption of the language extended to the college curriculum. Simms himself knew the Classics as well as any writer of his day, including Legaré. He called the classical Greeks "the most refined, intellectual race that the world has ever known" (Charleston *Mercury,* 25 December 1854). Simms said this in direct opposition to the popular Northern idea that modern progress in all spheres (including technological advances) have brought modern mankind to the zenith of civilization. As his book reviews of classical subjects reveal, Simms's knowledge of Greek and Latin literature extended to the scholarship they inspired, scholarship by Classicists like the best European scholars such as Niebuhr, Grote, Anthon, and Ashton, to name only a few (See, Kibler, *Selected Reviews*, 131). Particularly good examples are his "Literature in Ancient Rome" (1845), "Anthon's

Manual of Greek Literature" (1854), "Gurney's Translation of Apuleius" (1854), and "Conington's *Æneid*" (1867). The example of Simms is excellent proof of how deeply ingrained was the classical tradition in the South in the decades before the war.

Basil Lanneau Gildersleeve, another erudite Charlestonian, born in 1831, has been called the finest classical scholar America has produced. Educated at the College of Charleston, he taught at the University of Virginia, a bastion of the planter aristocracy and classical learning, as were the College of William and Mary, the College of Charleston, South Carolina College, and the universities of North Carolina, Georgia, Alabama, and Mississippi—indeed, the overwhelming majority of Southern institutions, large and small, up to 1861. Here, as we have seen, as was the case at South Carolina College, a reading knowledge of both Greek and Latin were required for entrance, and recitations and graduation addresses were delivered by students in Latin. This emphasis in the Classics had not abated by the time of the war in 1861.

What wonder that the Northern educator in a fast industrializing and urbanizing world would find the Classics uncongenial, if not subversive of their chosen way of life. Writers like Vergil in his *Eclogues* and *Georgics,* or Juvenal and Horace, in their satires of Roman city vices, or Homer in describing Laertes' consolations in cultivating the soil, all pointed to agrarians as the blessed ones, and their way of life the most conducive to health, contentment, intellectual pursuit, and stable civilization. Cicero became eloquent on the subject in *De Senectute*, a work which was a standard favorite in antebellum Southern colleges. At South Carolina College, for example, it was a primary senior class text that all students studied in the 1840s. (James Henry Carlisle/ S. M. Reynolds *De Senectute* S. C. College text with notes, JEKL).

Here in *De Senectute*, Cicero stated, "Nor does the farmer find joy only in his cornfields, meadows, vineyards, and woodlands, but also in his garden and orchard, in the rearing of his cattle, in his swarms of bees, and in the infinite variety of flowers. And not only does planting delight him, but grafting also, than which there is nothing in husbandry that is more ingenious." He concluded, "No life can be happier than the farmer's.... Of the verdure of the meadows, the even rows of trees and the beauty of the vineyards and olive groves, why should I speak at length! Nothing can be more abounding in usefulness or more attractive in appearance than a well-tilled farm" (*De Senectute*, XVI). Furthermore, Cicero made it clear that the honest and virtuous statesman sprang from those men who tilled the fields. He wrote *In agris erant tum senatores* – that is, "senators lived on farms" (XVI). This passage must have hit particularly hard on those who strategized for Northern ascendancy through government. Statesmen from the

South all came from farms. Fewer and fewer politicians were doing so in the North.

Even a writer like Xenophon in his *The Householder* (*Œconomicus*) lauded agriculture with copious eloquence. In the Classics, for the emerging New North intellectual such as Webster or Emerson there was little for cultural solace and urban-industrial validation. What wonder Webster and the Harvard professors savaged the study of the writers of Greece and Rome! Emerson found a celebration of steam power, railroads, and "industrial villages" the better subjects for celebration. Walt Whitman was to do the same. The Classics were major stumbling blocks to the implementation of their new materialist "progressive" utopias.

Pertinent also is the fact that the College of Charleston, Basil L. Gildersleeve's alma mater, was the last of the venerable American colleges to give up its emphasis on the Classics when it became a state university in 1970 and its enrollment quickly doubled the next year in 1971.

Caroline Winterer in *The Culture of Classicism: Ancient Greece and Rome in American Intellectual Life, 1780-1910,* noted that the classical texts which were central to the college curriculum imbued students like Legaré with the truth that Ciceronian participation in community and the agrarian nature of republics as defined by Cicero were critical for the perpetuation of their liberties (15). In this, Winterer would thus squarely contradict Noah Webster, and reveal how his anti-classical stand was another of the radical and revolutionary "progressive" schemes coming out of the North in the first half of the nineteenth century. Professor Gildersleeve proclaimed that it was Harvard University that destroyed the Classics in the academy. As potent symbol of non-Southernerness in *The Sound and the Fury*, Harvard is where Quentin Compson commits suicide, dogged as he was the day of his death by the factory smokestack with a savage and peremptory mechanism for regulating the factory workers' lives. The money for tuition had come from the sale of family farmland, Benjy's pasture, now converted to a golf course.

When Faulkner described the Harvard campus in *The Sound and the Fury*, he was actually using the buildings of Yale. He had not visited Harvard but knew Yale fairly well owing to visits there to his friend Phil Stone, a Yale law student. For realism's sake, he could have set the section at Yale. That he chose to make it Harvard, however, is very significant. To him, Harvard was apparently a more appropriate symbol of the Southern-other. To him, Harvard and its intellectual history, thus represented the antithesis of his traditional South.

When Faulkner created a courthouse town for his fictional Yoknapatawpha County, he called it Jefferson, not Hamilton or Adams or Franklin. He realized that the South grew out of an agrarian classical tradition, not an urban one, and his town's name reflected the fact perfectly.

Faulkner's great-grandfather, William Clark Falkner (1825-1889), was a planter and a true colonel of the Second Mississippi Regiment, which he raised and equipped with his own money. After the Battle of Bull Run, he also raised a Confederate cavalry regiment and helped General Bedford Forrest keep the U. S. troops from burning Nashville. He was a successful farmer, and well-to-do. His second wife, Faulkner's paternal step great-grandmother, Lizzie Vance Falkner, appeared on the Faulkner plantation house steps outside Ripley, Mississippi, in June 1864, to confront Union officer Colonel DeWitt Thomas.

General Forrest's biographer, Robert Self Henry, quoting from *The Official Records of the Rebellion* (Serial No. 77, p. 171), provided details of Mrs. Falkner's interrogation by the enemy. Col. Thomas described her as "a very intelligent person...wife of Colonel Faulkner [sic] of the Rebel Service." To Thomas' inquiry, Mrs. Falkner gave misleading information that General Forrest had 28,000 men. (He actually had only 5,000.) When asked where Forrest was, she replied that the colonel would find him soon enough. U.S. Colonel Waring called the ladies of Ripley "spiteful."

When Henry published the Forrest biography in 1944, he didn't seem to know much about William Faulkner's family background, for in a footnote, he wrote that the "distinguished Mississippi novelist" was the grandson of Colonel and Mrs. W. W. Faulkner. He apparently confused Col. William Clark Falkner, Faulkner's great-grandfather, with a Colonel W. W. Faulkner of Kentucky, killed in 1865 in Dresden, Tennessee. Henry's index incorrectly listed Ripley as being in Tennessee (Henry, *First With the Most' Forrest*, 297). Col Falkner's son, J. W. T. Falkner, called the Young Colonel, was born in September 1848. He was Faulkner's grandfather and his great aunt Bama's older brother. In 1861-1862, J. W. T. Falkner would have been thirteen, the right age for Bayard Sartoris in *The Unvanquished*. Again, in the *Official Records*, Colonel DeWitt Thomas noted that Mrs. Falkner fed him breakfast at her plantation the day of his visit, a detail that also squares with the novel.

There were other important similarities. In the novel, when asked by the enemy how many troops Col. Sartoris had, a family member, like Lizzie, also inflated the number, this time in the novel by even more than Lizzie had in life.

After the U. S. troops returned and burned the Falkner plantation, Mrs. Falkner and her children fled from the plantation as refugees. They moved to the town of Ripley and Colonel Falkner is buried in a rural cemetery there. Colonel William Clark Falkner survived the war to become a railroad builder. His tombstone, topped by a life-size likeness, as

Faulkner wrote in his first Yoknapatawpha novel, *Sartoris,* shows his carved stone eyes looking out across the valley to his railroad.

Faulkner's great-grandmother on his mother Maud Butler's side, Burlina Butler, the widowed proprietor of the Oxford Inn, pleaded with invading General A. J. ("Whiskey") Smith in August 1864, to spare the hotel, which was her only source of livelihood, but as Don Doyle reported in *Faulkner's County,* Gen. Smith, in a drunken rage, "replied very sneeringly and insultingly and went on with the burning" (Doyle, 248). Other families were treated similarly. The soldiers destroyed books, clothing, and food, and stole silver and jewelry. Author A. B. Longstreet, then president of the University of Mississippi, had his correspondence and manuscripts "of forty years" burned before his eyes. Longstreet reported that when he pleaded for them, a soldier used them as tinder to set fire to Longstreet's house to make certain they did not survive if the fires did not completely burn the dwelling. Longstreet reported that his friend, Presbyterian minister, the Rev. John H. Miller, was "murdered in cold blood" (Longstreet, "From Out the Fires," *XIX Century*, 2, Dec. 1869, 544-545).

In Oxford, thirty-four stores, the courthouse, Mason Hall, two hotels, and many more private dwellings than Longstreet's were burned. A contemporary described the scene: "The Yanks have ruined this country, destroyed the corn, killed all or nearly all the stock, burned the town of Oxford entirely up" (Doyle, 249). The town was left to starve and its citizens to live in the ashes. Starvation was a real possibility.

Oxford was thus still a heap of ruins two months after Step Great-Grandmother Lizzie Falkner had fled from the Falkner plantation. The extant dramatic photograph of Oxford's stark chimneys and the shell of the Lafayette County Courthouse speaks dramatically of the devastation. The town of Ripley where Mrs. Falkner and her children were refugeeing after the Falkners' plantation house was burned and its fields laid waste, was then also pillaged and burned and all food, livestock, and crops were destroyed. What wonder that Faulkner often referred to the war as an invasion.

Faulkner's great grandfather Colonel Falkner was the model for Colonel John Sartoris in Faulkner's novels, *Flags in the Dust-Sartoris*, and *The Unvanquished.* In other words, Faulkner was very much aware that he came from the Southern plantation culture that he depicted in his fiction. That was his heritage, and his heritage was agrarian. He knew from family stories the loss of their family land, and the subsequent struggle to survive. He understood invasion; and in Japan he was not shy about using the term in linking the youth of his Reconstruction South with the youth of post Hiroshima-Nagasaki Japan.

He said to them in 1955: "My side, the South, lost that war, the battles of which were fought…in our own homes, our gardens, our farms…. Our land, our homes were invaded by a conqueror who remained after we were defeated; we were not only devastated by the battles which we lost, the conqueror spent the next ten years despoiling us of what little war had left. The victors in our war made no effort to rehabilitate and reestablish us in any community of man or of nations."[1] It is little wonder, considering today's official version of the war, that this passage is seldom quoted in studies of Faulkner because it contains the taboo word *invasion*, the word denied out of a willful historical amnesia, conveniently preserving the American sentimental myth of righteousness. Faulkner, to his credit, did not succumb to that myth and its various hypocrisies. A close knowledge of his Southern cultural inheritance had set him free of national hubris. To use Millgate's words in a different context, Faulkner unlike the mainstream American of the dominant culture, did concern himself "with anxieties about its own identity" (Millgate, Place, 77). He had major questions about the American myth of self-righteousness, and mort particularly the Northern myth of moral superiority.

In 1936, in his excellent essay for *Who Owns America?*, Donald Davidson gave a similar view of Reconstruction in the South. He wrote that in 1865, "The South was defeated and was hauled back, in the status of a subject province, into the shell of the old Union. In that condition...the South has re-mained. For from the moment of Southern defeat, the regional imperialism of the Northeast began its effective reign" (117-118).

The Confederate monument in front of the Lafayette County Courthouse has a significant place in many of Faulk-ner's works. William was well aware that his own family had a role in its erection. The story of their involvement was perti-nent to certain details in the fiction. William's grandmother, Sallie McAlpine Murry Falkner (1850-1906), was a member of the United Daughters of the Confederacy who raised funds for a monument to the University of Mississippi Greys, all of whom were either killed or wounded in Pickett's Charge at Gettysburg. Faulkner's young narrator in *Intruder in the Dust* (1948) refers to Gettysburg in a description of deep local cul-tural memory, when he says he is speaking for "every Southern boy fourteen years old," that "there is the instant when it's still not yet two o'clock on that July afternoon in 1863, the brigades are in position behind the rail fence, the guns are laid and ready in the woods and the furled flags are already loosened and ready to break out and Pickett himself...waiting for Longstreet to give the word and it's all in the balance, it hasn't happened yet....*This time. Maybe this time* with all this much to lose and all this much to gain" (194-195). In other words, his people still relive that moment at this most crucial battle of the war and regret the forlorn hope of unrealized victory. They relive the moment again and again with all its possibilities as if frozen in time.

Mrs. Sallie Falkner was a part of the minority who wanted this statue commemorating the University of Mississippi Greys to be placed in front of the courthouse and to be in honor of all the local Confederate soldiers. It was placed instead on the university campus. The soldier on this monument has his left hand shading his eyes and his musket standing by his side. Foiled in this first attempt, Mrs. Falkner then led the UDC to erect a second monument in front of the courthouse to honor all the Confederate soldiers. The soldier on top of this second column is holding his musket with both hands in front of him. In some of his novels, Faulkner placed the University Greys soldier with the shaded eyes in front of the courthouse, as his grandmother had wanted. In fiction, he was rewriting history to give his grandmother the victory. Details such as this could only be appreciated by those who had a close knowledge of the local, and the minute specifics of the history of his family in this particular place.

Faulkner sometimes called himself a failed farmer. (See, for example, the 1951 interview in *Lion in the Garden,* p. 64). He was not altogether joking when he said so. First, his family had failed at it, through no fault of their own, being burned out and dispossessed. In 1938, he purchased the 320-

acre Old Joe Parks Place seventeen miles from Oxford, and owned it until his death (Parini, 223; John Faulkner, 177; Cullen, 29). He renamed it Greenfield Farm. Professor Meriwether told me that he bought the land partly to give his brother Johnnie a place to be drunk instead of in the eye of the public on the Square, and to give tenants a livelihood during hard Depression times.[2] Parini noted the important fact that the land had once belonged to his grandfather, the Young Colonel. In other words, he was reclaiming and restoring his family's "lost territory in a literal and figurative sense" (223).

I also see it as a symbolic gesture of solidarity with not only family tradition, but also the Southern culture itself—agrarian at its base from its beginnings. It was Faulkner's choice of staying and casting his lot with the central Jeffersonian tradition of his region. He was reestablishing his family's lost ties to the land and reclaiming their agrarian heritage.

As well, and perhaps even more importantly, Faulkner was identifying with the forms and codes of a landed gentry whose roots lay deep in Britain, from which his family came to the New World. In the failed farmer interview of 1951, Faulkner stated further, "I like silence. Silence and horses. And trees" (*Lion*, 64). The perceptive interviewer noted that this was "the only moment when pride touches the thoughtful, sensitive face." As Cleanth Brooks has stated in his important treatment of the similarities between Yeats and Faulkner, their honoring of an "aristocratic" land-based view of man stemmed not from caste and wealth but the codes of virtue, responsibility, self-discipline, honor, stewardship of the land, courage, graciousness, intelligence, and hospitality. These traits were the legacy of the squirearchy, when the squirearchy was at its best (Brooks, *Toward Yoknapatawpha*, 333-4). What wonder that we have left to us photographs of Faulkner mounted in riding habit on the grounds of Rowan Oak and on horseback in his last years in Virginia wearing a rider's formal silk top hat.

His first crops at Greenfield Farm were hay, cotton, and corn. He bred horses and raised, oversaw, and helped in the butchering of hogs. The farm was mule-powered. Faulkner knew mules and horses well. In *The Reivers,* he astutely contrasted their natures. According to Professor Meriwether, he had learned to love horses in his father's livery stable[3] and always kept two or three horses at Rowan Oak. To defray expenses, he raised some of their feed at the farm. He jumped horses up until his death. It was the mule he respected most, however. He understood hunting dogs and riding to the hounds—and particularly admired the courageous little mixed-breed dog called a fyce (*feist* in Upcountry South Carolina dialect). When Faulkner's daughter Jill married and moved to Charlottesville, she inherited her father's love of riding to the hounds. At one time, she held the position of "Mistress of the Hounds"—no small honor among the horsey set.

In restoring the land as a good steward, he planted trees on the hilly slopes. Faulkner loved and respected trees. He complained passionately when a magnolia tree was cut down in Oxford. When he bought the old Shegog place, one of the first things he did was plant four Rowan (ash) trees at the plot's four corners. He named the place after these trees.

Faulkner's critics and biographers often take Faulkner's "failed farmer" tag lightly and use this as an example of his humor, but I feel his Greenfield Farm purchase was very significant. It reveals a great deal about the man. Faulkner rightly identified the South with tilling the soil, and he was making his stand on that cultural base and the land-based codes before enumerated. That choice is a very serious choice if one knows and takes Southern culture itself seriously. If a person does not take the South seriously, he probably does not take Faulkner's choice seriously. This is why he can make light of it as a quaint gesture. I take Southern agrarian roots very seriously, so I regard Faulkner's choice to be not a pose or a joke, but something that had deep meaning for him, and properly so. Perhaps Wendell Berry has given a clue to that meaning. Berry writes, "To farm is to be *placed* absolutely."[4] That is a far different concept from the urban mindset of most academics who go where the job is. It is more likely that most of them agree with Karl Marx who spoke of "the idiocy of rural life."

We can gauge Faulkner's seriousness about a devotion to the soil of a particular home place by considering the section of *The Unvanquished* in which characters Bayard and Ringo barter for the snuff box of soil taken from the Sartoris Plantation that they have been forced to leave in front of invading troops. Granny has brought rose cuttings in her flight from the troops, hoping to reestablish them in whatever new home she is forced to live. The roses will be a tangible link to the place from which she has been uprooted. Stopping in their flight, the lads watch her water the cuttings at a spring and notice that there is a little soil still clinging to the roots. Bayard notices Ringo pinching off some of the dirt and putting it in his pocket. Feeling a little ashamed, he says, "I reckon I can save dirt if I want to," he says.

But Bayard has brought a snuff box of what he calls *true* Sartoris dirt, the soil where the two had made their play-landscape of Vicksburg and the embattled South. In discussing Faulkner and race, the critic misses this important scene, which to me says very loudly that Faulkner felt that both races are Southern and if they share the same love of place, they both belong to it. The ties that bind them are thus stronger than the difference in skin color that separates them. Ringo, watching

56

Bayard and the snuff box closely, says, "You brung a lot of hit," to which Bayard replies, "Yes, I brung enough to last" (62-63). Bayard then shares half of his true Sartoris soil with Ringo. To me, this is one of the most touching scenes in Faulkner.

Yes, I brought enough to last. If I had to choose a single sentence in Faulkner's writing that would go to the heart of his canon, I think this would be a good candidate. Young Bayard, Ringo, and all Southerners burned out by invasion and cut off from their farming roots, were going to require plenty deep remembrances of that lost familial soil to strengthen resolve and shore up the displaced and battered person torn from his or her cultural moorings. That knowledge was to be a key to retaining personal identity in the disorientation of trauma and a subsequent life in a time of chaos, alienation and deracination—those key words in describing Modernism.

Matthew Arnold's "struggle on the darkling plain" would be too tame a term to describe what many displaced and dispossessed Southerners in Faulkner's fiction had to endure. As the plight of Molly's grandson shows in *Go Down, Moses,* both races, but particularly the African American, had much to lose when the stabilizing ties and associations of place and family are snapped. The grandson is executed far from home for crimes he committed on the streets of Detroit. Molly makes certain he is brought home at last, for burial in Mississippi soil.

A traditionalist rooted in place and faced with the loss of it understands the poignancy of the passage in *The Unvanquished*. It is too moving not to have been felt by its author. So, we might rightly call Faulkner a son of the agrarian culture who valued it deeply. He understood the spiritual tie to the soil of his family's fields. It has been said that for the white South, the great Southern story is the loss of the plantation. If so, Faulkner tells it many times in many works, and the telling always has the ring of truth because he experienced it.

In that amazingly accurate historical novel *Gone With the Wind*, Gerald O'Hara teaches his daughter Scarlett this same lesson about the soil of Tara—the only thing that matters, the only thing "worth working for, fighting for, dying for," "the only thing in the world that lasts."[5] House servant, Elnora, in Faulkner's short story "There Was a Queen" understands well the difference between transients like the town folk and the landed gentry of and on the soil. She sniffs at Narcissa Benbow and her town ways and says with withering scorn and disdain: "Town trash!" For the Southern plantation culture, "town trash" is about as low as it gets. One is reminded of Southern author Havilah Babcock's declaration, "It ought to be against the law to let a boy grow up in a city" (*Best of Babcock*, 10).

Faulkner's fiction shows that he understood the cultural difference between town trash and the better classes of rural people. The story's ending proves that Elnora was correct about Narcissa, who chooses the sham show of respectability over honor and true virtue. On that subject, Elnora defines nobility this way: "Quality ain't *is*; it's *does*."[6] Faulkner no doubt agreed with Elnora, and with Thomas Jefferson before her. Aristocracy is a matter of character, and virtue best and more often resides with those who till the soil. Faulkner likely would also have agreed with Southern agrarian author Ben Robertson in his Upcountry South Carolina classic *Red Hills and Cotton* that in the traditional Southern culture, success is the *how* and not the *how much* of achievement.[7]

When not at Greenfield Farm and confined to town, Faulkner was both a keen vegetable and flower gardener. His brother Murry records how his brother, who did not tolerate most machines, was delighted with the gift of a motorized garden tiller. His tilling of soil was thus accomplished on both the large and small scales. Few major Southern writers have had such an intimate first-hand relationship with the soil and growing things.

Again in 1997 Fred Chappell listed one of the traits of the modern Southern poet: "a refusal to jettison rural topics" and to treat country folk, their language, and their folkways admiringly, or at least with respect and without the smug superiority of the local colorist interested in the quaint and picturesque.[8]

Perhaps John Cullen said it best in 1961 in writing about Greenfield Farm: Faulkner "keeps the farm because he likes the country, because he likes to see things grow and wishes to think of himself as a farmer" (49). Cullen, who knew him as well as anyone, took Faulkner's farming seriously. Whether or not he made money at it was incidental, Cullen said. Faulkner built a little one-room "office" there on the farm with his own hands, where he wrote in sight of his fields—the ploughed furrows of a working farm. Recognizing the significance of that fact would be a basic first crucial step in understanding Faulkner's fiction, the view of man this fiction presents, and the very man himself who wrote that fiction and held those views. He was not a man divorced from the land. He did not suffer from what has been called our modern machine culture's Nature Deficit Syndrome.

Faulkner's brother John agreed with Cullen in saying that Faulkner "had been a lot of different things in his life, ...but he always liked farmers and farming." Faulkner's daughter Jill commented, "Pappy loved horses, and he loved farming, and this was a way of bringing these two loves together" (Parini, 223). John Faulkner also noted that "Bill found more than just a farm out there. He found the kind of people he wrote about, hill people. They made their own whiskey from their own corn and didn't see why that could be anybody else's business" (John Faulkner, *My Brother Bill*, 177).

Perhaps Faulkner was thus not a *failed* farmer after all. If the proper definition of a farm is a place that feeds people, Faulkner's farm did so successfully. According to Cullen, who visited there often, it fed both those on the farm and provided occasional produce for the Faulkner family in town. Faulkner, to his credit, never fell into the trap of agro-industry or agribusiness and their wasteful and destructive methods in order to wrench the most profits from the soil and at its expense. He stayed true to the ideals of Jefferson, who wrote the Reverend James Madison on 28 October 1785, "The small landholders are the most precious part of a state." As Faulkner watched the rhythms of the seasons and fell in line with the gait of mules in the furrows, he was still a true farmer receiving from the soil more than a commercial livelihood. To me, that would qualify him as not just a farmer, but a successful one.

Faulkner's first published book was a collection of poems. He began his writing career as a poet. Chappell, in his collection of essays entitled *Plough Naked,* speaks of the origins of writing itself. *Verse*, he explains, comes from the turn of the plough at the end of the row. Anyone who has had the privilege of ploughing understands the relationship of the activity with seeing the ink spread across the page, stop, turn, and run again. The rhythm of ploughing was indeed a good elemental activity for Faulkner to watch from his writing office at Greenfield as his pen moved across the page.

Faulkner was neither what Wendell Berry calls a sweatless agrarian nor what others like Faulkner's friend Phil Stone named an armchair farmer. He was not a farmer in the abstract. His feet touched the soil. In our next chapter "Abstraction as Nemesis," Faulkner qualifies once again as centrally Southern in his refusal to replace reality with the disembodied idea.

It is fitting that today Greenfield Farm is still a small farm and is not swallowed up by a housing development, golf course, or an out-of-state mega-agri-industrial concern.

THREE

ABSTRACTION AS NEMESIS

> "The cold in clime are cold in blood."
> —Lord Byron, *The Giaour*

Indeed, Faulkner was no abstractionist. His concreteness of thought and language came from a long-standing intimacy with the land and a particular place. As seen in the previous chapter, he was close to the soil. Then the constant flow of family reminiscence and local tales of characters and events had consequences too. He learned much about human nature that way. Most traditional Southerners learn through talk. Theirs is not a Modernist society of isolated, alienated individuals who avoid eye contact and all that unfortunate habit represents of an inbred fear of human interaction. Theirs has never been a virtual reality.

The man-in-the-mass as idea or statistic was not Faulkner's concern. His essays detailed that he approached humanity on individual terms. For Faulkner, the individual is always sacred. His fiction shows it and many of his essays and speeches declare it unequivocally. In fact, almost all of them touch in one way or another on the topic. (See for example, *Essays,* 62, 66, 70-71, 147, 161-165.) Here Faulkner declared that the writer's key worth is to preserve the individual, to keep him human and not an idea. He continued that the writer's duty is "to save the individual from anonymity" (*Essays*, 165.) On this subject, Louis Rubin, a Charleston-born author and critic who made a life-long study of the region, accurately declared in 1979 in an essay "The South's Writers," that the Southern author has "a bias in favor of the individual, the concrete, the unique, even the exaggerated and outlandish in human portraiture."[1]

Author Julia Peterkin at Lang Syne Plantation in Calhoun County, South Carolina, declared in 1929 that in her rural community "Individuals are few, so each one counts for much."[2] That is a particularly apt way of saying that the Southerner is not desensitized by the crush of crowds into an abstractionism created out of necessity as a defense mechanism and a means to retreat from the world.

Critic and philosopher Richard Weaver understood this about Southern writers as representative of a Southern way of thinking, seeing, and living. He said that Southerners rarely attach to any abstractionist *ism* or *ology*. They do not abstract man into easy formulae (Weaver, 73.) As Chappell put it so effectively, they "refuse to theorize."[3] A Southern author myself, I can relate that one reason is that all theories are subject to change. All *isms* and *ologies* come and go, only to be replaced by other faddish *isms* and *ologies*. Southern writers, with their intimate knowledge of a long past, are preternaturally likely to have the long view which makes all the current rages look small-minded and myopic. A section of Andrew Lytle's essay collection, *From Eden to Babylon,* bears the title "The Long View." Strongly relying on Weaver's work, Eugene Genovese recently put it this way: antebellum Southerners "distrusted ideological nostrums and placed their reliance in a human experience that taught men to accommodate to natural law. From that natural law...human beings equip themselves with timeless moral truths that provide the standards for social life" (Genovese, 23-24.) Yes, indeed!

Faulkner is a very good case in point. One would never call him a determinist, a Marxist, a populist, an existentialist, a naturalist, a dada-ist, a feminist, a modernist, or a postmodernist. He may have dabbled for a time in one or the other, but never subscribed to any. That is not to say he did not understand theories or movements. He simply chose not to limit himself by embracing them as abstracts. As a result, he never fits comfortably into any category, and Weaver found that resistance to labeling to be centrally Southern and one measure of the greatness of the South's best writers.

As is often the case, we may look to the antebellum Southern writer, William Gilmore Simms, as an early corollary. He had a running war against the fanatical embracing of *isms* and *ologies*, especially as he saw those Northern authors who gloried in them. The antebellum North was an era of enthusiasms and fanaticisms, and the Southerner regarded the region as a strange and disturbing land. The Puritan zealotry of their background had now morphed into fanatical secular crusades. He described transcendentalists' vilification of the Puritans as leading to what he termed "Mamonism" (Charleston *Mercury,* 16 June 1859). Today we would likely term it secular humanism or something akin to Marxist-style social justice. The "Burned-over" districts of New York, a region looked on with disdain by conservative, old-fashioned James Fennimore Cooper, was a place of every conceivable *ism.* These Cooper said were imported from New England with hordes of settlers from Massachusetts and had run like wildfire across the country. The *isms* included socinianism, communism, fourieritism (forerunner of feminism), Mormonism, and abolitionism, to name only a few.

The recent collection of Simms's selected reviews and criticisms has traced the history of this central anti-*ology* aspect of his philosophy. Simms felt literature should be for all time. He felt that it transcends factions, intransigent ideology, polemics, the fanaticisms of various reforms, and the distortion of abstractionist oversimplification. Simms's reviews often took authors to task for betraying art by pushing various pet *isms* and *ologies* and thereby making the particularities of life and character into vague and flat generalities. The introduction to Simms's *Selected Reviews* is appropriately entitled "Literature's Long View."

In his October 1849 review of James Russell Lowell's *A Fable for Critics,* Simms wrote that Boston seemed to be the center of the schools of faddish programs. He wrote of Bostonians:

> They have a school of teachers, possessing large popularity, intense self-esteem, and considerable ingenuity, who, with new *isms* and *ologies* daily, will some day strive to throw down all their altars of belief. Were they a more inflammable race, with smaller [phrenological] bumps of caution, we might look for the advent among them of a Goddess of Reason, and a Reign of Terror, not imperfectly modeled upon those of the French (Simms, *Selected Reviews*, 98).

Simms concluded that were they not such thorough materialists and hedonists, "we should, in all probability, very soon behold a Temple of Reason in Boston, usurping that of Jesus Christ" (Simms, *Selected Reviews*, 98). Simms knew that this had happened in Paris during the French Revolution. In his reviews of the works of Longfellow, Emerson, and other New England worthies throughout the 1840s and 1850s, Simms also found didacticism and abstraction to be deep flaws in their literary practice. He declared that philosophy was "inferior to poetry in the discovery of truth" (Charleston *Mercury,* 20 February 1856). He felt this Northern propensity for abstraction and philosophizing to be the root cause of "the bookish coldness of New England letters" (Simms, *Selected Reviews*, 100). He rightly declared that Northern poets could compose no verse without philosophizing and preaching with tidy little moral tags.

Of the North, Simms wrote in 1837, "I am heartily tired of this region. It is physically and morally a cold one" (*Letters,* 1, 113). In 1838, he called the Yankee way "a mercantile and money-loving condition of things" (Kibler, "Prophetic Muse," 110). Throughout the canon of his reviews of New England authors, he used the words "cold," "cold-blooded," "frigid," "inflexible," "rigid in forms," and "arrogantly aloof" to describe the typical Northern materialistic manner (Simms, *Selected Reviews*, 25).

A century later, in 1933, Faulkner wrote at the height of his powers as a creative genius that the proper author is not the "cold intellect that can write with calm and complete detachment" (*Essays*, 292.) He declared that it is this kind of cold, intellectual clinical detachment that produces still-born fiction. Ever the one to phrase the idea succinctly and memorably, Chappell said of modern Southern poets: they turn *cerebration* into *celebration.* He continued that Southern poets do not write sociology tracts (Chappell address, 14 May 1997.)

On the same subject, Eudora Welty wrote an excellent essay, "Why the Writer Shouldn't Crusade." Here she said that many authors outside the South have sold their birthright for a pot of message. She placed the great writer and the crusader on "opposite sides." Restating her warning that the writer should not crusade in literature, she proclaimed that in fiction "generalities" and abstractions obscure truth, "for there is absolutely everything in fiction but a clear answer." She concluded, "Humanity seems to mean more to the novelist than what humanity thinks it can prove" (148-149). In his 1936 essay, "Literature as a Symptom," in *Who Owns America?,* Robert Penn Warren declared that the writer should not be political and have no party or agenda. He wrote that the good writer differed from the Marxist, Proletarian writer, whose aim was the future and was essentially propagandistic—to persuade to action or reform (272).

Another reason that G. K. Chesterton felt an affinity with the traditionalist South is made clear in his *Orthodoxy.* Here he declared, "The modern is not the man who has lost his reason, but has lost everything but his reason." Southern authors took their stand against "Mamonism" by making a distinction between America and the South. They distinguished the two by saying that in America, we speak of a standard of living, in the South, a standard of faith.

In 1960, Flannery O'Connor in "Some Aspects of the Grotesque in Southern Fiction," declared that the "Southern writer is forced…to make his gaze extend beyond…mere problems, until it touches that realm which is the concern of prophets…to keep for fiction some of its freedom from social determinism" (Collected Works, 818). She declared that the Southern writer instead of being a guide to topical reforms must be "the realist of distances" (819). By that she meant not of abstracts, but of the long view and the universals. She concluded that the novelist "must be characterized not by his function [as guide, crusader, and reformer] but by his vision" (Collected Works, 819).

The 2021 PBS "American Masters" remake of their documentary on O'Connor totally misses the point. The writers in fact dance around the real question with their view that O'Connor regrettably refused to meet with James Baldwin when he visited Georgia. They still attempt to make O'Connor into a critic of Southern racial attitudes, thus conveniently ignoring the rude son Julian of "Everything That Rises Must Converge" who with his cold and cruel attitudes to his "racist" mother causes her death. One notes that on the bus ride, O'Connor portrays Julian hiding behind a newspaper and "Behind the newspaper Julian was withdrawing into the inner compartment of his mind where he spent most of his time" (491). More often than not, any of her crusaders are portrayed as cold abstractionists who are good at only one thing—hatred and hating. Their hatred usually also entails hating themselves.

The list of these self-hating intellectual abstractionists who reject all but the idea of the world are legion: for example, Julian, Hulga in "Good Country People," the unnamed "ugly girl" in the doctor's office in "Revelation," and the do-gooding Sheppard in "The Lame Shall Enter First," whose fixation on saving a handicapped black juvenile delinquent, causes the suicide of his own son through neglect and abuse. Perhaps the most significant of these is the reclusive, over-educated, artist-dilettante Asbury Fox in "The Enduring Chill," whose coldness dooms him. For him, the dove of the Holy Ghost etched in ice with an icicle in its mouth refuses to descend to him. One is unkindly tempted to wonder if the writers of the PBS documentary were blind to the ways that these unfortunate characters are mirror-images of themselves. She certainly gets uncomfortably close to the truth.

For Welty, Warren, and O'Connor, like Faulkner, the author's birthright is far nobler than secularist crusading. For Faulkner, most especially, that birthright entailed keeping the *vision* of the whole man and woman intact—not going down the dead-end road of coldly analyzing a particular piece of fragmented psyche according to some theory. Essentially, then, we have been saying that these Southern writers all had the long view.

Weaver wrote that this vision of the whole man involves seeing him as glory, jest, and riddle—in his dual nature of both the angelic (capable of great good) and the fallen (capable of great evil) (*Southern Essays*, 70-73). He declared that evil for the great majority of Southern writers is found to be inherent in the nature of man rather than as external stimulus. The external stimulus school believes man has no free moral choice. So-called evil is only the product of economic and social forces, often with a bit of chance thrown in. Adjust the environment, then, and you do away with evil, which really doesn't exist any way. Politicians and social workers become secular priests in this way of thinking, and today that has become the paradigm in all the secular world, and even in a large part of the realm of organized religion. Faulkner would be horrified but not surprised. He had predicted it in fact, as we will see, in a discussion of his essays in the final chapters.

Once again, as described in our first chapter, most Southern writers have been out of step with the times, and thus outsiders in the National Eye. Their attitude toward evil clearly relegates writers like Faulkner and Flannery O'Connor to the "other." For them, Satan never sleeps and evil walks and has a face and a name. Evil is based both without and within, in the flawed nature of man. Understanding this view is an essential first step in knowing Faulkner and attaching him to his cultural hearth. James Cantrell in his brilliant recent analysis of Southern literature's Celtic foundation noted one trait often missing in the lists of traits that make a work Southern: a "spirituality that is often manifested in a recognition of the presence of evil in the world" (Cantrell, 83). As Simms wrote in his novel *Woodcraft* (1852-1854), "the devil is always at our elbow" and "hangs upon our footsteps" (410).

To see man in the Southern way, then, is thus to save the writer from attaching to various easy fashionable *isms* and *ologies*, and what Weaver called the partial, the "incomplete" view of man (69). Weaver continued that one of the chief strengths of Southern writing is that Southern authors have not been afraid to portray monsters capable of monstrous evil and that these writers deal squarely with sin (67). Weaver wrote, "one of the great merits of contemporary Southern literature is that it has faced the problem of sin." He went on to discuss Southern literature's portrayal of monsters (69).

"The denial of evil," Weaver wrote, "is a very great heresy" (52). Faulkner again is a good example. Simms in the nineteenth century is another. We could also quickly name twentieth-century authors, O'Connor, Warren, Davidson, Tate, Lytle, Elizabeth Roberts, Walker Percy, Foote, Caroline Gordon, Madison Jones, Cormac McCarthy, Harry Crews,

Katharine Anne Porter, Larry Brown, George Garrett, Barry Hannah, and a host of others.

Flannery O'Connor in fact made a pointed remark that applies centrally here: "What has given the South her identity" are "a distrust of the abstract…and a knowledge that evil is not simply a problem to be solved, but a mystery to be endured" (*Mystery and Manners,* 209). No *ism* can explain evil away. No abstraction can take away its lethalness and power to destroy. As most wise traditionalist Southerners understand, Satan uses man to destroy, but at the same time is destroying the destroyer, for Satan has no favorites.

As Weaver related, if man has no free moral choice in life's struggle between good and evil, then tragedy is not possible and literature is crippled, hamstrung from the start. That is why Southern literature with its frank dealing with evil can reach the plane of a *Macbeth* or *Lear.* That is why Simms in 1870 rightly saw himself to be a spiritual brother to Æschylus.[4] Without the ability to choose, life becomes abstract indeed. Man becomes only a case study of a type, a statistic, a victim, or a pawn—a passive creature buffeted by forces over which he has no control. In this severely diminished view of the world, the writer's primary duty is to change environment to do away with evil. Given that philosophy, crusading via the sociology tract is as good a way as any.

Weaver, like Faulkner, felt that preserving this complex view of the whole man in both his glory and his degradation was a way to preserve his humanity against easy sentiment and abstract simplification. For Weaver, that was the key reason Southern writers cohered as a group and made them celebrated worldwide. He declared that measured by the world's standards, it was the Southerner who was part of the norm and his American literary counterpart was the aberration—the abnormal one outside the pale (72). Weaver declared that it is the Southern writer who has reclaimed the great subjects of Western literature. This philosophy was responsible for Allen Tate's saying that we Southerners were the last Europeans, there being no Europeans left in Europe today.

Weaver emphasized the "riddle" aspect of the Southern writer's portrayal of man. A Southern humorist from the 1850s put it nicely. He has a rustic character say, "Human natur', Doc, is more amazin' than the seasins."[5] Southern writers say that one never can quite figure man out or pin him down with an *ology*. He never fits neatly into any convenient Skinner Box. He is a constant surprise that no science or pseudoscience can quite explain.

The Southern writer like Faulkner has thus been faithful to the view of man as glory, jest, and riddle, and there could be no better, improved, progressive version thereof. This has been and remains a priceless heritage to the Southern author.

The so-called Enlightenment that led to and relied upon the creation of *isms* might be deemed so much "Endarkenment." Homer, Horace, Vergil, and Aeschylus already knew that about the nature of man, and as such are Faulkner's contemporaries. Southern writers have often said that to them that is the only contemporaneity that matters. Two good current examples are Fred Chappell and Wendell Berry.

Faulkner understood clearly however that books in general, even the best, have their limitations. In *The Hamlet* he distinguished between a Southern and a Northern way of approaching the world. To do so, he used as subject, the homely goat. A Northerner comes to Yoknapatawpha to create a goat ranch but fails. His method for creating the operation was to first read a book on goats. Faulkner's rural Southerners had a simple solution. First get goats. Knowing goat nature, these locals believed that a goat farmer should work with nature and let nature take the lead. Goat nature would take it from there and solve the problem. As in so many things for the traditional Southerner, abstraction often kills.

The Northern and Southern divide relative to abstraction likely stemmed from the influence in the North of New England Puritanism, a way of life based on speculative abstraction. In the vast cousinage of Faulkner's world, reality was anchored in kinship, in flesh and blood, and individuals.

On 10 March 1988 I was privileged to witness a scene which clearly demonstrated regional differences on the subject of abstraction. It involved a Pulitzer Prize winning neo-abolitionist historian recently come South from Massachusetts and my friend Shelby Foote. The Honors Program at this Southern university had invited Mr. Foote to give an address, and the university was honoring him with a dinner. The director of the Honors Program, the president of the university, himself a recent transplant, the famous historian, and several university deans were present. I had not been invited, although I had helped get my friend to come. Upon the insistence of Mr. Foote, I was invited at the last minute.

The historian sat at the university president's right hand, I sat next to my friend. Both Mr. Foote and I were quiet, he most especially. The president had been on a "pro-active" mission to recruit African American students. The historian and he were excitedly discussing numbers and percentages getting more excited as they declared what totals they might reach—at a minimum the same percentage of the state's African American population. They debated what figure that was. The conversation did not let up and the excitement grew to a frenzy.

I felt how rude they were to ignore their guest of honor. Our eyes met several times in the mildly shocked recognition of this, until Mr. Foote finally asserted his presence by declaring how "uncomfortable" he was with the conversation, not because it was loud and rude, but because they were only talking figures and abstracts and forgetting the human element. They were dealing with numbers and not people. As I recall, in the slow Delta rhythms of his voice, he was quietly but forcefully eloquent.

One might expect those criticized would have felt sufficiently rebuffed to change the topic so as to include the rest of the dinner guests, but they did not. They returned to their abstractions. I looked at Mr. Foote. Without saying a word, we communicated that they were a lost cause, such was the intensity of their continuing dialogue. We ate our rubber chicken.

It is also pertinent to this chapter to note that this same Pulitzer Prize winning abstractionist historian from our dinner drama, in an address before a state historical society some years later, declared angrily in his zealotry that Confederate babies "should have been smothered in their cradle." Such is the end result of cold abstraction that lends credence to this chapter's overarching theme that Southern writers like Faulkner felt that abstraction kills—in this case most literally.

FOUR

THE BEST OF ALL TELLING: FAULKNER, THE

RACONTEUR

In *A Talent for Living* (2006), Southern literary and cultural historian, Barbara Bellows, saw that another connection between the Irish Literary Renaissance and the Southern "was the importance of language as a means of resistance to the modern forces of standardization" and "language, not mere accent, had long been considered one of the South's defining cultural traits." She declared that both cultures "treasured raconteurs." Bellows quoted Oscar Wilde's statement that the Irish "were the greatest talkers since the Greeks" (Bellows, 64-65). Bellows went on to cite Louisa S. McCord's criticism of Stowe's *Uncle Tom's Cabin* on many accounts, including "her Southern ladies and gentlemen talk rather vulgar Yankee-English" (65).

One of the most recognizable traits of the literature of the South is its oral quality. We see this most readily in the Old South frontier humorists like A. B. Longstreet, T. B. Thorpe, William Tappan Thompson, and George Washington Harris, and on to William Gilmore Simms and Mark Twain, down through Faulkner, Zora Neal Hurston, Welty, Lytle, and O'Connor, to today's best writers, Larry Brown, Harry Crews,

Cormac McCarthy, Wendell Berry, Fred Chappell, George Garrett, Barry Hannah, and others. Louis Rubin in listing this as a "distinctive" Southern literary trait, phrased it nicely as "a story telling bent, as compared with a concern for problems" (Rubin, "Changing, Enduring," 226).

This oral quality allows use of the local speech and breathes life into the page. There is kinetic energy in the language. Here again we see the results of Faulkner's choice not to be that "cold intellect" with clinical detachment standing aloof above his subject to abstract the world into ideas, *isms,* and *ologies.* Southern novelist George Garrett's *New York Times* obituary of 30 May 2008 singled out what reviewers of Garrett's works all agreed upon: that his works exhibited a "rapt attention to the sound of the voice."

In 1962, despite his praise of the power and energy of the imaginative folk language of George Washington Harris's *Sut Lovingood,* Northern critic, Edmund Wilson, was totally unsympathetic to Sut, whom he called "a peasant squatting in his own filth," "all that was lowest in the lowest of the South," "a malignant Tennessee 'Cracker,'" and a "dreadful, half-bestial lout" (*Patriotic Gore,* 507-17). As we have seen, Wilson was a prime example of the Northern establishment authors, editors, and academics who placed such Southern writers as Harris "outside the pale." Wilson's genteel sensibilities matched the genteel Brahmin caste whose members published

80

and puffed themselves and those like them. Wilson and his circle constituted the mid-twentieth-century American managerial literary in-group elite with its own brand of cancel culture.

Whereas both Faulkner and Mark Twain praised Harris's book, Wilson declared it to be the "most repellant" work he had ever encountered. Another of the reasons for what amounts to be righteous indignation bordering on hatred, was no doubt that Harris slew a lot of sacred American cows like the descendants of the Mayflower Puritans, pretentious and prissy New York sophisticates, effeminate New York dandies, "he-wimmen" Northern feminists, Wall Street hucksters, and greedy and ignorant Yankee merchants, to name only a few. Perhaps even Harris's worst offense was his hilarious treatment of "Old Abe Linkhorn" in *High Times and Hard Times*— a series of satires that makes Mark Twain seem tame and pale by comparison. Wilson called Sut's trenchant satire of Lincoln (a figure who must qualify as the most sacred of the sacred American cows) "not a satire" but a "libel." One indication of Mark Twain's eventual selling out to the Eastern Establishment of his day was his refusal to touch the idol into which Lincoln was being made. To his credit, Harris never sold out.

Faulkner, a great admirer of the language of Sut, the narrator of Harris's *Yarns*, commented very clearly on this point about oral narrative in 1933. About Southern writers, he was specific: "To talk, to tell" is our way, "since oratory is our

81

heritage" (*Essays*, 292). On another occasion, Faulkner declared that his style was the product of the twin marriages of the traditions of Southern-Rhetoric-and-Solitude, and Southern-Oratory-and Solitude (Blotner, *Letters*, 215-216).

What we know of Faulkner's Great Aunt Bama, Alabama Leroy Falkner (1874-1968) as keeper of the family story that she passed on to him by *telling* is pertinent here. Aunt Bama was the youngest child of the Old Colonel W. C. Falkner himself (1825-1889) and had long first-hand memories back to the fabled times. She died at the age of ninety-four and outlived William by six years. Faulkner always saw her as the unsung source of family continuity.

We also know from Faulkner's hunting buddy John Cullen that he went on long deer hunts largely for the stories told around the campfire. Cullen declared that the stories of the old hunters "are often the source of his tales." In this way Faulkner is indeed very close to the backwoods humor genre, for tales of hunting exploits are a key influence and comprise a big portion of the genre's canon. Cullen declared of Faulkner that in camp, "He always does more listening than talking." Cullen related that Faulkner in fact was always more of a listener than a talker, "even in grade school" (Cullen, 13, 15). Similarly, it is said that he visited the Memphis bawdy houses to sit downstairs and listen to the stories.[1] The novel *Sanctuary* lends credence to this assertion. Faulkner's fabled reticence likely stemmed from his habit of attentive listening to feed his art, for he no doubt knew that keen and careful observation was its primary source. One might say of him what was said of Flannery O'Connor: he was "as laconic as Cooledge." Like her, he was an excellent listener.

One might say of Faulkner's fiction that it is "the best of all telling." That is Faulkner's own phrase from *Go Down, Moses* for the stories of the hunt camp. The object of his art is to present life in all its concreteness and vitality. The reader hears the sound of the voice from the page. Southern writing is very much like Irish writing in that way. Cleanth Brooks declared that to both Yeats and Faulkner, "there was available an oral tradition—a fountain of living speech" (Brooks, *Toward Yoknapatawpha,* 339). Both the Celtic and the Southern way is usually a world apart from the tight-lipped and understated bookish English or New English manner. Yeats said it best: "It is through the dialect that one escapes from abstract words, back to the sensation inspired directly by the thing itself."[2] Yeats's aim was, as he said, "bringing all back to syntax that is for ear alone."[3] Faulkner and Joyce's celebrated stream of consciousness style is simply the mind talking on the page—a Shakespearean monologue writ large and long. Even there in the mind's associative meanderings, we have the force of strong narrative. We hear it rather than read it.

It has often been observed as a truism that the South's people are talkers, talkers more than readers. Julia Peterkin wrote in 1929 of the country store near her Lang Syne Plantation: "Printed words are scarce and so spoken words are all the more precious. News has to be passed on, old tales retold, present problems discussed and measured by old-fashioned wisdom. For old fashions are still in style here" (Peterkin, 12). In 1978, Cleanth Brooks concluded that the Southern "art of telling a tale is still very much alive" (*Toward Yoknapatawpha,* 339). Get Southerners together and trying to get a word in edgewise might often be impossible, for that is the nature of a gregarious, garrulous, and convivial society in which neighborliness, friendliness, and hospitality are more than just habits. A Southerner might say that these might in fact constitute an eleventh commandment.

Telling and *talking* are more than entertainment, though entertaining they usually are, and particularly when practiced by a teller skilled in the art. As Brooks observed, the South, like Ireland, is a land of talkers, and both always has had more than their share of excellent story tellers.

We Southerners tell stories out of many impulses and for many reasons. We tell stories to entertain. We tell stories in times of crisis to try to make sense of the incomprehensible and to make an attempt at explaining the unexplainable, usually all the time knowing it will be a failed attempt. We tell stories to create a pattern out of confusion—to get at least a tenuous hold on things we know we will never completely understand. We tell stories to console and comfort. We tell stories to capture character and human nature, to understand our families and friends, and maybe ourselves, in order to strengthen communal bonds, and to pass on values and what is important for whatever future there will be, to know about and from us. In these ways, stories are gifts from the teller woven out of his or her memory, experience, character, creativity, and the collective memory of his or her community. And as Faulkner phrased it, we also tell stories to put our "Kilroy was here" on the wall of oblivion (*Lion,* 252).

In his Nobel Acceptance Speech, Faulkner said he did not believe in the nuclear annihilation of man. What would be left over after a nuclear blast when everything else was gone was man's "puny inexhaustible voice, still talking"—still telling stories no doubt of what had just happened, trying to make sense of it—for the now and for a future (*Essays,* 120). In Faulkner's declaration, we have the plot, situation, and theme of Cormac McCarthy's recent novel *The Road.* From what we know of Southern garrulity and Faulkner's recognition of it, Faulkner no doubt concluded that the puny inexhaustible voice would have a Southern accent.

The passage in the Nobel speech could be viewed as Faulkner's saying that the necessary survivor would be a talker, a tale-teller required for mankind's survival as humans. If so, Faulkner felt that it is the oral narrator of Southern literary tradition who is the pillar and prop to help man endure and prevail—or at least it will be a talker from a future generation who has learned the Southern wisdom and way of telling from the culture that produced Faulkner.

I think Faulkner coded that message in his speech in faraway Sweden as an undercurrent of meaning for his own Southern people—and I wonder how many of his fellow Southerners have caught it. He traveled out of Mississippi to address the world, but also had his eye on home. Faulkner coded much in his fiction for a Southern audience—things he knew would be lost on the non-Southern reader. That is the way of subversive writing after all. If one is considered to be on the cultural margins or the "lunatic fringe" and "outside the pale" like a Sut Lovingood or other cancel culture victims, he or she has to get published, after all, and hopefully without selling out like a Mark Twain.

Southern readers of Faulkner must learn to be on the lookout for the coded words and phrases meant for his Southern readers. It is helpful to consider the fact that there are often two story lines running simultaneously for two audiences. There is a local undercurrent of meaning beneath the majority mainstream one. Perceptive as always, Cleanth Brooks was onto this in his sensitive common-sense reading of the fiction in his *William Faulkner: Toward Yoknapatawpha*. Once again, he saw close similarities between Faulkner and Irish writers who had to make their way in an essentially foreign, sometimes antagonistic environment.

Perhaps taking his lead from Cleanth Brooks, Professor Millgate suggested that Faulkner had two voices in his fiction, one for his regional audience, and one for his non-Southern, non-rural readers (Millgate, *Place*, 79). The result was thus a nuanced double line of narration. Unfortunately, Millgate, as an Englishman, felt that he was not capable of following this thesis to its logical artistic conclusion, as we have attempted to do here.

In this way of the oral narrative tradition, Southern writing stands out; and it is one of the great strengths of that literature. One never creates a lasting, living work from the upper stories of an office tower if he has the superior aloof attitude of O'Connor's Asbury Fox that he is infinitely brighter and better than his subjects. He must not hold life at arm's length, but enter it, and time's flow. He must be aware of himself as both outside of and part of the story. He has to be a part of the community's history, not just an observer and recorder of it. This kind of joining the human race allows what Louis Rubin saw to be a Southern writer's "uninhibited reliance upon the full resources of language" ("Changing and Enduring," 26-27). O'Connor predicts that aspiring writer Asbury Fox will never be a great writer and largely because he has failed to learn the wisdom expressed here. As one might imagine, "The Enduring Chill" is not one of O'Connor's stories that modern critics inside the pale care to treat. Perhaps it strikes too close to home.

The uninspired, omniscient, superior approach unfortunately is too often the typical way of modern academia and the writing done there, and of much non-Southern writing, which can degenerate to stuffy abstractionist agenda- and cliché-peddling and what I will call, for the lack of a better word, an abstract and evasive *Yankee-fied* way of seeing and doing. In the mid-nineteenth century, the *Yankee-fied* way of seeing produced the bookish coldness of an elegantly written *Walden*, for example, even in a time in which that kind of coldness was not popular.

It later produced the sterile clinical case-studies of pessimistic determinism called literary naturalism, heavily indebted to the works of Boston philosopher William James. It produced the stylistically brilliant works of a Stephen Crane, or the icy cold prose of a Harold Frederic, Frank Norris, William Dean Howells, Jack London, Upton Sinclair, or finally that most clinically detached of all semi-naturalistic writers— Ernest Hemingway.

Faulkner made it clear that he was not taking Hemingway's route. In his 1952 review of Hemingway's *The Old Man and the Sea*, he praised the book for its departure from its author's usual manner in that here Hemingway had found something greater and larger than Hemingway. As Faulkner said, in this book, "he'd discovered God, a Creator" (*Essays,* 193). To the consternation of Marxist critics in Establishment Literary America of the day, Hemingway had also discovered that Josef Stalin was an enemy of mankind, and that the individual was more important than government. If Faulkner knew this, he would have approved.

Again, Fred Chappell, in speaking of twentieth century Southern poets, stated that they have a strong narrative line and an oral quality both of which allow the author to have a respect for the vernacular. The memorable way Chappell put it, is that their language is not "prissy" (Chappell address, 14 May 1997). I might add "and not bookish." Chappell cited as examples of this non-prissy poetry the works of Donald Davidson, Robert Penn Warren, James Dickey, and George Garrett. And we must most certainly add Chappell's own verse and fiction. We always hear the sound of the voice in his writing—even in the non-narrative poetry. As it is in Chappell, that is one of Faulkner's great strengths. As said before, and worth repeating, Faulkner and Southern literature are recognized worldwide for this strength.

The opposite non-Southern way is to place too much control on the word and the words' march across the page—

"to want the word under complete control," as Richard Weaver put it in describing non-Southern writing. Weaver liked the Southern author's way of letting the words suddenly leap ahead and enter configurations not pre-planned. To do so, he said, shows "trust in the real creativity of language" and belief "in its vitality" (Weaver, 67). As Weaver noted, the Southern writer loves language and believes in its fidelity to truth. Its particularity rises from a rootedness and valuing of place and an immersion in family and community. How different from Hemingway, whose *A Farewell to Arms* deconstructs language to the point that words have no meaning at all, as his disillusioned main character declares. Wendell Berry's *Standing by Words* is another Southern writer's persuasive defense of saying what you mean and meaning what you say, and of a man standing by his words. It is a book-length treatment premised on the assumption that words have meanings.

Faulkner himself commented on the current dangerous use of language to obfuscate rather than communicate truth. His term "mouth-sounds" adequately portrays what language had become. He saw this inaccuracy in the use of language and the devaluation of it to be a frightening portent of worse things to come (*Essays,* 71-75). In 2022, we see it in the politico-babble of Washington and the refusal to answer a question, but instead to mouth word-sounds of evasion. The prophetic novel

1984 best details the destruction of language by Big Brother in the Ministry of Truth.

As usual, Brooks has gone to the heart of the matter. He cited particularly good examples of Faulkner's "living fountain of speech" in *The Sound and the Fury, Absalom, Absalom!,* and *The Hamlet.* Brooks concluded: "The ear does indeed rejoice in these passages. Moreover, even Faulkner's long, involved sentences, the syntax of which sometimes seems impossibly tangled, straightens themselves out when read aloud—perhaps *only* when read aloud" (*Toward Yoknapatawpha,* 340). Faulkner's way may indeed be described with Yeats' phrase, "bringing all back to syntax that is for the ear alone." [3]

Biographer Frederick Karl reported Faulkner's meeting with Albert Einstein at the home of Faulkner's editor, Saxe Commins, in Princeton in November 1953. Karl wrote that Faulkner "had nothing to say to the physicist, himself a shy man. They seemed to like each other without exchanging more than pleasantries" (868). Karl used the purported lack of conversation as evidence of Faulkner's extreme "self-absorption." Meriwether, however, who worked closely with Commins on his Faulkner bibliography at the time, reported that the conversation was far more than exchanging pleasantries. Meriwether told me that "Einstein asked Faulkner what it felt like when he was at the peak of creating successfully, and Faulkner answered, 'I hear voices.'"

I think it very significant for this chapter that Faulkner in answering Einstein, said he heard voices rather than saw faces, or images, or words on a printed page. It was a matter of hearing rather than seeing. The failure of Karl to understand the great import of this meeting is indicative at the least of the disappointing failure of the biography to grasp the greatness of its subject—and at its worst, to attempt to diminish him and his character. Are we in fact merely witnessing just another example of a milder form of cancel culture?

One may contrast Faulkner's rhetorical style and a love for and valuing the word with Ernest Hemingway's disdain for and distrust of words as expressed by his characters Nick Adams in *In Our Time* (1925) and Frederick Henry in *A Farewell to Arms* (1929). For them, words like love, honor, and bravery have no meaning. They come to trust only words on road signs. They both become masters of evasion. In these works, language is used as obfuscation of meaning. It is what that is not said that carries meaning.

The move among American realists like William Dean Howells, Harold Frederic, and the Northern naturalists of the late nineteenth century, at the time Faulkner was born, was to make a clipped factual account—the language a doctor or scientist would use in providing a case study. It was a No-

Nonsense language and valued brevity, terseness, and economy. Mark Twain, who wrote during that time, did not fall victim to that way. One may say that his Southern background saved him. His book *Life on the Mississippi* (1883) praised the Southern love of language and the mastery thereof by its raconteurs. The book's first half, the part most felicitous and worth reading, is an excellent example of what he meant. Mark Twain emphasized the Southern language's musicality and lyricism.

The Southern language was the only thing Southern with which Clemens found absolutely no fault. He successfully navigated his craft inside the Northern fortress pale and found favor with the Eastern Literary Establishment's managerial insiders by his ridiculing of Southern chivalry and honor, etc. But not language. Here he drew the line. He was an acute observer of the difference North and South in literature's most basic element. That is why his *Adventures of Huckleberry Finn* begins with his warning to the reader not to criticize him for inconsistencies in the dialect, for he was distinguishing numerous forms of Missouri dialect

In 1933, Hervey Allen, who helped found the Southern Literary Renaissance, wrote of the current American literature in an article in the *Saturday Review*, an article that must not have pleased all its readers inside the establishment pale. "People," he declared, "are tired of incomplete and inadequately phrased experiences, of shallow books...phrased in consti-pated staccato style" (Bellows, 155). "Constipated, staccato style" pretty well summed up the writing of Midwesterners Sinclair Lewis, Sherwood Anderson, and Anderson's star pu-pil, Hemingway. Faulkner satirized Anderson's grade-school primer-like style in *Sherwood Anderson & Other Famous Cre-oles* (1926), a fact Anderson never forgave. It is clear from the start that the primer-like style, an outgrowth of the stripped No-Nonsense language of the American Naturalist-Realists would not be Faulkner's way. As for Hemingway, he also par-odied Anderson's style in *The Torrents of Spring* but went on to imitate it. A lesson in Northern hypocrisy may be gained thereby.

A "constipated staccato style" rather accurately de-scribes what results from a machine culture dominated by sci-ence that distrusts language other than as stripped, statistical laboratory accounting of empirical fact. It is the language of business, the clinical case study, and the total triumph of pos-itivist science. It is most certainly not the way of Southern writing in the twentieth century. Most emphatically, it was not the way of William Faulkner.

Going back further in Southern literary history, one might contrast, for example, the way Simms saw writing de-veloping in the mid-nineteenth century North. In his review of James Russell Lowell in 1849, Simms wrote of the new language of the writers of the industrial North: "If the North's claims to poetry are to be founded upon her sledge and trip-hammers, her mills and machinery, she may grind verses to all eternity so long as she sets no one's teeth on edge but her own" (*Selected Reviews,* 97-99). This then is the mechanical "constipated staccato style" that sets one's teeth on edge. It is not *created* but "ground out." Here we also witness a warning about embracing the machine and eschewing flesh. In other places, Simms was to write of the machine as a cold mistress. At times for him it was more like the iron maiden of medieval torture.

Simms's description of mechanical language is a good way of defining what the *New York Times* praised as "brisk prose." Southern writers, Faulkner most especially, did not and usually still do not write "brisk prose." In culture and manners, as well as language, there is not a whole lot of difference between *brisk, brusque,* and *abrupt.* With *brisk*, we have the image of a cold winter splash in the face from a wave on Cape Cod or at the Hamptons in February. *Brisk* indeed!

Simms's reviews in his last decade to his death in 1870 showed that he was even more determined to retain Southern cultural differences, made even more crucial with the South's military defeat. Borrowing from Bellows in a new context, in Simms's last years, "To stroll the streets and alleyways of Charleston…was to feel like a tourist at Pompeii, to be made witness to a great calamity" (24). It was a time of somber and shadowy magnificence when the fortunes of the old Lowcountry families was hitting bottom. The most frequently used words in Simms's poetry of these years were *waste, loss, ruin,* and *ruined.* Interestingly, these are words also dominating the writing of Faulkner.

Against these ruins, Simms shored up words—words with meanings—words like *honor, gentleman, endurance, sacrifice, truth,* and *chivalry.* In his last review of 1870, Simms delivered the following philippic stating that the South still valued words like *gentleman, honor,* and *chivalry* and for Southerners the words had meaning. He said that in the North, the words *chivalry* and *gentleman* had finally become "a sort of scoff." He concluded that the "gulf between the two sections widens daily" and the land that does not value the meaning of words like *honor* and *gentleman* eventually "commits suicide." For Simms, it was the suicide of government, culture, and literature itself.

Here Simms stood in the line of descent from Thomas Gray's "The Bard," one of his favorite poems. The Celtic bard of the title is being hunted down and doomed to death by the invading English King Edward. Before he is exterminated and his land culturally cleansed and canceled, the Bard delivers the perduring curse of the poet. Simms knew much about the power of poetry through language. He knew his book of

Genesis and the Gospel of St. John on saying, creating through language, and naming. God said, "Let there be light, and there *was* light, and He *called* the light *day.*" Simms was aware that there is powerful magic in the creative act of naming allied to the charm of *making.* In the beginning, there was the word.

Celtic King Arthur's Druid Merlin most clearly understood this truth. The curse of the Celtic bard, whom Simms felt himself to be, is of a damnation that never fails. It is the final, most potent weapon in the writer's arsenal, used *in extremis,* when no other defenses are left. Thus, language in its integrity is the final defense. Such was Simms's belief in the word and the importance of the incorruptible integrity of language—not just the word's power, but as truth. Truth was an absolute for him, and not subject to twisting, obfuscation, and dissembling. In the temptation of Christ on the mountain, one should recollect who it was that twisted language and used it as subterfuge. One also should recollect that the root word of *Satan* is *lie.*

Faulkner said precisely the same about truth a century later. He called truth "that long clear clean simple undeviable-unchallengeable straight and shining line, on one side of which black is black and on the other white is white" (Essays, 72). He continued, that the relativist today has twisted truth "to an angle, a point of view having nothing to do with truth nor even with fact but depending solely on where you are standing when you look at it." Faulkner said that the object of relativism is to use language "to fool or obfuscate." For him, instead, the word was sacred; and a writer's duty was to ensure its integrity. So, we have come full circle in Southern literature to Simms's declaration: "The virtues of a people depend very much upon the incorruptible integrity of language" (Charleston *Mercury*, 20 August 1859).

The great twentieth century Southern Literary Renaissance fermenting in the 1920s in Charleston, Nashville, New Orleans, Oxford, Mississippi, and in any number of hamlets and rural communities South-wide, yielded an unusually powerful and remarkable body of writing that the world now celebrates. The world's two most celebrated novelists in the English language are Faulkner and James Joyce. Faulkner's reputation continues to rise, as Hemingway's declines. Faulkner and Joyce are testimonies to both their cultures' honoring the efficacy of the word. As for Joyce, it is pertinent here that one of his favorite pastimes as a lad was reading the dictionary.

In the generation after World War II, Southern author Walker Percy was perhaps the American writer most obsessed with language. His interests lay in its philosophical aspects— how it is formed, how it is shaped, its spiritual implications, and how it reflects the passage in St. John, "In the beginning was the word." As a master of language himself, Percy is an excellent example of the Southern mode.

The expert use of the Southern idiom is a great strength of modern Southern writers after Faulkner in authors like Percy, Flannery O'Connor, Chappell, Larry Brown, Harry Crews, and Cormac McCarthy. In general, Southern writers of the last half century are expert users of dialogue and of dialect. Like Faulkner, they were good listeners and had an ear for the word. In this way, these writers rely on the energy and vitality of the great Southern gift for language as it shows in Southern talk, a gift for gab which might at least partly trace its roots to the Blarney Stone and Faulkner's Butler ancestors. Faulkner likely would not have objected to this hypothesis, especially if the Blarney Stone could have also had a Scots counterpart.

FIVE

BLOOD TIES: FAMILY, COMMUNITY, & PLACE

> He's a countryman like the rest of us.
> He doesn't like to leave home.
> —Samuel Derieux, *Frank of Freedom Hill* (1923)

L ouis Rubin listed among the distinctive traits of Southern literature, the Southern writer's "strong sense of family" and his "awareness of the Past" *through* family (Rubin, "Changing, Enduring," 227-228). As in the great body of Southern fiction, Faulkner's novels and stories are stories of families and family connections. Southern novelist Mary Lee Settle's excellent title, *Blood Tie* (1977), is much to the point. Faulkner's Oxford friend, Stark Young's excellent novel *So Red the Rose* (1934) and Eudora Welty's classic *Delta Wedding* (1946) are perfect Mississippi examples of the same. Even in Caroline Gordon's hunting stories and Robert Ruark's *The Old Man and the Boy*, classic examples of the sporting genre, these Southern authors still focus on family.

One would be hard pressed to find a Southern author for whom family is not a central focus. I have often said that the history of the South is the history of individual families and their connections to one another—that the South itself is a close collection of families. Someone has called the South a vast cousinage, and I find this a particularly felicitous and accurate description.

Faulkner approached the world and entered reality through family. He related to the bigger historical picture of the South through his own family story. His first Yoknapatawpha novel, *Sartoris* (originally the uncut *Flags in the Dust*) makes essential good use of the stories surrounding his great-grandfather, Colonel Falkner. His eleventh novel, *The Unvanquished,* and his last, *The Reivers* are perhaps the best and most obvious examples of how he used his own family history.

Faulkner called his Great Aunt Bama, the Old Colonel's youngest daughter, the keeper of the family story. She bears strong resemblance to his strong, high-principled characters, Aunt Jenny Sartoris Dupre and Granny Millard, although there seems to be also much of Faulkner's stern Baptist maternal grandmother "Damuddy" Lelia Dean Swift Butler in Granny. Like Granny, Mrs. Butler would not be above washing out a grandchild's mouth with soap for cursing.

In all the novels, with the possible exception of *A Fable,* family is the center of the fiction—either when the family is working well (as in *The Unvanquished* and *The Reivers*) or in the fracturings and the dysfunctional—which is the case in most of the other novels. A major cause of that dissolution is often the impact of invasion, dispossession, displacement, and deracination, in other words, the modern malaise setting in.

The Sound and the Fury is an excellent example of this familial fracturing. Dilsey Gibson, who says she has seen the family's beginning and now its ending, is the Compsons' own particular keeper of the family story. In retrospect, Faulkner wrote of her in 1933 that Dilsey stood "above the fallen ruins of the family like a ruined chimney" (Faulkner, introduction to *The Sound and the Fury,* 1933, 294). For those attuned to the details of Southern history, it is easy to read this image as code for the invasion of hearth and home. The chimney stands for hearth and home, and it is in ruins— "Sherman's toothpicks" as we called such chimneys lacking their houses in South Carolina and Georgia, or "Chimneyville" as the citizens of post-Sherman-burned Columbia called their once beautiful city of gardens and avenues lined with magnolias and willow oaks.

Obsession with the war's dispossessions can have its own fatal legacy. The Reverend Gail Hightower in *Light in August* remembers too much and too often. His monomania with his family's story of loss eats up his entire life, drives his wife to suicide, and isolates him completely. It brings his family to an end. Monomania in Faulkner's fiction comes in a variety of forms, and although Faulkner himself could use his family's Confederate history for constructive purposes through balance and perspective, he portrays those who cannot. Quentin Compson in *Absalom, Absalom!* is another good example of one who dwells too much upon the sins and shortcomings of his family's past. Isaac McCaslin in *Go Down, Moses* is another. The past for Quentin and Ike is not regenerative, but death-dealing. Their guilt-and-shame complexes are as extreme as any created in the Southern self-haters of today. In both Quentin and Ike, guilt breeds sterility and brings their family line to an end. It is personal genocide writ large.

Besides being a work of consummate craftsmanship, *Absalom, Absalom!* provides the bonus to the fashionable critic of lending itself to being read as the ultimate Southern guilt-and-shame novel. It contains Quentin's testimony, "I don't hate the South! I don't hate it! I don't hate it!" said so many times with such passion that we feel he most certainly does. His declaration is among the most-quoted lines in Faulkner in a certain style of Faulkner criticism popular in today's academy. The motive in the political arena is power, gained by deconstructing the conservative South. For the literary Marxists, their engineered future is far more important than the work being discussed. To destroy the culture of a place requires redefining it in such a way that a people rejects it. Hence the destruction of Southern monuments to Southern heroes. It all begins with guilt and shame. The end game is a brand of cultural genocide, and Faulkner has often been used as a tool in the process.

It is more helpful to see that what many of Faulkner's novels portray is the undermining of family and familial bonds in a variety of ways and owing to a multitude of causes. The sum total is not a pretty picture. Faulkner faces the tragedy with unblinking fidelity. And we in 2022 are seeing the frightening results of the fracturing he portrayed. The traditional nuclear family unit has been under relentless attack from a number of sources, and the family's atomization holds the spectre of Western civilization's collapse, no doubt an even far worse threat than the much-vaunted fear-mongering over climate change and environmental crisis.

Related to the centrality of family is the importance in Faulkner of the collection of families we call the community. Cleanth Brooks' first work on Faulkner's novels, *William Faulkner: The Yoknapatawpha Country,* in my opinion is still the best book on the fiction. Its overriding thesis is that Faulkner put a premium on community and that his dramatization of the individual in family and community reveals a distinctively Southern way of seeing. In the traditional South, neighbors are viewed as extended family. Echoing Professor Brooks, Dr. Rubin rightly insists that a distinctive element of Southern writing is a "preoccupation with one's membership in a community" (Rubin, "Changing, Enduring," 226).

Faulkner's ideal man is never the *isolato*, the lone wolf, never the Natty Bumppo or Huckleberry Finn who are always striking out for the territories fearing communal or familial ties and civilization. He is not the misanthropic Thoreau at Walden, playing at and dipping into life, sojourning to get a book, then leaving place. He is not a cosmopolitan J. Alfred Prufrock or Eliot's model, Dostoyevsky's Underground Man. He is no Nick Adams. Southern readers are apt to question where the neighbors and grandfathers and grandmothers are in Hemingway's fiction. "Where are the Underground Man's family?" the Southerner might ask. "Couldn't Prufrock call on his father and mother for advice? Or maybe a wise grandfather or a devoted brother or favorite sister?" Both Faulkner's and the traditional Southern ideal is staying put in the bonds of family, having roots in place and membership in community and commitment to it. Even when he has disagreements with it, the individual is always part of a complex membership or memberships. The works of Wendell Berry, one of the most celebrated of Southern writers today worldwide, has this as his overarching main theme in both his fiction and verse. He speaks of his Port William community as the Port William Membership. He continues to do so in his just released *The Need to Be Whole*.

A character like Joe Christmas in *Light in August* or the monsters Popeye in *Sanctuary* or near automaton Flem Snopes in *The Hamlet* are the antithesis of this way. Their not belonging to any place is perhaps the worst thing that could happen to them. Faulkner's tragic characters are always without community. Jason Compson in *The Sound and the Fury*, even though he is in a real community, who knows him well, has no respect or love for it. The community knows that too, but still tolerates him. Jason is isolated in the midst of both family and town owing to his selfishness, egocentrism, and greed, so is still virtually the loner, whose isolation is rigidly self-imposed. Emily Grierson in "A Rose for Emily" eschews community. She walls herself away, even though the town in its own way respects her. The narrator's "rose" of Faulkner's title makes this quite clear. He has chosen community and prefers it. Alienation from community is a modern theme of twentieth century writers, and Faulkner portrays it well.

Belonging, failing to belong, refusing to belong, not knowing how to belong, and hopefully a learning to belong are primary considerations and a central focus of Faulkner's fiction. Brooks has treated community in the Yoknapatawpha works so masterfully well and thoroughly that I need only recommend his *William Faulkner: The Yoknapatawpha Country*. It is an obligatory read for anyone who seriously wishes to understand the springs of Faulkner's greatness. His follow-up volume on the non-Yoknapatawpha works, *Toward Yoknapatawpha and Beyond,* while not having the major works to inspire him, is even more useful in this current study, as the many references to it in this work will show.

What also needs saying, however, as an adjunct to Brooks' *William Faulkner: The Yoknapatawpha Country* is that Faulkner's understanding of the importance of community is quintessentially Southern. Simms, the father of Southern literature as he has been called, also portrays this drama of the individual in relation to his community. His novels *Woodcraft* (1852)*, The Golden Christmas* (1852), and *Martin Faber* (1833) are a few of many key titles that serve as good examples.

Professor Meriwether often said that to understand Faulkner fully, one must know Simms well.[1] In this placing of the individual in the family and community, the two writers seem to be close brothers, and a remarkable connection across a century's span. And this focus on community has been a Southern standard at least since Simms and John Pendleton Kennedy's *Swallow Barn* (1832), taking its best and most extensive current portrayal in the Port William fiction of Wendell Berry. Any number of the works by the Fugitives, and especially Caroline Gordon, Flannery O'Connor, Elizabeth Roberts, Jesse Stuart, Ellen Glasgow, Zora Neale Hurston, Eudora Welty, the early (Southern) novels of Cormac McCarthy, and Larry Brown provide other good examples. Harry Crews' fine memoir *A Childhood: The Biography of a Place* (1978) is one of the most incisive, gritty works on the subject.

Fred Chappell, once again in speaking of the traits of modern Southern poets, has said that they strongly emphasize community and that their voice is both communal and personal at the same time. This may be said of Faulkner as well. In the world of his fiction, alienation and isolation, although they permeate his works, are neither desirable nor inevitable. Community, whether intact or under attack, exists as the measuring stick by which to judge a character's actions. A character's relation to community is often what defines him.

No better work than "A Rose for Emily," (published the same year as *I'll Take My Stand*) shows this. The story's narrator thereby becomes an even more important character in the story than the title character herself. The Southern reader is likely to perceive this quicker than the non-Southerner who is more likely to be impressed with the sensational fact that Miss Emily has still been sleeping by the remains of Homer Baron. All manner of foolishness imaging Emily as the Old South sleeping with the corpse of its past should be contrasted to Southern novelist and critic Marion Montgomery's excellent treatment of the story's point of view (*Possum and Other Receits for the Recovery of Southern Being*, 124-134).

In 1953, in his essay "How Many Miles to Babylon," Andrew Lytle wrote that the Southerner "must have location, which means property, which means the family and the communion of families which is the state. Otherwise, as now, the individual is at the mercy of his ego" (*From Eden to Babylon,* 156). It all begins with the firm base of place and a rootedness there. Allen Tate, and English distributist economist Herbert Agar edited the 1936 collection *Who Owns America?* upon the premise that private land ownership, contrary to new Communist doctrines, was the primary means of providing stability, good stewardship, and love of country that would be the basis of patriotism (in his healthy meaning of the word.) Lytle's essay for this volume was entitled "The Small Farm Secures the State," and the title adequately states the essay's theme. *Who Owns America?* served as a second volume to *I'll Take My Stand,* and they both had thematic grounding in love of place.

It has been written that Charlestonian Basil Gildersleeve (1831-1924) was the "greatest American scholar of the 19th Century."[2] As the continent's first classical scholar, he knew the traditional South well, as proved by his justly famous essays "The Creed of the Old South" and "A Southerner in the Peloponnesian War." He wrote that "A man whose love for his country knows no local roots is a man whose love for his country is a poor abstraction." Here once again we see the Southern understanding that abstraction is nemesis. Further, the solid Southern grounding in place is an essential well-spring of civic virtue.

The importance of place as a major defining trait of Southern writing has become so well known now as to be a cliché. Dr. Rubin, in fact, listed "a firm identification with a place" as one of the distinctive elements that must be present ("Changing, Enduring," 226). Robert Penn Warren put it most succinctly in saying that the effective writer must define an appropriate "relation to a special place" (Tate, *Who Owns America?*, 272).

Faulkner is once again quintessentially Southern in this way. Place in his fiction is so tangible and important that it and its apotheosis in community becomes *a* if not t*he* central character of a work. Faulkner's knowledge of his community was deep and broad. His use of the local, anchors the fiction on solid ground. He is much like Thomas Hardy in this; and Hardy was a novelist Faulkner respected. At times I have gone so far as to see Hardy, with his intense localism in all things, was a Southern author living in England. Like Hardy, Faulkner's use of the local dialect, local customs, manners, traditions, history, and folkways is a reflection of his respect for place and its importance, what M. E. Bradford called a "piety for places" (Bradford, 91). Incidentally, here Bradford also noted that Donald Davidson felt that Thomas Hardy had affinities with Simms as preserver of oral history and an oral culture. In this oral tradition of passing on a piety for places, Faulkner displayed the Yeatsian Celtic heritage of the upland

South, for one of the chief duties of the Celtic bard was to sing songs venerating the local by attaching story, people, and events to a particular locale in order to humanize the landscape. It is interesting to add here once again that Michael Millgate, who did an early sensitive book on Faulkner, also wrote a fine work on Thomas Hardy.

The South, especially outside Virginia's tidewater, was largely settled by Irish, Scoto-Irish, Welsh, and Scots. Faulkner's North Mississippi was especially so, as his family's lineage reveals. Southern emphasis on place may indeed at least partly derive from the strong Celtic influence on the region. Among the Celtic Bard's chief duties was to honor place, sing songs in praise of place (*faoin dulraidth*) out of *duchas* (love of place engendered by legend and lore.)[3]

Faulkner's choice to stay in Oxford speaks also to the importance he put on place in his personal life. When given the choice between remaining in Oxford and a Hollywood career, he chose home. We may know the story of how Faulkner's boss at M.G.M. told him he'd done a good job that day and could go home, then for days, couldn't find him. Of course Faulkner took him at his word and went home to Oxford where, when the message came asking where he was, he replied that he was sitting on his back porch eating watermelon and watching it rain. Home was not an apartment in

111

Hollywood. As most Southerners would understand, a person can have only one home.

Faulkner did not like California. It was always sunny and never rained. To him it was the extreme epitome of the hedonistic anti-traditional culture. He felt it too transient, with nothing lasting, and no one staying put. His most telling comment was that he felt the place was so unstable that in a few years nothing would be left there but the iron "stobs" the Okies from the Dust Bowl drove into the soil to pitch horseshoes at. Of the movie industry itself, he advised others not to take it seriously, but to take the people seriously. He made friends with Humphrey Bogart, whom he admired because he was a craftsman and was good at what he did.

Malcolm Cowley, Ernest Hemingway, F. Scott Fitzgerald, Gertrude Stein, and other celebrated American artists went to Paris. After World War I, most of them returned home to find their hometowns boring. Cowley said that when he returned, he felt like an exile in the United States. Faulkner also went to Paris in 1925 during this crucial period. That same year Hemingway published *In Our Time* and Sylvia Beach had helped Irish expatriate James Joyce bring out *Ulysees* in 1922. Meriwether said that Faulkner went to the café that Joyce frequented. Later, when asked if he met Joyce Faulkner related that he only looked at him.[4]

The Wild Palms is Faulkner's take on the avant-garde, anti-traditional set. It is not a flattering portrait. Charlotte and Harry are his Bohemians. They seem to be playing at life, with disastrous consequences. They travel from New Orleans north then west before returning to the city. In doing so, they make a circle, and although constantly in motion, they get nowhere in the end. The novel's direct references to Hemingway ("set in a sea of Hemingwaves" for instance), as critic Thomas L. McHaney has explained, points the moral.[5] The novel's two lovers flaunt all the old mores. They want to escape all the limitations put on them of place, rootedness, marriage, kinship, parenthood, and community responsibility. They try to expatriate from society and live an endless honeymoon, but ironically end up with the whole world in bed with them when they have to sleep with a couple to keep warm in a home for which they cannot pay to provide heat. The novel's primary image is the dry wind (that thrashes the palms, or that is let in to achieve Charlotte's abortion). It provides the perfect symbol of modern sterility and the cult of death, and a culture of death. The bohemian rootless life *all for love* was not Faulkner's way. Although he could not often share his love of literature with his Oxford neighbors, he did not feel an exile at home or the necessity to escape it.

Of all the great American writers who went to Paris in the 1920s, he alone did not find the city and its artsy scene irresistible and invigorating. He was trying to be a painter as well as a writer and spent most of his days at the Louvre among the great art of the Western tradition, often taking an entire day to sit and look at a single painting. Picasso's Cubist way would not be his way. His early art tended, as seen in the University of Mississippi year books to which he contributed designs, tended to be in the style of the flat pen and ink drawings of Aubrey Beardsley, and not a Cubist or Abstract Expressionist's way.

The pull of home brought Faulkner back from Paris to the South, where in New Orleans he met Sherwood Anderson. Anderson encouraged him to write about that little postage stamp of land in North Mississippi where he was born and raised and which he knew so well, and Faulkner did precisely that before the year was out. Set in Yoknapatawpha County, "Father Abraham," the germ of the Snopes Trilogy which would occupy him off and on for the next three decades, was penned in 1926, the year after his return from Paris. (It was not published until 1983.) Indeed, Faulkner also went to the city of light in the 1920s, but oh the difference! And one might justly add, *Vive la difference.*

When Faulkner won the Nobel Prize, he seriously considered not traveling to Sweden to accept it. His daughter was a teenager however and wanted the trip, so he went to please her. After his young man's journey to Paris in the 1920s,

Faulkner eschewed travel. He intensely disliked the New York cocktail circuit encouraged by Bennett Cerf and his editors at Random House. When invited to the White House by the Kennedys to dine in that famous gathering of artists that included Robert Frost, he declined, saying that it was a long way to go for supper. His commitment to the soil of Greenfield Farm, as we have seen, is another indication of that commitment to place.

In his splendid essay, "The Regional Motive," Wendell Berry wrote in 1972 of the importance of staying put in order to know place: "Without a complex knowledge of one's place, and without the faithfulness to one's place on which such knowledge depends...the culture of a country will be superficial and decorative, functional only as...the affectation of an elite or 'in' group." "Superficial and decorative...the affectation of an elite or 'in' group" about sums up a goodly portion of the current literary scene today. I would add another image to Berry's—that what often passes for art in this non-culture is merely window dressing to sell a product with a hype and marketing glitz that attempts to mask the hollowness at the core. The great poet and critic Donald Davidson wrote perceptively in "A Mirror for Artists," his chapter in *I'll Take My Stand,* that American society was "merely gilded with culture and not permeated" by it (37).

William Gilmore Simms wrote a prophetic essay in 1840 entitled "The Age of Gold and Iron" in which he prefigured Davidson and Berry in a key critique of American society. With his long view of Western civilization achieved through wide reading and deep erudition, Simms stated that when a society leaves the land, forgets place, scorns the rural, and takes on the ways of rootless industrial empire, then its art languishes and dies. In prophetic words even more powerful than Berry's, Simms declared:

> The story is everywhere the same. It admits of no variation. The golden age is the age of agricultural preeminence. The nation whose sons shrink from the culture of its fields, will wither for long ages, under the imperial sway of Iron. It may put on a face of brass, but its legs will be made of clay. It may hide its lean cheeks, and all external signs of its misery, under the harlotry of art; but the rottenness of death will all the while be reveling upon its vitals, and a poisonous breath will go forth from its decay which will spread its loathsome taint along the shores of other happier and unsuspecting nations.[6]

Simms imaged a red-painted "harlotry of art" hiding the essential hollowness of the cheeks. As the industrial imperial iron culture rots from the inside, it breathes a "poisonous breath" to curse the world. "Unsuspecting nations" beware. The rotting Iron Empire is spreading the "loathsome taint" of poison cooked up by its own decay. Powerful prophecy indeed!

Most have likely heard the mantra of the American Public Broadcasting System from 2012 to 2014: "A great nation deserves great art." It would follow that if there is no truly great art being produced, then there is no great nation to produce it. At the root of the PBS mantra's problem is the fact that nations do not produce art; people rooted in places do. Gildersleeve again hit the mark in his essay "The Creed of the Old South." "If," he wrote, "the effacement of state lines and the complete centralization of the government shall prove to be the wisdom of the future, the poetry of life will still find its home in the old order and those who loved their State best will live longest in song and legend—song yet unsung, legend not yet crystallized."

In 1840 Simms's uncanny understanding of the rising Northern industrial machine culture and the horrific effects it will have, and Berry's 1972 essay both describe the unsettling of America into an essentially unstable, uncivilized state. Berry's essay was written ten years after Faulkner's death, and the situation has worsened since as Berry admits in *The Need to be Whole* (2022). Few stay put any more. To pick up and move is the norm. Houses are now popularly built on wheels and in a matter of minutes can be moved from site to site. Violation of place then comes as a result of not knowing it, except superficially at best. The Southern writer is still far less guilty of this shortcoming; and that is one good reason the South's literature has remained strong. In my own novels, I have tried to reverse the trend toward deracination by depicting the unsung lives of those coming home or of those staying rooted in place, or as in Thomas Gray's immortal line, "The short and simple annals of the poor."

Berry has continued to write on the importance of place and staying put. In 2002, a selection of his place-based essays appeared with the relevant title, *The Art of the Common Place.* In 2010, in his collection *Imagination in Place,* he declared that his fiction originated from "actual experience of an actual place" (4). He named Faulkner as one of his "literary mentors, exemplars, teachers, and guides" (5). This fifth chapter has perhaps explained at least one of the reasons why. In his 1990 collection of essays, *What Are People For?,* Berry declared, "Culture preserves the map and the records of past journeys so that no generation will permanently destroy the route. The more local and settled the culture, the better it stays put, the less the damage. It is the foreigner whose road of excess leads to a desert" (8). A reverence for place is the antidote to placeless, rootless America outlined in Berry's now classic *The Unsettling of America* (1977).

This proper valuing of place is also one major reason the larger body of Southern literature may be the continent's single greatest cultural legacy, or as some would have it, the continent's only one.[7] So let us put a twist on the Public Broadcasting System mantra, "A great nation indeed deserves great art. The South has produced and is producing great art, so the South, even without a government, is a great nation." PBS would not be amused.

This discussion of place in Faulkner and Southern literature may properly conclude with an excerpt from a poem in Faulkner's collection *A Green Bough,* published in 1933. Perhaps his best, this poem demonstrates Faulkner's attitude toward place more effectively than anything I can say:

...for where is any death

While in these blue hills slumbrous overhead

I'm rooted like a tree?

Though I be dead,

This earth that holds me fast will find me breath (67).

Antebellum Southern poet, Henry Timrod, had anticipated Faulkner very nicely nearly a century before:

Poet! If on a lasting fame be bent

Thy unperturbing hopes, thou wilt not roam

Too far from thine own happy hearth and home;

Cling to the lowly earth, and be content.[8]

SIX

HUMOR SOUTHERN STYLE

A nother quickly recognizable feature of Southern writing is its humor. The particular kinds of Southern humor are an expansive, hyperbolic, tall-tale variety, as well as the satiric and the darkly caustic, grotesque sort—everything but the humor of litotes or understatement. The last is a trait of the English and tight-lipped "down east" New English way. Chappell in 1997 found the prevalence of humor to be a distinguishing trait of Southern poetry. In 2006, James P. Cantrell also found it a key identifying feature of the literature—what he phrased nicely as "an appreciation and celebration of the wildly comic in life" (Cantrell, 83).

Although not properly known as such, Faulkner is one of the great American humorists. Novels like *The Hamlet* and *The Reivers* are obviously humorous; but even the grim dark worlds of *The Sound and the Fury, As I Lay Dying, Light in August, Go Down, Moses,* and *Sanctuary* are permeated with humor that is among world literature's best. Faulkner does not often get called a funny writer, but if one reads him closely and actively, he will find him to be among our most comic. It is often the humor of a Poe or Flannery O'Connor in which the grim, bitterly ironic, and grotesque mingle with the comic.

The young, already perceptive Shelby Foote in review-ing *Absalom, Absalom!* at the age of twenty, was among the first to point out the humor in this tragic novel. In November 1936, only a month after the novel's official publication (on 26 October 1936), Foote declared in a review of the novel in his University of North Carolina college literary magazine, "There is humor here but it is sardonic and not likely to make you laugh out loud." He then cited an example, with the com-ment that "there is no place for side-splitters in a work whose main intent is to look deep into the bowels of the human brain...past some folks' bearing" (Foote, "Fury," 30). Foote was often to tell me that he was a great admirer of Faulkner's various types of humor. He said that often in many works, there were indeed "side-splitters." He particularly appreciated the humor of *The Hamlet* and thought "Spotted Horses" supe-rior in humor to Mark Twain. When asked to give lectures on Faulkner, he chose this novel for his topic (Letter, Shelby Foote to James E. Kibler, Jr., dated Memphis 27 October 1969, Kibler Literary Collection, South Caroliniana Library).

Faulkner's humor was sometimes pervasive so as to crop up in unexpected places to surprise and delight. I was for-tunate enough to be able to share with Mr. Foote an instance of Faulkner's humor in *The Hamlet* that he had no way of knowing. At the time Foote wrote me about humor in *The Hamlet*, I had just completed research on the manuscript of the novel at the Alderman Library at the University of Virginia. There interlined in the manuscript, I found Faulkner's short note to his editors at Random House, concerning a rustic character's comment about poor unfortunate Ab Snopes' particular horse that was "the finest drove of a horse" he ever owned. Faulkner wrote in his usual careful pen over the word "drove": "Tell your high school proofreader to leave this alone. The man never had but one horse." With this humorous but caustic direction, Faulkner was making certain his Northern proofreader would not miss his down-home humor.

Wendell Berry seems to agree with Foote. On several occasions he has told me that the "Spotted Horses" section of *The Hamlet* may just be the funniest fiction ever penned by an American author. In this assessment he included Mark Twain. Berry makes a very persuasive argument, and especially since some of Berry's works might be distinguished contenders.

In 1984, Doreen Fowler's introduction to *Faulkner and Humor,* stated that Faulkner, who is "the recognized genius of tragic art, is a master of comic forms as well and, further, that neither mode, tragic [n]or comic, is ever very far from the other in Faulkner's world" (Fowler, ix). Not knowing Foote's critique, Ms. Fowler pointed out that Southern novelist Katherine Anne Porter was one of the first to note Faulkner's merger of the tragic and comic. In 1948, Porter declared that Faulkner "has the deepest and most serious humor in this country at present." Porter and Fowler understood that Faulkner "is always in touch with the potentiality of humor within tragic situations," thus creating a "tension between tragic and comic modes" (x). Spanish scholar Montserrat Ginés' recent treatment of Faulkner's similarity to Cervantes in seeing the intertwining of tragedy and humor in the human condition also reinforces this argument (*The Southern Inheritors of Don Quixote*).

Fowler's edition of *Faulkner and Humor* collected thirteen essays. The majority emphasized that same merging of tragic and comic and the dark side of the comedy. George Garrett's chapter "The Dark Side of Faulkner's Jokes" is particularly apt. But often Faulkner's humor is also unselfconsciously fresh in the rustic Old Southwestern humorist's usual countryman's healthy and happy tall-tale way of oral narrative. Cullen, Faulkner's hunting companion, again said it right in 1961: "In our county, there is a kind of salty, down-to-earth folk humor based on tall tales…and old frontier character" (Cullen, 130). No doubt Faulkner learned much about this humor first-hand from his and Cullen's hunt camp. Thomas McHaney's "What Faulkner Learned from the Tall Tale" explored this subject from the angle of "lying to strangers" and "that in lying, there is much truth" (Fowler, 110-133).

One particular thing that the humor of Faulkner has in common with that in Mark Twain, Cormac McCarthy,

O'Connor, and Fred Chappell is a common source in the antebellum Southern humorist, George Washington Harris (1814-1869), creator of the unforgettable character, Sut Lovingood Without Sut, there would be no Huck Finn, no *As I Lay Dying*, no Snopeses, no Virgil Campbell in Chappell, no Suttree in McCarthy, no Haze Motes in O'Connor, and no Triggerfoot Tinsley in my own fiction. Faulkner was asked at the University of Virginia and in his *Paris Review* interview who were his all-time favorite characters in literature. He answered quickly: Old Testament figures and Sut Lovingood. Faulkner declared, "I like Sut Lovingood, from a book written by George Harris about 1840 or '50 in the Tennessee Mountains. He had no illusions about himself, did the best he could; at certain times he was a coward and knew it and wasn't ashamed; he never blamed his misfortunes on anyone and never cursed God for them."[1] That answer must have been a real puzzle to the audiences. We can hear them whisper, "Sut who?"

Faulkner inherited a copy of Harris's *Sut Lovingood. Yarns Spun by a Nat'ral Born Durn'd Fool* (1867) from his great-grandfather, Colonel W. C. Falkner, and his father Murry C. Falkner. Murry died 7 August 1932. William signed the volume "Rowan Oak, 12 September 1932" (Blotner, Library, 35). This was done a month after his father's death.

Mark Twain reviewed *Sut Lovingood. Yarns Spun by a Nat'ral Born Durn'd Fool* in the year it was published; and the character Huck Finn is only Sut in a tamer, less funny guise packaged for a sentimental, genteel, mainly Eastern Establishment clientele. He would not be allowed to offend Victorian sensibilities or the so-called realism of his friend and supporter, William Dean Howells, whose dictum to writers was that they should never write anything that would cause a lady to blush. Of *Sut Lovingood's Yarns*, Clemens noted that the Eastern Establishment "will call it coarse and possibly taboo it," but outside the East, "it will sell well."[2] As evidence of his continued regard for Sut, Clemens collected Harris's "Sicily Burns's Wedding" in his *Mark Twain's Library of Humor* (1888). In his ground-breaking article on Mark Twain's debt to Harris, Hennig Cohen wrote, "The fundamental bond between Harris and Twain was their sense of man's predisposition to dehumanize himself" (21). Cohen also pointed out specific borrowings from Harris in *Huckleberry Finn* and *Tom Sawyer* (21-23).

Another indication of the division South and North on this question of Harris's brand of genuinely realistic humor appeared in 1962 in Edmund Wilson's celebrated study, *Patriotic Gore*. Here, as we saw in the previous chapter, Wilson called Sut sadistic, a "dreadful, half-bestial lout," "repellent," and a "peasant squatting in his own filth" (509-510). In 1962,

Sut was apparently still horrifying the Eastern Establishment. It was not until 2004, that James H. Justus published the first full-length study of the Southern humor genre in his *Fetching the Old Southwest: Humorous Writing from Longstreet to Twain.* Here, Justus accurately treated Southern humor writing as a kind of shadow canon in American literature. It is significant that Southerners Simms and Poe were among the genre's few important defenders in antebellum America.[3]

Faulkner's early Oxford friend, Stark Young, dramatized the antebellum popularity of Sut in the South in his novel, *So Red the* Rose (1934). It was Young who no doubt told him the Harris story of the bizarre country funeral (in Harris's story, "Well, Dad's Dead") that became the basis and central event of *As I Lay Dying.* The story did not appear in *Sut Lovingood's Yarns* and was known only through obscure newspaper circulation and oral transmission. Apparently it was still alive with Young in 1934.

We know Flannery O'Connor was aware of Sut because she referred to him in her essay, "The Catholic Novelist in the South." The reference appeared in the same paragraph of her oft-quoted comment, "I find that any fiction that comes out of the South is going to be called 'grotesque' by the Northern reader, unless it is grotesque, in which case it is going to be called 'photographic realism'" (O'Connor, *Collected Works,* 860). It is clear that the grotesquerie of both Poe and

Harris were primary influences on her fiction, and *Wise Blood,* in particular.

Cormac McCarthy's novel *Suttree* even has a main character whose nickname is Sut, and the antics of Gene Harrogate often sound much like Sut's and are good enough to have been written by the master himself. McCarthy's *Outer Dark* and *Child of God* also show Harris's strong influence. As fellow Tennessee writers with Knoxville backgrounds, Harris and McCarthy likewise have place, setting, and Cantrell's "wildly comic" humor in common.

An entire book could be devoted to this key subject of the continuum of the two modes of Southern humor, termed, for lack of better words, *genteel* and *rustic*. It is significant that humor is one of Southern literature's sterling traits providing healthy addition to an anti-utopian world view that is far from the "yea-saying," rosy, and buoyantly optimistic view of a Ralph Waldo Emerson or a Walt Whitman.

Interestingly, to be so optimistic about everything, these Northern writers are usually completely lacking in humor. "Deadly serious" would be too mild a phrase to describe their writing. No wonder that drab Whitman is called the good *gray* poet, for gray seemed to be the color of his temperament. And Melville had it right when he said that Emerson's brain went down into his neck and inhabited the regions of his heart. No place for humor there. During the period of what F. O.

Matthiessen called the American Renaissance (that is, the decade of the 1850s), there was only one major humorous novel published, and that was Simms's *Woodcraft* (1852-54), arguably one of the best works of its decade, and a very good example of Southern humor.

Humor is still not a dominant trait of Northern writing. The hard-bitten effect of an efficient, dour and oftentimes intolerant culture whose roots go back to Puritan New England, a time that outlawed fiction (synonymous with lies), dance, card playing, bright colors (except for the occasional scarlet A), music in church, and even Christmas, seems still to be having its influence. One need only view the black attire and black masks of the poorly lit parking lot in Wilmington Delaware where Biden held his bizarre victory celebration on 7 November 2020.

Nathaniel Hawthorne at least thought that the gloom of Puritanism still dominated the New England of his day when he declared that strong roots of that Puritanism intertwined themselves with his own. One with such a serious world view as the Puritan has no time to waste with levity. For the Puritan type, a tall tale would not be tolerated because it exaggerated the truth and was thus a lie.

Levity was not tolerated. To quote one of the Northern Founders, time *is* money, after all, in a business-oriented, cash-nexus society, and not to be wasted in the concerns of those with a cash-register evaluation of life. Simms, in fact, said this of Benjamin Franklin and the Northern way: "To insist that a penny saved was a penny gained, was just the sort of lesson to convert thrift into avarice, to freeze up all the generous sensibilities lest they become expensive as indulgences and to make wealth precious for its own sake rather than its uses. Such teaching is too much calculated to sharpen the instinct of acquisition into a passion, such as must...swallow all the rest." He continued, "It is this wretched sort of schooling...which has done so much towards making the national character so selfishly eager—so hardfavored in its intensity—so proud of merely material results—so entirely adverse to the refining influences of art—so easily persuaded to regard, as frivolous, all pursuits which promise neither wealth nor aggrandizement" (*Poetry and the Practical,* 102).

In reviewing Thoreau's *Walden* in 1855, Simms wrote that this "queer, well-written book" was a curious volume of Yankee philosophy that taught how stinginess and not hospitality was a virtue. Simms wrote that *Walden* was

> a somewhat queerly conceived narrative of a
> Yankee philosopher, whose question is upon
> how little he can live and be virtuous; feed and
> be charitable; clothe himself and others; and test
> both parties; first in what they can endure in the
> way of privation, before he bestows upon either

of them a shirt or a supper. The conception is that of a pure Yankee. It could be made by no other. It is carrying out the antique Puritan philosophy to its proper results, in all social matters (Simms, *Selected Reviews*, 141-142).

Simms's buoyant and convivial Southern nature could not fathom that reasoning.

Two decades earlier, Simms had referred to Franklin's negative influence on America in his "Philosophy of the Omnibus" (1834), calling Poor Richard's maxims "miserable and miserly." In his Hudibrastic satire on New England Puritanism, "The Father Abolitionist" (1850), Simms wrote, "With maxims pitch'd on the Franklin plan,/ He who can get is the noblest man." There is no room for levity and humor in this "great get and grab" way of living!

In 1866, Harris in his "Sut Lovingood on the Puritan Yankee," has Sut declare that the "rale, pure puritan, yankee" is truly strange cattle. He concluded in exasperation, "Powerful ornary stock…powerful ornary"[5]

The two literatures of the two regions often divide very clearly on the subject of humor. Most Southerners usually made time for it. Most Northerners usually found it frivolous because not making money. The subject is just another one of those cultural divides that demarcate two distinctly different literary traditions. In the nineteenth century, Simms saw clearly and perceptively that this was the case. He noted that Northern character was like the English, tending toward the gloomy and cold, like their climates. Southern character, like the Southern climate, was ebullient, warm, extravagant, and lively, and manifested itself in its humor. He went so far as to say that in England, attempts at humor were so lame that their humorists, so-called, were often more guilty than their gray weather in being the cause of suicides (*Selected Reviews,* 25, 29-30).

I would be remiss in closing this chapter without mentioning Faulkner's early seldom-mentioned series of humorous "Al Jackson" letters written in the broadly, wildly-exaggerated humorous dialect mode of the frontier humorists—or the comic dialect poem "Ode to the Louver" and its accompanying letter of 1 November 1925 written under the pseudonym of Ernest V. Simms to H. L. Mencken for publication in his *The Smart Set.* If it ever reached Mencken, he was apparently not pleased. At any rate, he didn't publish it, perhaps thinking it was serious and not a spoof at all, coming as it did from the Southern Sahara of the Bozart. If this was the case, Faulkner's ode would be another example of a countryman's gulling of a greenhorn city-slicker. A few lines of the six stanza poem should suffice to illustrate:

> The Louver was built by a king named Lou
> In 15 hundred and 22

After he seen in Milano

A church that somebody built & so

He come to France and settled down

To build himself a big town

And the Louver.

In the accompanying notes and hilarious letter to Mencken, Ernest V. Simms refers to the "orthur"—a comic dialect misspelling straight out of Sut Lovingood—who always says either "orfer" or "orthur." (Louis D. Brodsky, *A Comprehensive Guide to the Brodsky Collection,* Items 54 and 55.)

SEVEN

THE CREED OF MEMORY & ENDURANCE

> If the land is made fit for human habitation by memory and
> old association, it is also true that by memory and associa-
> tion, men are made fit to inhabit the land.
> --Wendell Berry

A historical consciousness that realizes the continued presence of the past is recognized as a hallmark of Southern writing. Donald Davidson described this attribute effectively with the felicitous phrases "the folk-chain of memory" and "the creed of memory." Allen Tate called it "memory carried to the heart." For the Fugitive-Agrarians, memory became a much-needed key to combating the "new provincialism," which they defined as a provinciality of time— hedonistic modern man locked in the moment.

In his essay, "The New Provincialism," Tate stated that to have only time present with no past in the way of deracinated moderns is the true narrowness, the true provinciality, and a serious bad thing. Provinciality of place, on the other hand, could be a good thing because it generates and enhances memory and prevents the provinciality of time. This provincialty of time was a result of narcissism and the isolated individual cut off from family, community, place, and history—in essence, imprisoned in himself (*Collected Essays*, 282-293).

Writing from New Orleans in 1932, Grace King (1852-1932) began her memoir by treating the Southerner's recognition of the importance of the past, especially in a time of war-induced poverty. She began, "The past is our only real possession in life. It is the one piece of prosperity of which time cannot deprive us; it is our own in a way that nothing else in life is. It never leaves our consciousness." She declared, "In a word, we *are* our past; we do not cling to it, it clings to us." She then treated the Southern concept of memory, saying "memories do not date merely from our childhood. They go back far beyond our experience, out of sight of it, to fasten upon parents and grandparents. Blessed are the children who have parents and grandparents who can relate the stories of their own pasts and so connect the younger with the older memories" (King, *Memories*, 1). Faulkner's *The Reivers*, published a short thirty years after King's statement, comes immediately to mind. King's comments on telling stories are also relevant to our Chapter Four on Faulkner the raconteur.

Cleanth Brooks concluded that Southerners are "good rememberers" and that Faulkner in particular "found the past alive and meaningful" (*Toward Yoknapatawpha,* 338). Brooks felt that in so doing, Faulkner's works are "suffused with history—not as barren antiquarianism, but as a record of the striving of man" (341). Like Tate, Brooks saw the end result of such a deep historical consciousness to be the recognition that mankind over time is "unchanging," but allows the individual to "realize his true self by rising above his habitual self" (341). This knowledge (let us call it wisdom) frees the possessor of the prison of egocentrism and the provinciality of time that the Fugitive-Agrarians felt to be so prevalent in modern America. Theirs was a minority report that, sadly, was largely only scorned by the present-and-future bound momentary men of the American intelligentsia elite of the day.

Southern writers dramatize the importance of the past in shaping the present, and it is memory that makes this possible. Memory is the effective means to short-circuit the linear-progressive scientific construct of rigidly chronological time. It is no accident that among Wendell Berry's best works of fiction are his novels *The Memory of Old Jack* and *Remembering*. As their titles suggest, memory in both works plays a key role in preventing the deracination of society and provides the base for human ties and community. Remembrance is at the true heart of the matter. It can lead to a reverential view far removed from the brattiness of arrested development—so that man becomes the child forever, never growing up to the understanding that there are others in the world besides himself.

The young narrator of *Intruder in the Dust* declared, "yesterday today and tomorrow are Is: Indivisible: One…. Yesterday wont be over until tomorrow and yesterday began ten thousand years ago" (194). In Faulkner, the past is present as a palpable reality, and it was so from his first Yoknapataw-pha novel, *Sartoris-Flags in the Dust*. In this work, objects such as coin-silver spoons are worn smooth from use. Door thresholds are cupped with wear by the passage of generations of feet. Bricks are worn smooth from touching. The effect of this impress of time is to provide a rich full texture of deep time and to show the impress of man on place. Empirical matter is thus humanized and personalized. Associations through memory provide meaning.

Memory is also another product of all those oft-spoken stories, all that telling. Memory is required both to tell stories and remember them so that they can be retold. George Garrett was a more recent good example of the continued focus on remembrance in the next generation of Southern writers after Faulkner. The overarching concern in his career of ten novels, seven short story collections, eight books of poetry, and nine collections of essays is the exploration of memory and especially that "hazy place where truth, fiction, and memory meet."[1]

It is this veneration of the past that explains Davidson's use of the word "creed" to describe the proper attitude toward memory. The connotation is of sacredness, a faith by which one lives. For the Southern writer, it is just that crucial a component of the human psyche. M. E. Bradford got it right when he declared that for Davidson, to be deprived of "deepest remembrance" was a form of death. Bradford wrote, "Historic empathy—remembrance rooted in 'affection, kinship, piety, and above all religious belief,' is central to life" (87). Here Bradford quoted from one of Davidson's last essays, "The Center That Holds" (1984).[2] Davidson's essays are a great gift to us, and this last piece was one of his best and most significant. Unfortunately, it is one of his least known.

When I wrote my novel *Memory's Keep*, a thirty-year flashback from the previous work *Walking Toward Home*, I chose its title to emphasize the key role of memory in keeping mankind human in an era of increasing emphasis on empiricism bred out of the triumph of science and technology in every phase of life. The "keep" of the title, echoing a line from Appalachian poet, Byron Herbert Reece, has several meanings, including the castle's keep, the central place to be defended at all cost, a sacred space not to be violated. It is that last stronghold to be protected against all the dehumanizing forces of modernity. I also had in mind "memory-keeper," that is, the stewarding duty of the writer-story-teller-poet to pass on the legends and stories that provide the continuity of society, or, to use Davidson's words, to shape "the long continuities of time and place into transcendent memory" ("The Center That Holds," 18). That is a key role of the Southern writer, whose duty is to be a kind of vatic bard, the insurer of man's continuing humanity by telling him stories that create identity.

In 1977, English critic, Richard Gray, devoted an entire volume to the importance of memory to modern Southern writers, including Faulkner, in his *The Literature of Memory.* Here he spoke of Faulkner's "land haunted by memory" (231). In Faulkner criticism itself, recent critics like Lee Anne Fennell have furthered Gray's elucidations by focusing on "the central and unifying role of memory" to Faulkner's work, "how memory directs the flow of time," creates "the sense of fate, doom, and determinism" in his fiction and has the power "to transcend death and loss"[3] These studies expand the sound base given us by the inspired creative genius of earlier generations of still unsurpassed stellar Southern critics like Tate, Ransom, Brooks, Lytle, Warren, Davidson, Weaver, Chappell, and Garrett.

Modern critics, however, are more apt to look at a down-side to memory, in a way deconstructing its salutary effects. There is certainly ample reason to credit its dangers when one considers a host of characters like Rider in "Pantaloon in Black," Quentin Compson, the Reverend Gail Hightower, Joanna Burden, Drusilla Sartoris, Isaac McCaslin, and others. For every Jenny Sartoris Dupre who is bolstered and strengthened by memory, one finds a Reverend Hightower who is harmed and debilitated by it. Faulkner understood the regenerative force of memory and its necessity for health and the long view that is essential to creating civilization itself, but he also saw how the narcissistic modern can pervert its ends. As usual in Faulkner, the outcome depends on the character of the individual portrayed.

What Faulkner did not feel, however, was that humankind should be locked in the present, and into the eternal gratification of the moment, an attitude that only yielded writing that was a product of the "glands." His Nobel speech made that very clear. Glandular writing had no past, as it had no future, and it grieved "on no universal bones." Memory was a key to keeping mankind human in an abstractionist machine-age technocracy, and a necessity for literature that mattered.

The continuum of Southern writers reveals an understanding that memory is a powerful weapon in the fight against the dehumanizers. These progressives, so-called, would severely truncate history and claim that the now is the zenith of civilization—only to be bettered perhaps, by tomorrow. In this philosophy, we hear echoes of the words of Ralph Waldo Emerson and of Henry David Thoreau's "earth is a morning star" mentality. Memory would be a roadblock to a brave new world in which only the latest program mattered. Too often, for the non-Southern sensibility, all else was baggage that needed jettisoning.

Memory also helped man survive. A long span of knowledge of experience could put the present in proper perspective. If times were bad, there was recollection of a year when it was worse. If there was a drought or a cold or a heat, there was the story of a worse drought, a colder cold, or a hotter heat. Memory prevented egocentrism and a feeling that one is the only person to have experienced a thing. The communal fund of memory made it easier to endure.

Endurance was one of William Gilmore Simms's key topics[4] and has been arguably one of the most recognizable themes in Southern literature over its long span. Understandably, after 1865, when surviving became triumph enough, the theme of endurance became even more pronounced in the works of Joel Chandler Harris, Charles Egbert Craddock, Grace King, Ellen Glasgow, Josephine Pinckney, DuBose Heyward, Julia Peterkin, Elizabeth Allston Pringle, Elizabeth Madox Roberts, Havilah Babcock, and Archibald Rutledge, to name only a few of the lesser-known authors. Faulkner's Nobel address is on this subject. He learned the value of endurance from the common Southern experience of his own family and of Southerners who survived the great trauma of total war and its aftermath. Simms said of Southern women on the home front: they behaved nobly under their insults in the hour of trial "when nothing can be opposed to the tempest but the virtue of inflexible endurance."[5] This description sounds much like Margaret Mitchell's Scarlett O'Hara and, of course, the women of Faulkner's *The Unvanquished.*

The Nobel address is not just a period piece of the Cold War era as it is sometimes seen to be, but more a summation of the strengths of Southern culture in its chivalry: honor, pity, pride, compassion, sacrifice, and most especially endurance. Reynolds Price, the contemporary Southern novelist phrased it nicely: "Surviving, not flourishing, has always been a Southern specialty."

In May 1970, I visited Rowan Oak for the first time. Faulkner had been dead a little less than eight years and I had just come from his grave at St. Peter's Cemetery where the clay still showed red through sparse grass healing over the dug grave. I was twenty-five years old and just completing my dissertation on *The Hamlet.* This was an important pilgrimage for me. Faulkner's reputation had been growing steadily in the 1960s, but he was far from being the towering figure he is recognized to be today.

Faulkner's house itself was not disappointing. Most literary shrines are, but here the visitor felt the writer. His khakis on the little single bed by the battered typewriter looked like he had just put them there. It was if he had stepped out for a bit and would come back any moment. He might already be behind you entering the door. The experience was just that real. A spring breeze circulated through open doors and windows, blowing sheer white curtains to and fro. A faint but distinct fragrance of Faulkner's favorite sweet-shrubs from the dirt swept garden could be detected over the smell of an old house recalling my own Grandmother's. Faulkner had walked these paths a short eight years ago. Were some of the spadings and diggings in the garden soil his own?

In the house itself, there were no climate control mechanisms, security systems, or glowing red EXIT signs, so destructive of the *genus loci*. There was no hermetic sealing with storm windows or doors or vinyl siding on the old heart-pine clapboards outside. The floors were honest native pine, unsanded and devoid of encasing in polyurethane. They yielded to the feet and bespoke the feet of many others before. This was not a museum but a home, the home of a special individual.

Faulkner was a good and devoted gardener. Dr. Meriwether, at the time my dissertation director, had told me so. In fact, as I have said in the introduction, in the 1950s, Meriwether had hired on with Faulkner to assist him in gardening when he himself was doing his dissertation on the author.

Indeed, in the yard, among the field rock borders and swept dirt paths, there were a dozen or more *Calycanthus*, called variously in the South, sweet-shrub, Carolina allspice, or bubby bush. It made me feel at home immediately. My aunt had a large one at the water spigot at the edge of her vegetable garden, and I had transplanted cuttings to my parents' yard, not yet having a place of my own. The sweet-shrubs were blooming as they would be at home. Where the sun struck them this morning, their peculiar spikey reddish-brown flowers were giving off their unforgettable scent.

But it was an old blasted and dying pear tree in Faulkner's back yard that attracted my attention. In my meanderings, I kept circling back to it. It, or what was left of it, was about seven feet high. The soot-black rough bark was brittle. The twisted trunk had no hint of life. The tree leaned at an angle of forty-five degrees and would have fallen for sure were it not for the support of a cedar post inserted at an angle in what remained of a cleft in the trunk where branches had been (Haynes, 37).

It was remarkable that there was one new green joyous shoot at the top. I felt that the tree seemed to be singing life in leaves, although they were few. The young man who was the keeper of the house and grounds shared my admiration for Faulkner and was generous with his time. He said, yes, it was indeed Mr. Faulkner who had honed the cedar post to smoothness and placed it there. It was done not long before he died. That is what I needed to know.

In 1992, Jane Isbell Haynes in her *William Faulkner's Lafayette County Heritage,* included a photograph of the pear tree stump with the caption, "Faulkner would not allow its removal. The remnants of this stump finally disappeared around 1984." In Isbell's photograph, taken less than fourteen years after my visit and my own photograph, Faulkner's cedar post was gone.

What significance did this tree have for Faulkner? Maybe some family associations gathered around it. Perhaps he had planted it thirty years before when he first came there to the dilapidated old house. I rejected the latter possibility when I considered its age. Like the house itself, it must have preceded the new owner. Pear trees do not usually live to be ancient, but this one may very well have been more than a century old. If Faulkner thought so, then the tree would have been witness to the burning of Oxford. The fire's cinders may have floated there to nourish it. It may have been witness to the fire's glare that leveled the town.

For whatever reason, Faulkner helped it to survive. Apparently others wanted it removed, but, as Jane Isbell Haynes reported, he would not hear of it. Many gardeners and most landscape crews would have deemed it an eyesore. But I conjecture that Faulkner must have admired its will to survive, and the fact that with very little future, it still put forth leaves. Even here, despite odds, the life force was strong and the struggle to go on was intense. He must have felt that he could at least show respect for it with the carefully planed cedar post. Cedar it would be, for cedar would last beyond him.

I like to think of it as a living symbol for Faulkner's own burned land surviving and carrying on. I wonder if

Faulkner did not see it the same way. In the Nobel address of 1950, in speaking of the writer's duty, Faulkner used the words "pillars and props to help man endure and prevail." Here in his backyard he had fashioned such a physical, literal prop. I have no doubt that he understood the symbolic implications of his act. Here was the tangible propping that mirrored what he had done for forty years with the round wooden stylus that had spread ink on the page, making words that themselves were written so carefully to have endured. Honing cedar to smoothness is just another kind of craftsmanship after all, just in a different medium. As an amateur carpenter, Faulkner, like his character Cash in *As I Lay Dying*, understood the meaning of "I made it on the bevel"—so that it would not let the water in and last.

Here follows the simple poem I wrote in May 1970 after seeing the struggling pear tree propped with Faulkner's cedar. The scene struck me as being well worth recording. Both tree and prop have been gone now for several decades and few are left who recall it, hence the poem's additional last stanzas.

IN FAULKNER'S GARDEN, 10 MAY 1970

It made triangle:
Pear tree leaning hard toward death;
The base, home's soil itself,

Hypotenuse a polished cedar prop
Placed at a cleft to shore tree up
For one more year of life renewed.

The man who placed support
Often spoke of props
Helping man endure, prevail.
It was his cast of mind,
This shoring up of things
Bespeaking struggle in a struggling time.
He knew the process well.
The fall-out ashes of war-wasted town
No doubt had fed the tree
That may have even felt the glare of August 1864.
It was a link in time,
This living-tissued monument,
Become the artifice eternity
In shaping shoring hands,
A more than prop—a solid pyramid immutable.

Half century has passed.
Today the tree is gone
Succumbed to drought, or wind,
Or just a gardener's tidying up.

But it remains like truth
Because I saw it there,
Still see it clear in memory—
The one green joyous shoot atop,
Singing life in leaves though leaves were few;
And in these lines
Prop it again
With cedar-penciled memory,
Poor words the leaves of life
Replenishing the branch
Into a hemispheric tree
Bearing perfect fruit.

EIGHT

FAULKNER THE PRESERVATIONIST

> Greed is the resort of the uninspired.
> —William Gilmore Simms

Faulkner purchased a dilapidated antebellum plantation house in April 1930. It was known as the old Shegog place, built on the edge of the village of Oxford by Robert B. Shegog, an Irish emigrant from County Down, in 1844 (Parini, 155). The home had been a handsome plantation great house but had been deserted and become decayed. The windows upstairs had rotted and fallen out and termites had been busy in the floor joists. Faulkner was a fairly good and careful carpenter and did most of the restoration work with his own hands. This was to be his and his family's home until his death over three decades later.

Faulkner moved into the dilapidated old house the summer of 1930. His actions caused many of the locals' heads to shake—Count-No-count was at it again. The work of restoration was not just cosmetic or planting geraniums in a window box. It involved jacking up sagging sections of the house and replacing rotten and termite-riddled beams. Faulkner did the restoration sensitively. He kept to a minimum any alteration that would violate the home's original integrity. He patched and retained the cracked walls' hard plaster, including a star-shaped plaster ceiling medallion that remains today in the hall. He repaired and hung operable exterior shutters at the windows, upstairs and down. This was his effective air conditioning system. When he first moved in, lacking electricity, he used oil lanterns and had no plumbing. The Faulkners used an outhouse. They drew their water from a well in a well-house (Parini, 155).

1930 was a year when Faulkner had no money to spare. He had just married his now divorced childhood sweetheart in June 1929. His wife brought two children to the marriage. Faulkner's own first child was born in January 1931. She was named Alabama after Faulkner's great aunt. The little girl died less than two weeks later. There were many bills to pay. His second child was born 24 June 1933. As is often the case, monetary restraints no doubt helped encourage Faulkner to keep his restoration pure and honest. He was certainly not interested in seeing his house featured as some do today as a *Southern Living* photo spread.

As one indication of how some literary scholars have not quite understood Faulkner, one might consider Dr. David Aiken's recollection of a Faulkner seminar at the University of North Carolina in the summer of 1968 in which the Southern literary critic Professor Louis Rubin, often quoted here in this work, called Faulkner foolish for restoring the old house. He said that it took too much of Faulkner's creative effort in an impractical, romantic gesture.[1]

Rubin was echoing his time. In the history of America, the post-World War II generation was perhaps the most destructive of the built environment in its embracing of the new, artificial, and mass-produced. This is the era in which the main streets of many towns lost their brick façades to aluminum encasements. This is the era of "The Jetsons" on the new televisions that were becoming the rage with rich and poor alike. The members of this generation deemed an out-with-the-old and in-with-the-new philosophy to be the ultimate "practical" approach. In the eyes of some, this work of restoration was simply impractical. A sensitive critic of his canon would find Faulkner's big project fitting. Faulkner's love of the old and genuine pervaded all his work as a constant.

Faulkner enjoyed carpenter work, and the imagery and diction of carpentering and woodworking suffuses his writing. It is particularly prevalent in *As I Lay Dying*, a novel he was writing during his early work on the house. As mentioned in the previous chapter, carpenter Cash Bundren's famous "I built it on a bevel" when referring to his craftsmanship in making his mother's coffin, is a case in point. Even two decades later in the Nobel address Faulkner imaged writing as craftsmanship akin to woodworking: "leaving no room in his workshop for anything but the old verities and truths of the heart" by which to erect props and pillars to help man endure. Of the materials from his life which he used for his fiction, Faulkner called them "the lumber in the attic" (Cullen, vii). Faulkner was thus a hands-on preservationist in a way that was in keeping with his anti-abstractionist philosophy, as discussed in chapter three, "Abstraction as Nemesis."

We see his honoring of the past so clearly in his respect for the old structure that was to become Rowan Oak. It has only been recently that the house was "climate controlled" with air conditioning and central heat. Faulkner never considered storm windows or doors or that scourge of preservationists, vinyl or aluminum siding, all the rage after post-World War II's progressive, anti-traditional push to make everything "convenient," efficient, and modern. No need to repaint! How simple and natural was the opposite way of thinking for Faulkner. A true, deep honoring of the past created for Faulkner the preservation guidelines that prevented making wrong choices. His good preservation "theory" was just instinctive.

In 1947, Faulkner wrote the following to his local newspaper:

> Bravo your piece about the preservation of the courthouse. I am afraid your cause is already lost though. We have gotten rid of the shade trees which once…bordered the Square itself, along with the second floor galleries

which once formed awnings for the sidewalk; all we have left now to distinguish an old Southern town from any one of ten thousand towns built yesterday from Kansas to California are the Confederate monument, the courthouse and the jail. Let us tear them down too and put up something covered with neon and radio amplifiers (*Essays,* 202-203).

The first Lafayette County Courthouse was built in 1840, then burned by U. S. troops under Gen. A. J. Smith in 1864. It was rebuilt in 1874. George Stewart has written accurately that Faulkner "had a profound regard" for the courthouse, its "symbolic social value, and the durability of its architecture and history" (9). In this way, as we will see later, he is much like his character Sarty Snopes in Faulkner's story "Barn Burning." Sarty looks at a great columned plantation mansion and compares it to the courthouse, both symbols of order, justice, and high aspirations. For Sarty, these structures are worth preserving against the fires his arsonist father sets, and he saves the mansion even though it means he must lose his father.

Faulkner continued in his letter to the editor that Oxford's old buildings

will go the way of the old Cumberland church. It was here in 1861...the only building on or near the square still standing in 1865. It was tougher than war, tougher than the Yankee Brigadier Chalmers and his artillery and his sappers with dynamite and crowbars and cans of kerosene. But it wasn't tougher than the ringing of a cash register bell. It had to go—obliterated, effaced, no trace left—so that a sprawling octopus covering the country from Portland, Maine to Oregon can dispense in cut-rate bargain lots, bananas and toilet paper (*Essays,* 202-203).

Faulkner concluded, "They call this progress. But they don't say where it's going: also there are some who would like the chance to say whether or not we want the ride."

In 1834, over a century before Faulkner wrote his letter to the editor, Simms wrote that progressive Northern "levelism" and "that love of change which is the delirium of unaccustomed license" was a powerful force that once begun was like a large New York City omnibus going down hill and gaining speed as it went. Without brakes, it smashed everything in its path. Simms cautioned that all the old and genuine, from buildings to manners, would be obliterated. His wise advice from his Southern way of seeing was to "Spare that which time would spare." He concluded, let us "preserve the memorials which are true to taste" and "not destroy, with headlong

153

stupidity" the past's temples and "high columns—the vaulted grandeur of its dwellings," for these are tangible embodiments of the "spirit that was great and glorious in the history of the past."[2]

A good poem also on the respect due these grand memorials of the past is Simms's "Veneration," written in 1839. Here Simms, with the tone of anger rising in his voice, said of the one who, with all the gifts bestowed by the past, destroys and gives nothing to the future:

> Thou hast been false to both [past and future], hast lived for neither,
>
> But to the selfish present hast devoted
>
> The rights of time—go, profligate—make answer
>
> To the eternity, and hear thy doom.
>
> As thou hast lived but for thyself, go perish. [3]

Simms's selfish egocentric individual locked in the present is the perfect portrayal of Allen Tate's provincial of time, of Andrew Lytle's "momentary man" living only in the moment, and of Tate's and Lytle's prediction of the doom that awaits him.

The authors of *I'll Take My Stand* understood the materialistic, self-centered bourgeois boosterism of the New South that would level everything in the path of progress like Simms's runaway city omnibus. The momentary men who lived for the gratification of the moment were the antithesis of what they deemed Southern. These materialists had the stereotypical Northern mindset that C. Vann Woodward called "a cash-register evaluation of life." Such men veiled their motives with the shimmering word "progress," that amounted to a virtual religion in the new century. It is remarkable that Woodward, no traditionalist himself, could conclude that the protective barrier that the antebellum South was erecting against such a philosophy of "money as measure" and "progress-for-the-sake-of-progress" was "blown to pieces by the guns of the Civil War."

Despite the New South materialists, the first zoning ordinances for historic preservation in America were written first in Charleston and then New Orleans, setting up the first historic districts in America. The New Orleans ordinance is particularly pertinent to Faulkner because he was living in the city during the decade when the ordinance was conceived, discussed, and hammered out. These two famous ordinances were preceded a decade earlier by the founding of the Society for the Preservation of Old Dwellings in Charleston and the Society for the Preservation of Virginia Antiquities, themselves preceded by many years by the preservation of George Washington's Mount Vernon, America's first national shrine to be saved, and as a result of the tireless work of a plantation lady from Upcountry South Carolina born in 1816.[4] In 1853, after the federal government refused to buy the house and grounds, that lady, Pamela Cunningham, wrote her famous letter "To the Ladies of the South" asking for support, which came, and the home was saved in 1856. Shortly before her death in 1875, she plead to let at least one spot in this country be "saved from 'change'!" And so it has been done by the Mount Vernon Ladies Association, largely as a result of Southern foresight and devotion.

The popular, perhaps too-quotable quote, "Too poor to paint, too proud to whitewash," is sometimes used to explain why Charleston saved so many of its early buildings. I have even heard a prominent speaker on the city's architecture say that it was as if poverty preserved her like a beetle in amber. While no doubt true in some instances, this explanation does not give Charlestonians proper credit for their honoring of history and the valuing of the genuine and true. The city's 1783 Latin motto on her city seal, after all, declares: *Aedes mores jurasque curat*— "She protects her customs, laws, and buildings." There is nothing equivocal about that.

Another proof is an antebellum article in a Charleston newspaper which I encountered many years ago researching Simms's poetry. I recall what an impact it made on me from its shadowy microfilm image. The essay was on St. Andrew's Episcopal Parish Church on the Ashley River Road just outside the city. The early colonial structure was built in 1706 and was about a century and a half old at the time of the article. It was showing the stress of age and was too small to house its congregation. Despite the reasons for demolition and rebuilding, the movement to preserve the church was successful, and it should be noted, nearly a century before the enacting of Charleston's preservation zoning ordinance.

Although ransacked and vandalized by invading troops in both the Revolution and 1865, and badly damaged by the earthquake of 1886, the city of Charleston survives today as a testament to long-term Southern preservation. The initial movement to save St. Andrew's Parish Church came in flush antebellum times, so poverty obviously does not explain its preservation. It was saved in both boom and bust times and now serves an active congregation. One other similar example in Charleston is the preservation of the city's Old Exchange, the old customs house of 1767—an elegant Palladian structure where patriots were jailed during the Revolution, the United States Constitution was ratified, and President Washington was entertained with a great ball on his Southern tour in 1791. It was damaged by Federal bombardment in 1863-1865 and further weakened by the earthquake of 1886. The federal government was on the verge of demolishing it during Reconstruction, when Charlestonians, in the most destitute of economic times, stepped in and prevented the beloved structure's demolition, bolted the brick walls together with earthquake bolts, and preserved the building. It was again threatened with demolition in 1912, but preservationists again succeeded in saving it. The Old Exchange underwent extensive restoration in 1976 and sits proudly today with its cupola restored, at the foot of Broad Street, a sturdy survivor of Hurricane Hugo in 1989 and a testament to Southern preservation despite the wasteful national throw-away society's rage to destroy and replace.

Unfortunately, however, the recent demolition of the Calhoun Monument in Marion Square is another story. The tides of political change exemplified by a sign that replaced it is telling. The sign read "Vote Socialist." Above it, were the shadowed removed words of the Monument awaiting bulldozing and hauling away: "Liberty, Justice, and the Constitution." A disregard of the past more destructive than war, earthquake, and wealth had succeeded in accomplishing this frenzy of vandalism.

Preservation, despite such unfortunate aberrations, is a Southern tradition, as might be expected in what has always been a predominantly traditionalist society. Faulkner had other options in 1930, but his decision to take on the saving of the dilapidated antebellum mansion which became his home and today is arguably the nation's most important literary shrine, signifies just how traditionally Southern he was in this respect.

Critics Brooks and Millgate both understood that Faulkner's impulse to preservation of the built environment extended to the Southern culture itself. In distinguishing the difference between the love of place shared by Faulkner and Thomas Hardy, as opposed to Faulkner and William Butler Yeats, Millgate made the important point that Hardy's world that he wished to preserve in his fiction had already passed and was a thing of only the past, unrestoreable except on the printed page, but both Faulkner and Yeats insisted "upon the necessary preservation into a foreseeable future of a regional distinctiveness that remains, in [their] own day, a cultural and political reality" (Millgate, Place, 79). This is a very important distinction.

Allen Tate in his 1949 essay, "Ezra Pound and the Bollingen Prize," provides my favorite quotation on the traditional Southern impulse to conserve, salvage, and preserve. Tate declared, "The task of the civilized intelligence is one of perpetual salvage" (*Essays of Four Decades*, 512; *Collected Essays*, 536). The key words in Tate's sentence are "civilized" and "perpetual." The shifting flash-fads of Andrew Lytle's "momentary men" are the diametric opposite. The way of the momentary men is generally the American way. Faulkner's, Lytle's, and Tate's way of perpetual salvage is the Southern way. Tate, quite the anglophile (of what was left of the landed gentry, at least) understood well the sources of the impulse. Southerners like Tate and Faulkner no doubt intuited from their breadth of history what Sir John Kenneth Galbraith meant when he declared that "Preservationists are the only people history invariably proves right."

James P. Cantrell accurately designated as a salient trait of Southern writing, "an awareness of man's role as despoiler of God's nature that is decidedly non-transcendental" (83). An as yet little-known Southern author, Adam G. Summer (1818-1866), wrote eloquently on the need to preserve forests, soil, and other natural resources. As Andrea Wulf has written in *Founding Gardeners,* contrary to many sources on environmental writing, the literature of conservation did not begin in New England in the 1860s. Summer's criticism of American wastefulness, disregard of the future, mania with getting rich quick, and disregard of the long-term results for Chamber of Commerce style short-term gains predates both Henry David Thoreau and Scotsman John Muir.

Summer had much to say about the "insanity" of materialism and a throw-away society. His preservation theories included his statement, "We are averse to all big things." He advocated "sustainability" as a goal and used the word at least twice in his writing. His localist approach to nature sounds very current today. An edition of his nature writing, *Taking Root,* was published in 2018 by the University of South Carolina Press and prefaced by Wendell Berry's forward.

Although we see it throughout his canon, *Go Down, Moses* is Faulkner's clearest critique of man's careless destruction of the natural world. The wanton disregard of nature is reflected in Roth Edmonds' shameful treatment of the woman he has gotten pregnant. Often in Faulkner, the way a character treats nature is mirrored in the way he treats women. In the "Delta Autumn" section of *Go Down, Moses,* Faulkner describes the break-down in morality, sexual and otherwise, leading into World War II. What had been unwritten laws concerning hunting game now have to written down and enforced by game wardens. The law is now seen as a uniform and a badge, made necessary by man's lack of honorable personal codes.

In *The Hamlet*, Eula, a strong life force in a materialistic realm, is not appreciated. Mirroring this lack of appreciation is man's despoiling the landscape even down to cutting the dogwood trees to be made into cotton spindles for cotton mills. Eula is the mythic "eternal feminine" "waiting for no one"—that is, for no proper man to call. Instead, her father barters her to Flem Snopes, the impotent one, the embodiment of ruthless acquisitiveness—a man who goes from farmer to clerk to merchant to real estate dealer to bank president in his Horatio Alger Chamber of Commerce achievement of the American Dream, the debased version thereof, in Faulkner's mind, having nothing to do with the Southern way of seeing. Faulkner would have equated Flem's way more with a New South (No South) way.

Eula and Flem's story is the old one of Venus married to the impotent Vulcan who cannot appreciate her. Faulkner understood the ancient story well and cast the myth in its proper twentieth century context against a backdrop of wasted land. The fertile natural world becomes the legal property of the cold, metronome-like, mechanical man, who can only desire profit. Greed thus becomes the resort of the sterile, uninspired, impotent, unnatural man. Flem, like his other Snopes kin (except little Sarty and poor, unfortunate Eck), thus moves over the countryside, as Faulkner said elsewhere "like mould on cheese, destroying everything of beauty." Armstid, in the novel's final scene, is made insane by greed and digs himself into his own grave hunting nonexistent buried treasure in the middle of a ruined garden. This garden was once a thing of beauty in the antebellum days when beauty was appreciated.

Like Eula, fertile Lena Grove, in *Light in August,* is also unappreciated. She is pregnant and in search of her lover, who stays one step ahead of her, fleeing her and responsibility. The novel's story is played out against a backdrop of the stumps of giant trees in a pocked and barren landscape denuded by saw mills. In *Absalom, Absalom!* Faulkner has Thomas Sutpen rip out of the wilderness a great house debased and doomed by a faulty abstract "design" very different from the gentry's model that sustained the culture of England for four centuries. What wonder the house is burned down at the novel's end.

As Brooks points out, Sutpen's "design" is not Southern at all. It originates in the mind as an I-centered abstract, the Southern nemesis, in a most un-Southern way. The great house does not represent a place of family and high motives, but the abstract selfish imposition of a man's egocentric will on nature. Women are thus also only abstracts, objects necessary to Sutpen's design. The literary critic often sees Sutpen as Faulkner's symbol of the Old South, not crediting the fact that Sutpen hails from the mountains of West Virginia and is not accepted by the members of the settled truly Southern community he comes to—the real representations of the Old South in the novel, if one must find them. Realizing Faulkner's Southern values allows the reader to see that Sutpen, like Jason Compson and Flem Snopes, is one of Faulkner's most un-Southern characters.

Passages describing the ruthless destruction of nature crop up everywhere in Faulkner's fiction. Often the abuse of people is parallel to the activity of sawmill camps and logging operations in *Light in August.* As we will see later, the drama in the lives of characters is played out against a landscape dominated by a burning plantation house debased by an abolitionist Puritan Calvinist New England family turned secular into zealous crusading and diametrically opposed to Southern traditions, by illicit and perverted love trysts in the Sacred Grove of the overgrown great house garden, and by falling trees in a disappearing wilderness. The logging train snakes through the Big Woods in *Go Down, Moses* where the cries of a few of Faulkner's "Lord God birds," the ivory-bill wood-pecker, get rarer and rarer.

Faulkner no doubt knew the great controversy over the ivory-bill. It was brewing and in full force as he was writing the sections of *Go Down, Moses*. The bird was being studied and filmed in the late 1930s. At the same time, logging in-creased in the Singer tract on the Tensas River in Louisiana where the last birds were being sighted and studied. The log-ging of trees really heated up in 1940, two years before the novel was published. In response to pleas from ornithologists and the governors of Louisiana, Mississippi, Arkansas, and Tennessee to spare this area, the Chicago Mill and Lumber Company instead sped their logging into high gear. Louisiana governor Jones raised $200,000 as an initial pledge to pur-chase the tract, but was refused. The Audubon Society got in-volved, but to no avail. As Faulkner's novel came from the press in 1942, the tragedy was almost accomplished. The Singer Sewing Machine family of Chicago who owned the land refused to sell or intercede, and the last bird was sighted in 1944 in a small part of the tract yet to be denuded. The or-nithologist who had sighted the bird fled rather than see the tree that held a nesting pair of birds felled. A touching and enlightening account of this event appears in Tim Gallagher's *The Grail Bird.*

While Faulkner did not usually agree with him, Ike McCaslin's vision of the future for the exploited Southern wilderness of Faulkner's childhood has the sharp edge of Faulkner's own passion. The passage is reminiscent of the prophetic Celtic *aisling*, or prescient dream-vision. McCaslin, as an old man, lies in his hunter's tent shaking from the cold and listening to the rain:

This Delta, he thought: This Delta. *This land which man has deswamped and denuded and derivered in two generations so that white men can own plantations and commute every night to Memphis and black men own plantations and ride in jim crow cars to Chicago to live in millionaires' mansions on Lakeshore Drive, where white men rent farms and live like niggers and niggers crop on shares and live like animals, where cotton is planted and grows man-tall in the very cracks of the sidewalks, and usury and mortgage and bankruptcy and measureless wealth, Chinese and African and Aryan and Jew, all breed and spawn together until no man has time to say which one is which nor cares....*No wonder the ruined woods I used to know dont cry for retribution he thought: The people who have destroyed it will accomplish its revenge (*Go Down Moses*, 364).

As Faulkner expressed it himself in his interview with Ed Kimbrough in 1951, he loved farms, horses, silence "and trees"—and trees most particularly (Faulkner, *Lion,* 54). In Faulkner's fiction, logging trains, imaged as winding like snakes in Eden, carry their dead remains away. It was not just forest trees that he loved. We recall earlier in this chapter, that he complained about the town's cutting trees around the courthouse in Oxford.

Throughout Faulkner's canon, one is startled by the shocking juxtapositions of his veritable great hymns to nature and the atrocities of destruction committed by the rapacious ones. Here again, one finds the author's contrasting of a bourgeois mercantile petty and short-sighted mindset that spreads its blight over the countryside "like mould on cheese destroying everything of beauty," and its opposite ideal of civilized stewardship of the land that salvages, conserves, and preserves rather than destroys.

It is clear to me that Faulkner understood what was at stake in the struggle. *Go Down, Moses* should as surely stand in the forefront of social history depicting the horrors of the industrial revolution's rape of the land (and people) as do Mrs. Elizabeth Gaskell's *Cranford,* Thomas Hardy's *Tess of the D'Urbervilles*, or some of the novels of Charles Dickens. From a thematic standpoint, they tell similar stories. Among Faulkner's own Southern literary contemporaries and confreres, the works of Ellen Glasgow, Caroline Gordon, Andrew Lytle, Robert Penn Warren, Harriet Arnow, Archibald Rutledge, Havilah Babcock, Elizabeth Allston Pringle, Julia Peterkin, and Flannery O'Connor also come quickly to mind. Among Faulkner's heirs to whom the mantle was passed are Ron Rash, Fred Chappell, Wendell Berry, Harry Crews, Cormac McCarthy, and Larry Brown.

O'Connor's "A View of the Woods," written in 1957 and published in her *Everything That Rises Must Converge,* is perhaps her most dramatic and masterful treatment of the destructive potential of the machine, first on nature which then leads to human self-destruction. The story ends with only one survivor—the "big disembodied gullet," of the "one huge yellow monster…gorging itself on clay" (*O'Connor,* 525, 546). Once again, it is the traditional Southern story of man's attempting to play God, as we will explore in our next chapter on Finitude. Man's tool here is the machine. "A View of the Woods," for me, is one of O'Connor's premier masterpieces, even though little read. No doubt one of the reasons it has not achieved its proper due in anthologies is that it criticizes too sharply and meaningfully all the assumptions the materialistic technocratic nation is built upon. It as well hits a little too closely to home in its revelation of the flaws in the personal value systems in a large number of Americans. The subject is certainly one of the central interests of the literature of the South in the twentieth century, and Faulkner was deeply and centrally engaged in its portrayal.

In *The Hamlet* Faulkner commented on the denuding of lush Southern land when even the dogwood trees are cut to make cotton mill spindles. He could have used no better symbolism to point to the war upon nature and her beauties as a result of the industrial revolution.

Larry Brown's fine novel *Joe* (1991), set in Oxford and the countryside around it, also draws parallels between the brutalizing of people and the brutalized landscape. The novel's title character is a tree poisoner employed by a timber company. He is injecting poisons into unwanted saplings on a clear-cut at the same time he is injecting the poison of alcohol into his own body. John Crowe Ransom in his introduction to *I'll Take My Stand* writes that the American way is not to make peace and coexist with nature "but to wage an unrelenting war on Nature" (7). That is the not-so-shining Puritan legacy of shining cities on hills, a legacy that prepares for Singer Sewing Machine Companies and Chicago Mill and Lumbers. The virgin forests of Louisiana may have lined city pockets and built structures in the Midwest, but at a tremendous cost. "How much is a species worth in dollars and cents and shareholders' profits?" we can hear Faulkner ask in his fiction. It is the same war against nature dramatized by current Southern novelist Ron Rash in many of his celebrated recent works, the most famous of which are *Serena* (2008) and *Saints at the River* (2004).

The once grand formal garden of the great house in *Light in August* is profaned as the site of illicit love trysts. The columned home is debased even further from the Southern ethos that built it with ownership by descendants of New England Puritan zealots. It is the pillar of smoke from this burning house that is seen at the beginning of the novel. In *Absalom*, the great house in its overgrown garden burns to the ground at the novel's end. The fine antebellum formal garden of the Old Frenchman Place in *The Hamlet* is being destroyed by treasure hunters digging for buried gold; and the shell of the deserted plantation great house itself is being stripped for firewood and building materials for shanties. In the late twentieth century Mississippi novels of Larry Brown, not even the vestiges of great houses exist to remind the desperately impoverished inhabitants of the land that the grand houses were once there, and of what they might represent of a better way. The place is now a cultural blank slate where the word "barren" would be too mild a description.

Faulkner understood well the great house tradition (Bradford, 84-91). His sensitive restoration of one such antebellum great house proves that he chose to be an active preservationist, not just an advocate. Lady Gregory's Coole Park was such a great house to Yeats, as were Penshurst to Ben Jonson, Appleton House to Andrew Marvell, Fair Saxham to Sir Thomas Carew, Pemberley to Jane Austen, Penhally to Caroline Gordon, Monticello to Jefferson, Stratford and Arlington to the Lees, Drayton Hall and Magnolia to the Draytons, Middleton House to the Middletons, Woodlands to both Simms and Donald Davidson,[5] and Hampton Plantation House to Archibald Rutledge, to name only a literary few—all structures representing humane order and enduring values, stewardship, and true community—the high point monuments of Western civilization to their builders and those blessed enough to live in them.

Richard Gil's *Happy Rural Seat: The English Country House and the Literary Imagination* (1972), and Mark Girouard's *A Country House Companion* (1987) treat the South's historical English counterparts. As seats of family established on the land and stewarded for generational continuity, these buildings have been depositories of art, literature, and history. And more than archives and museums, they are the tangible representations of the family itself in such a Southern way. Their absence in Larry Brown's late twentieth century rural Southern world is thus all the more poignant. He portrays the results of a terrible war of invasion having damaged the agrarian Southern world irreparably. In losing their cultural monuments and continuities, the people lose their identity and their moorings. They then become easy prey for all manner of predators, big and small. Cultural genocide awaits.

Larry Brown's monument of the Confederate soldier in front of the courthouse in Oxford is one monument his characters have left them, but the soldier (unlike Oxford's actual monument) has a rifle whose bayonet is broken off at the heft. This small detail easily missed by the reader is symbolically significant. For Brown, there is no defense today against the invasion of savage and alien un-Southern ways, demonstrated most obviously and pervasively as the despoiling of forest landscapes in clear-cutting and chemical poisonings by outside timber concerns. A quick look into the early twentieth century history of Brown's community, Tula, Mississippi, not far from Oxford, reveals the shocking, poignant story of a great ancient forest denuded and hauled out on logging trains. The despoiling of a place effectively reduced to desperate colonial status is the result of a culture kicked to pieces.[6]

Faulkner's most recent biographer has stated that "Faulkner in particular always yearned to replicate the Big House that his grandfather lorded over. His characters are always in awe of fine houses, always yearning for land…. He knew these feelings intimately, and he wanted something grand and glorious, an imposing house that would reify his

171

internal sense of self" (Parini, 155). While there is truth here about Faulkner's desire to preserve a great house, Parini's spin seems colored by an attitude at best ignorant of the great house tradition itself and Faulkner's Southern sensibility that understood it fully. After all, it was his birthright. He did not want a place to "lord over" or by which to "reify a sense of self." It was not a materialist's robber baron snobbery that led him to pull out rotten beams and rehang windows in vacant slots, but a Southern way of feeling, seeing, believing, and acting that was Faulkner's center. In this way, in the long view, he also connected to the highest aspirations in Western culture. As such, his impulse transcended Southern culture while it connected it to its own roots. Parini's treatment is just another example of how the biographer and critic can be misled if they do not know the culture which bred Faulkner and his conscious connections to it.

In comparing Faulkner and Yeats, Brooks understood the proper significance to these writers of great houses and the squirearchy that built and stewarded them. Of Yeats and Lady Gregory at Coole Park, Brooks says that it was not Lady Gregory's title and wealth (which was minimal anyway) that Yeats valued, but "rather the courage, self-discipline, magnanimity, courtesy, graciousness—in short, the aristocratic virtues.... Such, too, were the qualities and virtues that Faulkner admired in the Old South" (Brooks, *Toward Yoknapatawpha,* 335). The great house became the physical symbol of these virtues in both men's work, particularly Faulkner's.

A Yeats scholar has said for Yeats what may also be said of Faulkner: the attraction of the great house tradition was more a quality of intellect than class (Torchiana, *Yeats and Georgian England,* 89-90). Brooks has expanded the concept to include literature, a code of self-discipline, responsibility, and effort, and a marked resentment of the bourgeois ethic of materialism—the "leveling, rancorous, rational sort of mind," to use Yeats's phrase[7] or again, to quote Yeats, of those who "fumble in a greasy till/ And add the halfpence to the pence" until they've "dried the marrow from the bone." There is no better description of Faulkner's Jason Compson or his Snopeses.

We may also add to what Faulkner felt the great house to represent, the central idea of harmony and order amidst a tangled disorder. One of the few good Snopeses, Sarty Snopes in "Barn Burning," is perhaps the best spokesman for this view. As we have already said, Sarty declares that the beauty and grandeur of Major DeSpain's classical columned mansion reminds him of the courthouse. He has to make the hardest choice of his young life when he goes against his father in order to protect the house from burning. Outlawry, violence, hatred, Marxist-style class envy, and the chaos they cause stand against and threaten the very fabric of an ordered, civilized society, which Sarty sees represented in the courthouse-great house itself. With no formal education, Sarty has only to look at the house to understand the essentials of what the great house has represented throughout time. Thomas Jefferson would no doubt have included Sarty among his natural *aristoi*.

I think Brooks rightly concluded that both Yeats' and Faulkner's view of man "is on its positive side aristocratic and heroic" with "close affinities to the orthodox classical-Christian view of man" (*Toward Yoknapatawpha,* 343). As usual, with a few words, Professor Brooks has gone to the heart of the matter.

Six days after her son's seventh birthday, Faulkner's mother, Maude Butler Faulkner, penned this note in his King James Bible: "Just after his 7th birthday, William & Muddie [his grandmother Lelia Butler] were studying the Sunday School lesson. In reply to Muddie's question… 'William, what would you rather have than anything else?' he answered, after a moment's thought, 'I'd rather have honor and do what's right.' Saturday—Oct. 1—1904."[8] Here already present in the young Faulkner is the old chivalric code represented purely in its "aristocratic and heroic" positive side.

Brooks noted that the "history of man is the history of the creation of such codes and man's struggle to live up to them or his failure to do so." He continued, Faulkner's heroes struggle mightily to do so. His villains like Flem Snopes,

Popeye, or Jason Compson are men who "deliberately disavow not only the aristocratic code of the Old South but any fully human code" (*Toward Yoknapatawpha,* 342). When Lancelot Snopes' un-Snopesian mother, names him after the most chivalrous knight in King Arthur's court in a valiant attempt to counteract the lethal Snopes inheritance, the child is so ashamed that he changes Lancelot to the more comfortable and appropriate nickname, "Lump."

It is fitting that Flem Snopes, the epitome of bourgeois American materialism, is seen sitting in the barrel "throne" in the ruined formal garden of a once fine great house gone back to weeds and briars at the tragic end of *The Hamlet.* Will Varner, another materialist who trades him the property, bought it out of curiosity just to try to see why any man would need all this just to eat and "lay with his wife in"(28). Snopes now has title to the land and ruined house, but like Varner has no idea what they represent. One step even lower than Varner, Flem is quintessentially the deracinated hollow modern who has been coldly dehumanized in his disavowal of an honorable code and the human feelings that inspired it. Yeats' fumbler in the greasy till, adding the half-penny to the penny until the marrow is dried from the bone would accurately describe him and those of his world obsessively bent on material progress devoid of higher values than the cash-register evaluation of life.

When Faulkner created Flem Snopes in a short story in 1926, he called the piece "Father Abraham." The rail-splitter's popular nickname, log cabin beginnings, and Horatio Alger rise to prominence are clearly drawn upon to parallel Flem's life and career. For those twentieth century unreconstructed Southerners who would not even allow a car with the name of Lincoln on their property, Father Abraham represented the antithesis of the aristocratic values and, with the great war he had fomented and relentlessly waged against the South, he was seen as their destroyer. Faulkner was writing in an age when Lincoln could not be criticized, and to do so would have brought down the anger of the entire Establishment upon the poor offender's head. He would have been so far outside the pale that his New York publisher Random House would not have touched him. "Father Abraham" was not published until 1983 and is still rarely spoken of.

It is interesting to speculate if Faulkner was not echoing the unreconstructed Southerner's sentiment with the comparison of Flem to Lincoln. At any rate, Faulkner clearly envisioned the Snopeses as the bourgeois opposite of the patrician Southerner and the destroyer of Southern patrician values. In one of his first interviews, Faulkner described the contrasting families of Sartoris and Snopes. The Sartorises and Compsons were his patricians, now down on their luck, cuffs frayed, and shabby genteel. The Snopeses, he said, creep over the countryside like "mould over cheese and destroy its traditions and whatever loveliness there was in the place" (*Lion,* 39). For Faulkner, that beauty included all the embodiments of the virtue and taste of the gentry and squirearchy: the great house, a fertile green landscape of ordered rows and pastures, formal gardens, a revered and carefully stewarded natural world, and the ordered justice of the columned courthouse. English author Adam Nicolson's *Gentry: Six Centuries of a Peculiarly English Class* (2011) is a perfect description of how the ideals of the English country squire were imported to the agrarian South in a sensibility like Faulkner's.

In *The Hamlet* (1940), Flem takes ownership of the ruined great house and its ruined formal garden but pawns it off on another in his way up his twisted Horatio Alger American rise to material success. In *The Mansion* (1959), at the Snopes trilogy's end, Flem now owns the Sartoris bank and the bank president's mansion. There he sits alone with his shoes propped on the elaborately carved high mantel. He is cold and as colorless as a dead fish and accepts his violent death without a struggle. The imagery that has surrounded him throughout the trilogy is of the machine. In his last moments, he is the automaton, man transformed to machine, flesh frozen into metal. Such is the process of complete dehumanization charted over the three novels.

Faulkner understood that patrician values did not reside exclusively in the patricians, however. As we have seen, Elnora and Sarty obviously have them, and Jason Compson is as much a Snopes as Flem. A character's attitude toward the values which the great house represents is often what determines a character's status in a most Jeffersonian-Southern way—a version of Jefferson's natural *aristoi.*

Readers should keep in mind that while Faulkner was writing all these novels in which plantation great houses are burning, being profaned, dismantled, or allowed to rot down, he was laboring to preserve and restore one with his own hands. The old heroic culture in shambles and still under attack, would have that one pillar and prop that was a restored Rowan Oak and the creative literary activity that would take place inside. After all, as Brooks noted of Yeats, the great poet associated the manor house itself with literature—as did all the poets in the great house tradition before him.

Faulkner's 1954 essay entitled "Mississippi" described the despoiling of the old growth Southern forest in the early twentieth century at the hands of wealthy Northern interests like the Singer Family. Faulkner depicted a colonial economy in which rich natural resources are milked by men "from Chicago and the Northern cities" where the cash was, "setting up with their Yankee dollars the vast lumbering plants and mills" leaving "stump-pocked barrens" (*Essays,*

20-21). When able to do so in the 1930s, Faulkner did his active share in planting new trees at Greenfield Farm. Just as he was no abstract preservationist, he was thus no armchair conservationist. Perhaps he recalled his early mentor Phil Stone's comment about the Nashville Fugitive group as the "sweatless agrarians" and was making sure this would not be his way.

Wendell Berry in our time, like Faulkner, has exhibited a most Southern attitude to conservation. Although his politics might sometimes be suspect, Berry has always said he was not much of a joiner. It would be fine to belong to a conservation group, he declared, but even better to go pick up trash by the side of your own road. With him, as it was for Faulkner, conservation thus begins at home and in one's own back yard. As traditional Southerners have often said, abstraction is usually the enemy of action. Berry affirms this truth in his *The Need to Be Whole* (2022).

1. 1ˢᵗ Edition Jackets

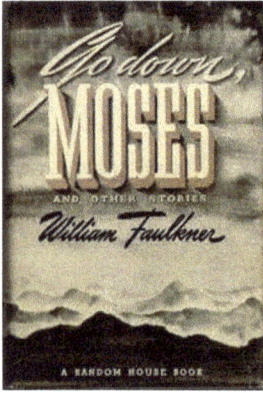

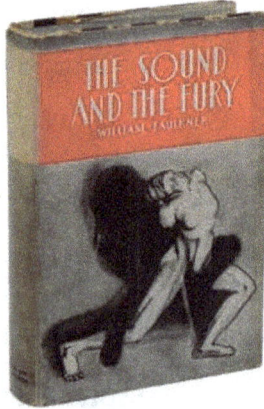

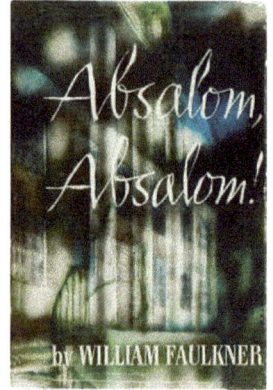

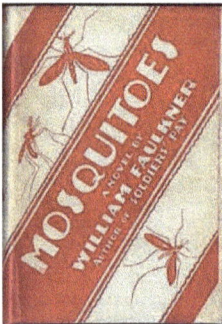

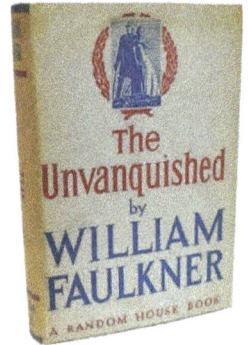

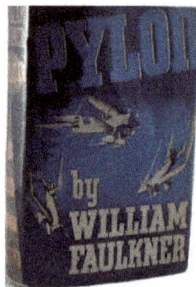

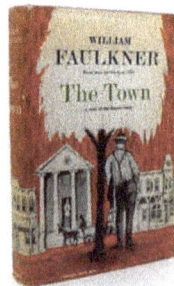

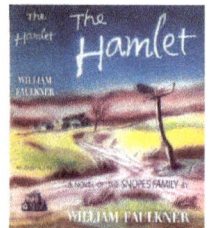

2. The Courthouse in Oxford, Mississippi in December 1862, before it was burned two years later. Here we see an Illinois regiment guarding twelve hundred Confederate prisoners.

Photograph from Henry W. Elson, *The Photographic History of the Civil War* Vol. 2 1911.

3. Oxford, Mississippi in ruins following the raid of Gen. A. Smith, August 1864. View from the northeast showing Court-house chimneys on the right.

4. Faulkner's bedroom with his khakis on the bed as he left them.

5. Faulkner's desk and typewriter in his "office" where the outline of *A Fable* is written on the wall. The pocket New Testament was found in the desk drawer by the author in May 1970.

Self portrait of Faulkner with his mule at Greenfield farm. Pen f ink line drawing in a letter to his stepson. (Pen f ink copy by the author.) Courtesy of The author.

6. Faulkner pen and ink self-portrait plowing with mule.

7. Faulkner, who referred to himself as "a farmer who likes to write," accepting the Nobel prize for Literature in 1950 (it was awarded in 1949).

8. Rowan Oak.
Photo by the author, 10 May 1970

9. The struggling fruit tree at Rowan Oak. Faulkner placed the cedar prop at the base and would not permit its removal. The remnants of the stump were removed around 1984.
Photo by Jack Harbeck, 10 May 1970. Courtesy of the author.

Yours Respectfully
W. C. Falkner

10. Colonel William Clark Falkner, great-grand-father of William Faulkner. Engraving from the frontispiece to Falkner's *Rapid Ramblings in Europe*.

11. Colonel Falkner's monument in Ripley, Mississippi cemetery. Note the stack of books at his left leg almost as a prop to steady him.

12. The Confederate Monument in front of Lafayette County Courthouse of 1871 replacing the one burned by U.S. troops in 1864.
Photo by Hubert A. Lowman c. 1965.

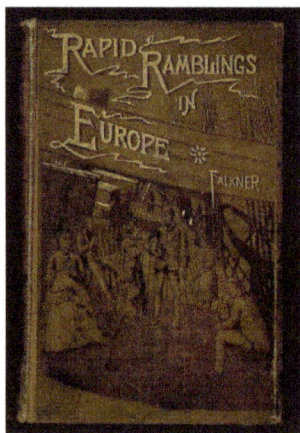

13. Cover of Col. Falkner's *Rapid Ramblings in Europe* (Philadelphia: Lippincott, 1884).
Courtesy of the author.

14. Hunt breakfast at Rowan Oak, 8 May 1938. Ned Barnett (center) is wearing Col. W.C. Falkner's blue frock coat with the brass buttons, as described in Faulkner's "Mississippi."

Photo by Cofield

15. Frock coat detail.

16. The University of Virginia Years

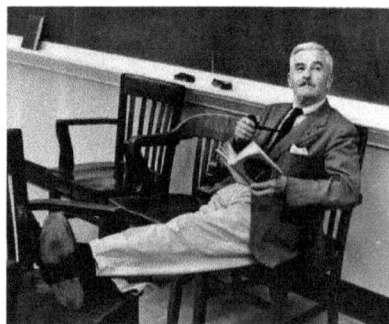

17. Faulkner and Grover Vandevender at Farmington Hunt, 1960.

Photo by George Barkley

18. Faulkner with hunting horn at Farmington Hunt Club, 1960.

19. "There is something about jumping a horse over a fence, something that makes you feel good. Perhaps it's the risk, the gamble. In any event it's a thing I need."
As quoted in "Visit to Two-Finger Typist" by Elliott Chaze in LIFE magazine (14 July 1961).

20. Faulkner with his horse at his log stable at Rowan Oak.

21. Five-foot scroll signed in 1955 by Japanese scholars in appreciation of Faulkner's visit to Nagano in 1955. It was presented to Faulkner, then inherited by Faulkner's stepson Malcolm Franklin. It was returned to Nagano by Dr. J. B. Meriwether in 1987.

Photo courtesy of the author

NINE

FINITUDE & THE MACHINE CULTURE

Ole man Know-All died las' year.

-Uncle Remus. His Songs and Sayings (1880)

In *Go Down, Moses,* the character Ike McCaslin in his usual idealistic and irrational ramblings, full of non sequiturs and wishful thinking, declares that man "isn't quite God himself yet," implying that he is on the way (*Go Down, Moses,* 348). He is the modern progressive who sides with Hegel in declaring that man is always progressing. Richard Gray, in his 1994 biography of Faulkner, says that this is "the voice of Faulkner, already preparing for his Nobel Prize acceptance speech" (275). Gray ignores the response to Ike from the reasonable Wyatt, who asks McCaslin, "When will he be?" To that question, Ike answers that when a man and woman have sex ("it don't even matter whether they marry or not") "the two of them together were God." To that, Edmonds answers, "Then there are some Gods I wouldn't want to touch, and with a damn long stick." Edmonds then looks at Wyatt and adds, "And that includes myself."

Edmonds has gotten a woman pregnant; she is looking for him, and he is running. "Some God!" the good and perceptive reader should conclude. Critics of the wishful-thinking school of New Humanism like Gray would create Faulkner in the Emersonian-Hegelian mold that man possesses infinite possibilities—to the extent of even replacing God. (Karl Marx would be doing back-flips of joy at the realization.) Unfortunately, however, Faulkner's latest biographer is mistakenly following the tradition of earlier misguided Faulkner criticism in this respect.

The traditional Southerner has always understood that man is flawed and his earthly possibilities are finite. Faulkner subscribed to the Delphic motto "*Gnothi sauton*," "Know thyself"—that is, know your place as the created not the Creator. This is a far cry from the modern Emersonian translation that knowing thyself means self-reliance and cultivating the divine spark of the Oversoul within, to such a degree that man, who is already a God in ruins, if he only knew it can create a heaven on earth. Conversely, man's limitations have been fully impressed upon the Southerner by his culture in two ways.

First, the traditional Southerner has had the lesson taught by farming and his agrarian culture that the farmer cannot control the weather. As Andrew Lytle put it succinctly in his essay in *Who Owns America?,* when man becomes "vainglorious and thinks he can conquer nature" and "forgets his right role in nature" religion grows weak. The farmer's relation to his creator only gets stronger. Of the philosophy that man is in control, Lytle declared, "This the good farmer knows to be nonsense" (247-248).

A second lesson in man's finitude came as the result of a lost war which other parts of America did not experience. It may be argued that the non-Southerner has developed a hubris of unlimited success to the point of attempting to play God with the world. The secular *Humanist Manifesto*, framed by Northern academics and intellectuals in 1933 and again in 1973, is proof of this attitude. Written by a benevolent techno-cratic managerial elite ("scientists elevated to the status of priests," as Margaret Mead put it in a 1959 issue of *Daedulus*), its thesis ran thus—since there is no God, man must take God's part and engineer the future. The methods would be through a technocracy of reason and science, even science applied to the mind. The Skinner Box, thus became a reality. Francis A. Schaeffer has treated the subject ably in "The Humanist Reli-gion" in his volume, *A Christian Manifesto* (1982). In order to fill the void left by denying God, one instead creates a social do-goodism and a do-goodism government as a feel-good re-placement.

The South told a different story about man's unlimited powers to her children. From the South's history, the South-erner developed a tragic sense, not a blithely optimistic one. In one of his most discerning essays, Richard Weaver called the American attitude of "no limits" that of a petulant adolescent spoiled by getting everything he desired, and very different indeed from the Southerner matured by hardship and hard realities (72). One recalls Quentin Compson's saying in *Absalom, Absalom!,* "I am older at twenty than some people who have died."

Weaver wrote that "A dominantly Christian point of view has preserved in the South the idea that man can fall. This is why Southern literature, within the context of Southern belief, has been able to recover the theme of the greatest literature." Weaver continued, "Tragedy is probably the most deeply educative experience; it is in a sense, the typical experience…Southern writers have told much of that tragedy, and in doing so they have told us important things about the human condition" (72). Hence, we have yet another reason for that literature's appeal worldwide. The violence of two world wars in Europe that occasioned an Amazon of blood, it is hoped, has become an educative experience in finitude for that continent. It is not surprising that Faulkner was discovered by French literary critics and philosophers after World War II. The American establishment only began to take notice of Faulkner after the French made him fashionable. Robert Penn Warren had much to say on this discovery.

Donald Davidson wrote Charleston poet Josephine Pinckney in 1930 that traditional faith in America had been edged out by all the various "*isms.*" He declared:

195

"progressivism, which has all along linked up with transcendentalism, idealism, industrialism, efficiency—they all go together. Emerson, John Brown, Whitman, Wendell Phillips, Rockefeller, and Harry Emerson Fosdick, are all spiritual brethren, in the same line of descent" (Bellows, 134). Davidson understood the difference between this radical Northern way and the philosophy of the traditional South. He was clearly in the Southern line of descent, and his work proves and establishes a strong link in the continuity of Southern thought. Twenty years later, Richard Weaver's criticism of American "*isms*" and "*ologies*" in his essay on contemporary Southern literature merely restated and amplified Davidson's position. Today's identity politics with its socialist secular zealotry is a modern outgrowth.

Perhaps Flannery O'Connor put the nature of man's finitude most succinctly. The Southern writer does not explain mystery, she declared, but instead deepens it (Preface to the second edition of *Wise Blood*). In 1957, in her essay "The Fiction Writer and His Country," she wrote, "to know oneself is, above all, to know what one lacks…. The first product of self-knowledge is humility" (Collected Works, 806).

This was certainly nothing new in Southern letters with O'Connor, and the roots of its wisdom ran deeper in Southern literature and culture than the loss of war in 1865. Southern realist Thomas Bangs Thorpe in 1854 described his Southern hunter Jim Doggett of "The Big Bear of Arkansas" in much the same way as O'Connor. The un-huntable big bear awes him to "a grave silence" owing to the "mystery" of the thing that "he could never understand." Thorpe called it "some superstitious awe...a feeling common with all 'children of the wood.'" Thorpe perceptively caught and portrayed the Southern sense of awe at the unexplainable infinite that is a source of what is essentially a religious response to nature.[1]

Wendell Berry's most recent poems, like "Sabbaths 2009," for example, bring us down to the present in seeing the Southern writer's rejection of modern man's insistence on trying to pin down existence into quantifiable certainties. He writes, "in a time/ gone mad for certainty, 'maybe'/ gives room to live and move and be." Berry's "maybes" presuppose "how little I know in my widest/ waking." The poem's speaker is aware of the world as a "great weight he has no way of weighing...the unweighable/ weight that registers only/ on his heart." The speaker completely rejects his "time's rage for quantification" (*This Day,* 332, 342). Berry's epigraph to poem XII, in fact, bears tribute to Faulkner with a quotation from "Race at Morning": "'Maybe,' Mr. Ernest said. 'The best word in our language, the best of all'" (342).

Berry's book-length *Life Is a Miracle* (2000) is a formidable debunking of uninspired and arrogant science's cult of empiricism, and of playing God with the world—in its own way a technocratic brand of superstition, as Berry persuasively argues. Here, Berry wrote, "To experience life is not to figure it out or even to understand it, but to suffer it and rejoice in it as it is" (9). So much for crusading to the tune of any scientific *ism* or *ology*! Walker Percy's statement comes to mind that the problem with science is that it cannot tell us what something *is*. As discussed in chapter three, Fred Chappell's *Cerebration* thus becomes the Southern writer's *Celebration*.

In questioning God's punishment of a good man, Job gets answer from the voice in the whirlwind, an answer in the form of a question: *where were you little man when I hung the stars and laid the foundations of the earth?* That is all Job needs to hear and know. Wisdom follows in the way of Delphi. He learns his little place before the Infinite I am. Many Southern writers have shared Job's wisdom. As Weaver wrote, the Southern loss of war underscored that understanding, but it was there before 1865. It was natural for William Gilmore Simms to begin his *Sack and Destruction of the City of Columbia* with references to Job. Fred Chappell in a crucial scene in his novel, *I Am One of You Forever,* has the voice in the whirlwind quiet the egos of his characters with the proper reverence of silence. For once, the novel's characters all stop talking. The hubris of taking God's place has not been the way of wisdom for writers of the South.

Cleanth Brooks once again read Faulkner brilliantly. He traced the long continuum of American (non-Southern) millennialism in Northern literature from its secularizing under Emerson, Whitman, and even Hawthorne in *The House of Seven Gables.* Brooks wrote that the powerful force of no-limits, no-boundaries idealism and the declaration that one can accomplish anything if he works hard enough and sets his mind to it, is to this day referred to "rather fondly as simply the American Dream."

Brooks concluded that "the issue of millennialism is, however, one that sets Faulkner off from a great many other American writers" (*Toward Yoknapatawpha,* 281). Brooks quoted historian C. Vann Woodward to good purpose. Woodward wrote, "An age-long experience with human bondage…and later with emancipation and its shortcomings did not dispose the South very favorably toward such American popular ideas as the doctrine of human perfectibility."[2] Not to mention, becoming God on earth!

Brooks rightly declared that Faulkner was particularly concerned that the United States might be "undone by her sometimes overweening faith in the future, by her belief that progress was inevitable," by reliance on technology, sociology and sociological solutions, and "most dangerous of all, by her unprecedented record of military victories" so that non-Southerners might get the impression that they "were immune to defeat, loss, and evil," an "innocence" that "might in the end prove disastrous"(*Toward Yoknapatawpha,* 282-283). The idea that man can play God has always had disastrous results. Anyone who reads the Greek tragedies has known this truth right away. And it is pertinent to say here that traditional Southerners, as was the case of Faulkner, studied their Latin and Greek, early and late.

Southern writers as a group have questioned the secular humanistic stance that since there is no God, it is left to man to act as God and engineer the future. Perhaps Southern author Archibald Rutledge phrased it best in his little book, *Life's Extras*, published in 1928: "I have often heard people say that they would like to remake the world. Well, I am glad we don't have to live in a man-made world…how impossible would be an earth and a scheme of life man had made." Rutledge continued that it is the "sophisticated" persons who dream so, but he feels that sophistication "instead of being a proof of enlightenment and culture" is "the evidence of ignorance, and perhaps of folly…. The great trouble with a sophisticated person is not that he knows too much, but that he knows too little" (35-36). Rutledge apparently had no problem with the proper understanding of the Greek motto at Delphi.

In *My Colonel and His Lady* (1937), Rutledge, sounding very much like Faulkner, wrote that the "modern boasted progress" may be valiant, but "not especially interesting; for no material greatness can ever satisfy the heart….it cannot live by bread alone" (77). In Rutledge, we again see the old patrician values of the landed gentry in play against a bourgeois value system based on material wealth at the expense of the civilizing virtues. Likewise, Rutledge made light of the new technocracy that took itself so seriously. He was a man who lived on the land, lived according to nature's rhythms, and never aspired to remake the world in man's image. Rutledge's South Carolina contemporary, the underrated sporting writer, Havilah Babcock (1903-1964), said much the same in his canon of five well-loved books beginning with *My Health is Better in November* in 1948. It is not surprising that Professor Babcock preferred the company and conversation of rural people to academics.

In his brief review of Hemingway's *The Old Man and the Sea,* Faulkner observed that in this novel, Hemingway had for the first time "discovered God, a Creator"—something greater than physical man himself. Heretofore, Hemingway's characters "had made themselves, shaped themselves out of their own clay." Here in this review, as at every turn in his fiction, Faulkner showed that he was acutely aware of the limitations of man and understood that man, no matter how heroically striving, cannot create himself in the way of modern progressive secularism. He does not try to elevate man to the

Creator's throne or believe man can shape himself out of his own clay.

O'Connor's *Wise Blood* provides a brilliant corollary to Faulkner in the image of the man-made replacement of God's throne on which modern man sits and holds sway over his dominion. The throne is a gilded toilet and the man who sits thereupon is a shrunken hollow mummy filled with sawdust. Although it is gilded, it is still a toilet. Allen Tate, on the subject of such gilded thrones, said that flush toilets were good things if one did not have to kneel down and worship them.

Faulkner saw man as imperfect by nature and unperfectible, but also possessing an indomitable spirit and will to endure, and capable of courage and bravery, of "love and honor and pity and pride and compassion and sacrifice." Man's dual nature is often expressed in his characters in Faulkner's justly famous phrase, "the human heart in conflict with itself"—a heart imperfect and unperfectible, and man (as Weaver phrased it) the "riddle, jest, glory and unquantifiable mystery" (69-73).

Not too long before Faulkner was born, that wise Southern philosopher, Uncle Remus, himself commented on limits and the real danger of overreaching reasonable bounds. He warned, "Watch out w'en you'er gittin all you want. Fattenin' hogs ain't in luck" (Harris, 177, 158). Remus was speaking out of the old-time wisdom of the conservative South, and very much out of fashion in his Victorian Gilded Age of American buoyant optimism and excess. Restraint (classical or otherwise) has never been an American virtue. Southern wisdom teaches it as a basic, however. No doubt Faulkner, like so many Southerners of his day, had often heard General Lee's advice to those who had power over the weak and helpless, that having that power is the very best reason not to exercise it. Richard Weaver's view of gentlemanly restraint entailed humble submission to tradition and was the opposite of the bratty superiority complex of thinking one can do whatever he strives to do.

This view of finitude and limitations is certainly diametrically opposed to the modern liberal-progressive premise that man is by nature essentially good and perfectible by utopian means, what Eugene Genovese came to call "The Left's rosy view of human nature" (xi). So many of Faulkner's critics and biographers apparently have shared that rosy view. Genovese, in fact, drew attention to the Southern conservative understanding that man is finite before the infinite I Am, a legacy of this society's Christian underpinnings. In "The Catholic Novelist in the Protestant South," Flannery O'Connor became eloquent upon the subject. She wrote: "What has given the South her identity are those beliefs and qualities which she has absorbed from the Scriptures and from her own history of defeat and violation: a distrust of the abstract, a sense of human dependence on the grace of God, and a knowledge that evil is not simply a problem to be solved, but a mystery to be endured." The first collection in which this essay appeared was appropriately entitled *Mystery and Manners.* In her usual succinct, incisive way, O'Connor's essay pin-pointed several traits of the Southern writer discussed in this volume, traits she, Faulkner, and the majority of Southern writers have shared in common throughout the years.

One reason for the modern idealism of an unlimited rosy future and of man becoming God is man's great triumphs in science and technology. A questioning of the cult of technology and its machine culture, however, has been an abiding theme in Southern literature at least from the time of William Gilmore Simms in the antebellum period, and on down to the present in such a novel of ultimate and repulsive absurdity, as Harry Crews' *Car.* In this novel, published in 1972, the main character loves that American symbol of technology so much that he wants it inside him, and thus eats a Maverick—before television cameras, and complete with televised defecations of car bits. The painful feat does not satisfy, however, and only the promoters profit. This American love story with the car is a futile attempt to find meaning. It ends in severe pain and frustration.

One is again reminded of Simms, who wrote in 1842 that not "all the steam power in the world can bring happiness to one poor human heart" nor "all the railroads in the world can carry one poor soul to heaven."[3] He wrote that "improvement in Rail-roads or Steam Engines is spoken of as a great moral improvement—a discovery in physical science, which may increase the powers of machinery, wins all the palinodes of the press; and we constantly deceive ourselves in this way by confounding the idea of a cunning or an ingenious with a great people. This seems to be the whole amount of our national idea of progress." In 1844, in his novella, *Castle Dismal,* Simms declared that for "a man of moderate understanding and invincible self-esteem…it is fashionable…to disparage the claims of the spiritual world. Science, so-called, that coldest and vainest of all modern pretenders, is particularly hostile to everything, and every thought, which you cannot analyze in the crucible, or estimate by the square and compass. Its professors believe nothing which they cannot see and feel…. They know nothing but what is kindred to their own eyes and fingers" (151-152). Donald Davidson in his tribute to Simms in his poem "Woodlands" understood Simms well, when he wrote, "We are a century of no belief, and cannot read your stories Gilmore Simms."

In *The Machine in the Garden*, University of Minnesota and Amherst College professor, Leo Marx, wrote that in nineteenth century America, "The locomotive, associated with fire, smoke, speed, iron, and noise, is the leading symbol of the new industrial power" (17). The year before Simms made his statement on the locomotive, Ralph Waldo Emerson wrote his essay "History" in which he used Prometheus, the fire-stealer, to show how "advancing man" with the "invention of the mechanic arts," makes progressive strides toward utopia, actions that, in the words of John Stuart Mill, "carry the feeling of admiration for modern, and disrespect for ancient times." As Leo Marx phrased it, for the man of the industrial North, "To see a powerful, efficient machine in the landscape is to know the superiority of the present to the past" (192). Marx ably presented the regnant New England establishment views on industrial progress.

John F. Kasson, in *Civilizing the Machine* (1976), presented a more nuanced view of Emerson as he went from exhilaration over the possibilities of machines in his first ride on a locomotive to a questioning in his last works of what effects embracing the machine might have on the life of the imagination. Still, Kasson found that Emerson never rejected his essential faith in technology as vanguard of progress, and makes no mention of Simms, any other Southern writer, or the possibility of a Southern minority report. This total disregard of "the other" is symptomatic of the usual manner of American intellectual history that has helped create a monolithic, flat version. By extension, this exclusivity has contributed to a misguided historical perception that the South had no intellectual life.

When fairly considered, the Southern minority report looks very good by comparison.

The Machine in the Garden, hailed by reviewers as "major," "impressive," "brilliant," and "exciting," also treated American thought by using Northern authors exclusively and without looking at their dissenting Southern counterparts. It is this myopia (and perhaps establishment elitism) that opens the book to the criticism of superficiality. It is clear that scholar-gypsy academic Marx had no conception of what constitutes a traditional land-based society with life fixed in one place, that society's understanding of the value of continuities, or of how that society felt that the past informs the present. First published in 1964, there are no references to Simms, any other Southern writer, and only five passing mentions of Faulkner. In a book devoted to the cultural ramifications of the industrial versus the agrarian visions, it is astonishing that there is not even a passing mention of *I'll Take My Stand* (1930).

Like Simms, the Fugitive-Agrarians of *I'll Take My Stand* questioned the "Cult of Science" and industry through-out their work. Here, they fought what Donald Davidson called in 1958 "the new barbarism of science and technology controlled and directed by the modern power state" (*Southern Writers*, 45). Many of the essayists of *I'll Take My Stand* came together once again in 1936 to publish a second collection of essays, *Who Owns America?* In this second volume, the authors called the modern power state the Technocracy. To-day, *Who Owns America?* (also either unknown or ignored by Marx) is still one of the most important underutilized collections of twentieth century essays in the Southern canon.

Ralph Waldo Emerson recognized the great difference between the men of the North and the "mannered" men of the South. In bitterly bewailing the political dominance of America by Southern statesmen, he explained Southern success by saying that "Northerners knew how to control steam and machines, while Southerners knew how to control men" (Powell, 10). He also said that the North had engines but no engineers. It is appropriate to observe that when the dominance of government shifted to the men of the machine culture, America changed dramatically.

In 1993, Eugene Genovese explored the traditional Southern critique of bourgeois materialism and what he called the "cult of scientism" and paid special tribute to the Agrarian authors of *I'll Take My Stand.* He saw their stance to be representative of the tradition of Southern conservatism through the ages. Frank Lawrence Owsley in his chapter "The Irrepressible Conflict" summed up a primary theme of *I'll Take My Stand* on the differing attitudes toward the machine North and South. What he found to be irrepressible in the conflict between the regions that erupted into war was the South's rejection of the machine. This was anathema to the Northern progressive and a stumbling block to his vision of the future and its material gains, so "The South had to be crushed out, it was in the way; it impeded the progress of the machine" (91). He and the book's other authors declared very wisely that industry, commerce, technology and the machine that drove them must remain life's servants and not its masters.

Genovese wrote, Southern conservatism "has from its origins constituted America's most impressive native-born critique of her national development, of liberalism, and the more disquieting features of the modern world" (1-2). And the modern world reacted in typical fashion by ignoring them at best and ridiculing them at worst. It was the cancel culture of their day. Leo Marx is thus merely one of many. A study of this rejection of *I'll Take My Stand* would be very revealing of sectional division. Although Faulkner, in the hands of his biographers and critics, has not usually been mustered to the side of the Southern tradition, he most definitely deserves to be there.

Faulkner wrote in 1946 that "maybe a group of Dismal Swamp or Florida Everglades Abolitionists will decide to free the country from machines." In discussing the Northern war upon the agrarian South in 1861, he declared, "the machine that defeated his [the Northerner's] enemy was a Frankenstein which, once the Southern armies were consumed, turned on him and, removing him from a middle class fixed upon the land, translated him into a baronage based upon the slavery...of machines" (Faulkner-Cowley File, 80). Faulkner's statement sounded very much like Owsley's in the previous decade, and Wendell Berry's most recent work *The Need to Be Whole*, where his attack on mechanization has intensified. I find it sad that Berry does not know how close he is to his tradition, and especially its expression in the antebellum South. Perhaps, had he known so, he would not have been so hard on his planter ancestors.

One should note carefully Faulkner's words, removing him from a life *fixed upon the land*. As shown in chapter two, Faulkner's purchase of Greenfield Farm reestablished that tie to the soil and for Faulkner reversed the process of deracination. What his family had been removed from, he returned to. The phrase "fixed upon the land" is of particular relevance to that commitment. Like Wendell Berry, Faulkner was a great advocate of staying put, as we have seen in chapter six. A century before, Simms's primary thesis in his *The Social Principle* was that Southerners should not leave their ancestral places. "How could one leave the graves of one's people, after all?" Simms asked. For him, staying put was the foundation of civilization.

As critic of the machine culture, Faulkner was certainly out of step with an America assured of infinite and unlimited progress through technology, the universal panacea. When that technology was admitted to create problems, then the defenders always put forth more technology as the cure. Few questioned the sanity of that reasoning. When one considers the national love affair with cars and gadgets from electric can openers to salad-shooters and I-phones, this was yet another way Faulkner was bucking the American technocratic consensus. Wendell Berry too has been our current major questioner of the efficacy of the machine and has practiced what he preached in ploughing with draft horses, eschewing the television, computer, and the plethora of gadgets most twentieth and twenty-first century progressive Americans have considered to be not only luxuries but essentials. In the twenty-first century, however, there are an increasing number of questioners, but in their day in America, Faulkner and the Southern writers stood virtually alone. In England, there were counterparts like G. K. Chesterton, J. R. Tolkien, and Hillaire Belloc.

In his beautifully written 1967 memoir, Faulkner's brother Murry, described his brother William as a man who refused electric gadgets at Rowan Oak. He never owned, or watched a television, for example. Murry wrote that "radio and television struck him with horror… he mentioned that he never watched one work and had no intention of doing so." Faulkner laughed and said that he had seen an article in a paper relating that some people in a large Eastern city who lacked television sets "would buy and erect sprouts (as he termed the antennae) on the roof so the neighbors would assume the presence of a TV set beneath." This he said was "beneath his comprehension" (197-198). He only had a telephone at Rowan Oak as a concession to his wife and daughter. Murry wrote, "he had a natural and sustained aversion to the telephone, anywhere, anytime, and under any conceivable circumstances." He would not use it, and the one time Murry called and Faulkner answered, Murry was so shocked at hearing Faulkner's voice on the line that he hung up "before I could get my breath and identify myself" (197).

Murry, however, did describe his brother's joy at purchasing a garden tiller for the Rowan Oak vegetable plot. Murry said he was like a child with a new toy at Christmas. Then there was Faulkner's love of the airplane and flying (as dramatized in his 1935 novel, *Pylon*). He drove a car—decidedly not new, and out of fashion, but a car nevertheless. Murry wrote, "With him an automobile was solely a means of transportation, to get him to some place too far to walk.... He had an old Ford touring car for years.... He later had a cloth-topped Jeep and after that a fiery red Rambler station wagon" (194). Although he feared man's dependence on and obsession with the machine, he was no Luddite. As usual, as in most things, Faulkner did not take a fanatical stand on his disdain for the machine. What he scorned was the culture built around it and that worshipped it. That was the true fanaticism. It was the matter of misplaced priorities that distressed him.

Faulkner wrote a letter to the local newspaper in 1946 after his daughter's dog was run over by a speeding motorist. The letter shows so many of the traits of Southern writing enumerated in this volume that it deserves quoting at length. I regard it as one of Faulkner's better pieces of prose showing a Southern countryman's concrete understanding of nature coupled with an indictment of nature's destroyer. What makes it quintessentially Southern is that the philosophy is unfolded in personal rather than abstract terms out of a particular event in which he was centrally and emotionally involved. Faulkner wrote:

> His name was Pete. He was just a dog, a fifteen-months-old pointer…He expected little of the world into which he came…food (he didn't care what nor how little just so it was given with affection—a touch of a hand, a voice he knew even if he could not understand and answer the words it spoke); the earth to run on; air to breathe, sun and rain in their seasons and the covied quail which were his heritage long before he knew the earth and felt the sun, whose scent he already knew from his staunch and faithful

ancestry before he himself had ever winded it. That was all he wanted. But that would have been enough to fill the eight or ten or twelve years of his natural life because twelve years are not very many.... Yet short as twelve years are, he should normally have outlived four of the kind of motorcars which killed him.

After this little jab at the shoddy throw-away society, Faulkner continued,

But Pete didn't outlive the first of his four. He wasn't chasing it.... He was standing on the road waiting for his little mistress on the horse to catch up, to squire her safely home. He shouldn't have been in the road. He paid no road tax, held no driver's license, didn't vote…The driver was in a hurry…Perhaps he…was already late for supper. That was why he didn't have time to slow or stop or drive around Pete. And since he didn't have time to do that, naturally he didn't have time to stop afterward; besides Pete was only a dog flung broken and crying into a roadside ditch…. But Pete has forgiven him. In his year and a quarter of life he never had anything but kindness from human beings; he would gladly give the other six or eight or ten of it rather than make one late for dinner (*Essays*, 200-202).

Here we note Faulkner's withering disdain for the regimentation of road taxes, driver's licenses, and the like, all considered more important than courtesy, responsible action, decency, and a respect for life. And for Faulkner, "hurry" seemed to be the new way that prevents civility and neighborliness.

Finally, there are those academics who grant that Faulkner is Southern but would have him a New South progressive. Perhaps this is a way to make a Southern writer more acceptable to certain circles of academia; or perhaps it is wishful thinking. Academics might ask, "After all, how could a great genius not be progressive *like me*?"

To address that issue, we may let Faulkner speak for himself in an essay he wrote as an introduction to a new edition of *The Sound and the Fury* in 1933:

> There is a thing known whimsically as the New South…, but it is not the South. It is a land of Immigrants who are rebuilding the towns and cities into replicas of towns and cities in Kansas and Iowa and Illinois, with skyscrapers and striped canvas awnings instead of wooden balconies, and teaching the young men who sell the gasoline and the waitresses in the restaurants to say O yeah?

And to speak with hard r's, and hanging over the intersections of quiet and shaded streets where no one save Northern tourists in Cadillacs and Lincolns ever pass at a gait faster than a horse trots, changing red-and-green lights and savage and peremptory bells (*Essays,* 291).

The impersonal and mechanical command of *savage and peremptory bells* indeed! Faulkner had already been critical of "cash register bells" in his defense of old buildings in the previous chapter. Here, the bells may have extended to railroad crossing bells, fire engines, city trolley cars, or pedestrian crosswalk bells—the usual barrage of noise-makers in an urban environment. Faulkner valued silence tremendously, as his writings often reveal. (See his interview in which he declared, "I like silence," *Lion,* 64.) The urban and suburban assault on the senses raised his ire. He felt that a culture and society that devised such peremptory bells were themselves savage and peremptory and only deserving of his scorn. In the tone of this passage, one hears the withering disdain of his wise character Elnora, saying "Trash. Town trash." A man, consciously heir to the old squirearchy as Faulkner was, would certainly be able to deliver the indictment quite effectively, knowing precisely what he was indicting and why. As we have already said, Havilah Babcock went even further by saying that raising a boy in the city should be a capital offense.

Once again, Simms provided a striking corollary to these twentieth century Southern writers. He felt that in 1865, defeat in war left the old Southern ideals of civility and chivalry in tatters before a triumphant, impersonal, burgeoning industrial-urban machine culture that only valued getting rich and getting ahead at all cost—in other words a vulgar and boorish (and very un-Southern) Chamber of Commerce mentality. It should be noted that the Chamber of Commerce is a national organization, really a business with a CEO, and local chapters pay their dues to the headquarters in Washington, D. C. For this, the locals receive very little, except attacks on the Southern heritage which the locals usually believe in and support. A thinking person might well wonder if this is not a bad business deal, and bad business practice. I am certain that Faulkner would have.

Near the end of his writing career in January 1870, Simms predicted that a people who forswear chivalry and high ideals in their rush to power and materialism will fall into tyranny and commit cultural suicide. Simms hurled the curse of the poet on the victors for whom the words "chivalry" and "gentleman" have become "a sort of scoff, especially as they perpetually heard of these beautiful virtues, from European tongues, as especially belonging to the South." Simms concluded, "There was an awful consciousness, among many of them born yesterday, and with no other capital of character

217

than a fashionable tailor could supply—assisted by some stolen crest from some English gentleman's carriage—that there was a very substantial difference in the training and development of the two sections" (*Selected Reviews*, 192). Instead of coming together as one people, Simms felt that the gap between the two sections would widen, and one reason for it was this essential difference in values. A "cash-register evaluation of life" is the way historian C. Vann Woodward phrased the Northern manner. In Faulkner, that cash register would have savage and peremptory bells that would wind up controlling lives.

When Faulkner wrote his indictment of the New South in 1933, he did so one year after the death of Grace King. Miss King's works had been known for their author's outspoken declaration that the New South was inferior to the Old owing to the materialistic Northern influence upon it (Powell, 31). Faulkner's comments in 1933 showed he agreed with her and his reasons for the agreement were the same as hers. The urban, machine culture of the New South would be a place of savage and peremptory cash-register bells, complete with the savage and peremptory urban value system that drove it.

Georgia essayist John Donald Wade in his chapter in *Who Owns America*, wrote of the un-Southern arrogance of the city in feeling superior to the country. Size, machines, and technocracy had made the city dweller proud. Wade wrote, however, that "the principle of metropolitanism is basically parasitic…it leads man to the folly of thinking man is invincible…. The validity of his understanding rests in size and number and not in quality and spirit." Wade, along with the traditional wisdom of many Southern writers including Faulkner, concluded that "the essential thing about human endeavor is not how large it is but how human it is." Wade declared that man was not to shape his humanity after the machines he has made, because the machine model leads to a "devouring torture chamber." Wade found it even more disturbing to see the trend of the country beginning to "idolize" the city and its ways. For Wade, this admiration meant "going after spuriousness and vulgarity" and "independence paying tribute to parasitism, and humanity becoming cold and unfeeling" (256-258). These last descriptions of the drift of the new way are a good statement of what Faulkner and most writers in the Southern literary tradition did not do, and a description of the values of the Technocracy they have rejected.

Their humanity and insistence on keeping mankind human is one of the greatest legacies of the Southern writer. It is certainly a basic attribute of their writing that will remain pertinent and timeless. This in no small way is at the center of the greatness of Southern literature, and it stems from the recognition of man's finitude.

TEN

RACE

W hen an early version of this study was presented as a four-part Abbeville Institute lecture at Seabrook Island, South Carolina, in the summer of 2010, I left out a treatment of race, mainly in reaction to the near obsession with the subject among current academic writers on the South. Some extremists have gone so far as to say that the only Southern subject worth treating is race. Just as foolish and myopic are a growing number of historians who say that the teaching of American history should begin with the civil rights movement and all else is but prelude. The obsession has increased with the 1619 Project and shows no signs of diminishing. Once limited to treatments of the South, the focus now includes the whole of America from its founding as "systemic racism"— the new buzz word of the Left in 2020-2022.

In 2010 I thought it an object lesson to my listeners to exhibit my own contrariness (see Chapter One), and to show them that there is much more to Faulkner than race. One of the most gratifying rewards in giving that series of lectures was that thirty or so students and I in extemporaneous discussion after and between the lectures contributed the ideas that became the outline for this chapter. Those dialogues provided its basis.

Zora Neale Hurston (1891-1960), arguably the greatest African American author of the South, was speaking for more than herself when she said that in the North, blacks were coolly thought of as a group and in the abstract, and thus kept at a distance. She declared from experience that Northerners preferred not to be around black individuals; whereas in the South, the Southerner approached race on the individual level, and was thus more likely to develop genuine affection. She caught a lot of grief outside the South for making that distinction, but her understanding was derived from long custom and experience and certainly applies to Faulkner. So does her focus on rural life and folk wisdom as the repository of cultural knowledge. Her autobiography *Dust Tracks on a Road* (1942) was published the same year as *Go Down, Moses.* Her novel *Moses, Man of the Mountain* (1939) invites worthwhile comparison to the Faulkner novel.

Faulkner approached race in Hurston's Southern way of individual personal relations. His closest association from childhood, about as close as any could be, was with the woman who helped his mother and grandmother raise him and with whom he was in daily communication for thirty-seven years until her death in 1940. She was Mrs. Caroline Barr Clark (1840-1940), called Mammy Callie by Faulkner and what he called "her white family." As Faulkner wrote in his appreciation of her, she had been born in slavery and served the family faithfully for her entire life. If born on the Falkner plantation near Ripley, she would have been twenty-one when the war began and would have seen Colonel Falkner in his prime. She would have likely witnessed the burning of the plantation and the destruction of the village of Ripley where the family was refugeeing. When the Falkner family lost all their belongings and went hungry, she did as well. As Faulkner put it in the words he said at her funeral, she passed "much of her early maturity…in a dark and tragic time for the land of her birth" (*Essays,* 117-118).

Of Mrs. Clark, Faulkner wrote that it was she who taught him his manners, to be gentle with his inferiors, to have respect for his elders, and to be honest and truthful. It may be claimed that Faulkner's novel *Go Down, Moses* is as honest and sincere a treatment of black-white relationships as has been written. The novel for good reason was dedicated to Mrs. Clark with these words:

To Mammy

CAROLINE BARR

Mississippi

1840-1940

who was born in slavery and who

gave to my family a fidelity without

> stint or calculation of recompense
>
> and to my childhood an
>
> immeasurable devotion and love.

Faulkner began the novel in the year of Mrs. Clark's death and published it two years later in 1942. The book is in a sense a posthumous gift to her.

In the novel itself, the character Cass Edmonds pays tribute to Aunt Molly, the woman who raised him, with similar words to Faulkner's in his funeral sermon for Mrs. Clark. Edmonds declares that Molly had

> surrounded him always with care for his physical body and for his spirit too, teaching him his manners, behavior—to be gentle with his inferiors, honorable with his equals, generous to the weak and considerate of the aged, courteous, truthful and brave to all—who had given him…without stint or expectation of reward that constant and abiding devotion and love which existed nowhere else in this world for him (*Go Down, Moses,* 117).

When Faulkner restored Rowan Oak in 1930, Mammy Callie was ninety years old, and had outlived her children. As the eldest of the Faulkner sons, he took the responsibility to make her a home in his back yard. Faulkner felt that the privilege had passed to him. As he phrased it, he was "the oldest of my father's family." In the old social code, he was thus

"Master," but Faulkner was quick to add that "the relationship between us never became that of master and servant" (117, 275). Faulkner, thus from duty, privilege, and affection, stood by her until her death, and actually past it, for it was Faulkner who arranged for her grave marker at St. Peter's Episcopal Cemetery in Oxford where he himself is buried. The inscription, dictated by Faulkner, reads: *"Callie Barr Clark. 1840-1940. 'Mammy.' Her white children bless her."*

Outside Faulkner's novels and stories, we have only brief glances of the relationship between Faulkner and Mammy Callie. Hunting companion and childhood friend John Cullen recalled that when butchering was done at Greenfield Farm in the 1930s, William carried Mrs. Clark the thirty miles to the farm to give her choice of the cuts of meat. They would be laid out for her so she could make her selections (Cullen, 79). Faulkner always kept her supplied with pipe tobacco. Such small amenities and day to day personal considerations were Faulkner's way.

Faulkner's brother John Faulkner wrote perceptively that "It was by the yardstick of the memory of Mammy, I think, that Bill measured integration." Sounding very much like Zora Neal Hurston, John continued, "They say we love the Negroes as individuals down here and hate them as a class, while up North they love them as a class and hate them as individuals. I know we loved Mammy."

Mammy was apparently a stern disciplinarian. John wrote that if God didn't admit her white children into heaven, He would have to answer to Mammy. God Himself would finally relent and say, "All right. Let them in." John concluded, "I expect even He has learned by now not to argue with Mammy" (John Faulkner, 51-52).

It is often said that Dilsey Gibson of *The Sound and the Fury* has many of Mammy Callie's sterling qualities, and this is true; but it is *Go Down, Moses*, not *The Sound and the Fury*, that is her book. The Phi Beta Kappa, Harvard- and Heidelberg-educated Gavin Stevens is a well-intentioned local do-gooder. He sees Aunt Molly in his own white image and in the abstract. He assumes she will want her grandson's funeral to have the coffin, hearse, and flowers of a white funeral. Stevens thinks Molly would not want it known that he was executed for murder and he thus succeeds in keeping the story out of the local newspaper. Stevens, as we have said before, is the intellectual abstractionist, so antipathetic to Faulkner's Southern way of seeing. His abstraction prevents his really knowing the flesh and blood Molly and what she wants. When Stevens is confronted with the raw grief of the grandson's wake, he panics and flees. A mourner tells him that leaving is fine, because "it is our grief"—implying "and not yours." Throughout the novel, Stevens always keeps life at a safe distance.

Aunt Molly does not value the white man's trappings of respectability, and most definitely *does* want his full story "put in de paper. All of hit" (*Go Down, Moses*, 383). The *all* is inclusive. The *all* involves her family story several centuries back to beginnings. A chain of failed responsibilities has led to the grandson's displacement from his home and family to an alien Detroit or Chicago where his crimes are committed. The novel is Faulkner's way of "putting it in the paper, *all of hit.*"

Gavin Stevens, for all his education, is no Moses, even though he may see himself as such. Neither is Ike McCaslin, even though admirably trained in the mysteries of nature. Neither man takes the proper responsibilities nor has the deep understanding of the complex continuities of intertwined black-white relationships. The key to that relationship is personal mutual respect and caring. Molly, still on Faulkner's mind, was to appear briefly a final time six years later in his *Intruder in the Dust* (1948).

When Mrs. Clark died in January 1940, Faulkner said the words over her coffin in the parlor at Rowan Oak as she had requested. In her funeral address, he said that from childhood on, she was a fount "of active and constant affection and love.... She was an active and constant precept for decent behavior. From her I learned to tell the truth, to refrain from waste, to be considerate of the weak and respectful of age. I saw fidelity to a family which was not hers, devotion and love for people she had not borne" (*Essays,* 117).

Faulkner thus approached race most literally through his own back yard. Mrs. Hurston's description of race relations in the South could not be more accurate in Faulkner's case. As in other ways, his views and attitudes started with the concrete and individual— "the lumber in the attic," as he phrased it— with that material closest to heart and hand. It started with the personal, individual, local, and familiar and only then fanned outward to the general and universal.

Faulkner had more than Mammy Callie in his immediate household in 1930. Biographer Jay Parini described how "a staff began to gather around" Faulkner at Rowan Oak "almost inadvertently" (156). Mammy Callie, who had helped raise William, was not alone. There among the "staff" was Uncle Ned Barnett, a "man with a fine sense of style" who "wore a tie every day, even when he would help Faulkner take care of the three horses" (156). Ned doubled as waiter, serving the Faulkners at dinner. Another retainer was Josie May, who had been a cook for Estelle's parents. Mammy Callie helped take care of Estelle's two children by her former marriage and helped Estelle with the baking in a wood cook stove (156-157).

Uncle Ned Barnett deserves extended treatment here. He was Born in 1865 in Ripley and was the servant of Col. W. C. Falkner. In the 1930s he became a tenant farmer at

Greenfield Farm and worked as the dignified butler at Rowan Oak until his death in December 1947. A month later in January 1948, Faulkner put aside the work he was writing to write *Intruder in the Dust*. Just as Mammy Callie inspired *Go Down, Moses*, Uncle Ned inspired *Intruder*.

Doreen Fowler writes that Faulkner "elegizes" Ned as Lucas Beauchamp in *Intruder* ("Beyond Oedipus," 815). An even more powerful eulogy appears in Faulkner's moving, dramatic essay "Mississippi" written in 1954. Faulkner wrote:

remembering: Ned, born in a cabin in the back yard in 1865, in the time of the middleaged's great-grandfather and had outlived three generations of them, who had not only walked and talked so constantly for so many years with the three generations that he walked and talked like them, he had two tremendous trunks filled with the clothes which they had worn—not only the blue brass-buttoned frock coat and the plug hat in which he had been the great-grandfather's and the grandfather's coachman, but the broadcloth frock coats which the great-grandfather himself had worn, and the pigeon-tailed ones of the grandfather's time and the short coat of his father's which the middleaged could remember on the backs for which they had been tailored...so, that, glancing

idly up and out the library window, the middleaged would see that back, that stride, that coat
and hat going down the drive...and his heart
would stop and turn over (Essays, 39).

Faulkner's tribute to Ned is also a remarkable instance of his
very personal recognition of how past and present merge into
one. When Faulkner saw Ned in three generations of his ancestor's clothes, he could feel that the men who sired him were
ever present in the person of Ned. In this same way, the races
merge in remembrance. Robert Hamblin has detailed the pro-
visions Faulkner left for Barnett in his 1940 will ("Lucas Beauchamp and Ned Barnett," 281-283).

The paragraphs following the description of Ned details
the last months of Mammy Callie's life in her little house at
Rowan Oak. She refused to use electricity and opted for kerosene lanterns. She roasted sweet potatoes on her hearth and
was piecing a quilt by firelight with Faulkner's little daughter.
After her stroke, she moved into the big house and in her last
days she sat where she wanted her body laid out and her funeral preached in the parlor (Essays, 40-42). It is clear from
this essay that Ned also helped take care of Mammy Callie,
who liked to walk into town. One of his duties was to prevent
this by picking her up and driving her. These last few pages

are among Faulkner's best, and "Mississippi" in my opinion ranks very high in the canon of Faulkner's works.

Perhaps through close association, Faulkner was more typical than not of Southern writers in his individual, non-abstractionist manner of regarding race. Arguably the closest to his attitude and upbringing among African Americans is Archibald Rutledge's, as shown in the numerous works in which he pays tribute to the friendship and service of the Alston family retainers who lived with him at Hampton Plantation. The entire volume *God's Children* (1947), appearing only five years after *Go Down, Moses,* is upon the subject. The sentiments expressed there are the same as Faulkner's and each author helps a reader understand the other. Before writing on Faulkner and race, or race in general, a critic might benefit from reading and deeply considering Rutledge's *God's Children.* Wendell Berry's *The Need to Be Whole* would have benefitted greatly from it.

Faulkner, born in 1897, and Rutledge, born in 1883, were both heirs to the patrician antebellum tradition of the gentry's code of noblesse oblige. The Bourbon aristocracy after the war, perhaps best exemplified in South Carolina Governor Wade Hampton III, was their heritage. The Vardamans and Bilbos in Mississippi and the Tillmans and Bleases in South Carolina were the antithesis. Appropriately, Faulkner named two sons of his poor white Snopes and Bundren families

Vardaman and Bilbo. A Bilbo Sartoris or a Vardaman Compson would be unthinkable, unless as irony.

As we have seen in previous chapters, Faulkner himself characterized the Snopeses in an interview in 1939. They
are "a tribe of rascals," numerous and growing in number.
They move across the country "like mould over cheese," destroying its traditions and everything of beauty and loveliness
there is in the place. (*Lion*, 39-40). They represent a predatory,
rapaciously material bourgeois mindset diametrically opposed
to the old traditional codes of the landed gentry and the values
of the squirearchy. It is they who elect the Vardamans and Bilbos. The old planter patricians are out, and with them most of
their values.

Cleanth Brooks noted that historian C. Vann Woodward wrote that the Old South had no Jim Crow laws. These
were passed by "the poor whites—and the people who opposed the laws, fruitlessly, were the descendants of the old
plantation masters." Brooks continued, "The descendants of
the old plantation owners when they rode the cars had their
black servants right along with them—they lived with
them...Thy felt their own superiority or their own difference
so fully that they weren't threatened by them—by proximity
to them" (Brooks, Interview, 157-158). Woodward made it
clear in his work *The Strange Case of Jim Crow,* that racial
segregation was introduced to the South by Northern

progressives in an effort to turn the white proletariat against their traditionalist conservative aristocratic leaders. When Faulkner questioned the fairness of racial segregation in the 1950s, he, in effect, was following the lead of his planter's landed-gentry heritage.

Mississippi poet William Alexander Percy's memoir *Lanterns on the Levee* (1942), Rutledge's two works, *Home by the River* (1941) and *God's Children* (1947), and to a lesser degree the works of Havilah Babcock and Ben Robertson's *Red Hills and Cotton* (1941) are also good examples of this same traditionalist Southern patrician value system. Today, Percy's, Rutledge's, Babcock's, and Faulkner's attitudes might be scorned by some as patronizing and condescending, but the sincerity of these authors' words still resonates from a time when, despite segregation, the races lived more closely together across the line of abstraction. The much-vaunted civil rights era has brought much needed legal rights, and Faulkner was all for that, but it has also sometimes brought as well the disconnect of distrust, fear, and animosity on both sides of the color line. Faulkner had predicted these consequences if his warnings "to go slow" with integration were not heeded. He predicted government forced associations would sometimes leave unhealable scars. Abstraction kills affection and separates, as he knew well.

Alabama author, Harper Lee's *To Kill a Mocking Bird* (1960), a treatment of small town Southern racial and religious bigotry and the search for racial justice, won the Pulitzer Prize, became a Literary Guild and Book-of-the-Month Selection, was made into an Academy Award-winning film, and has become a standard reading selection in high school English classes. The timing of its publication when the South was being criticized in the media for segregation and racial prejudice, and its overt sermonizing on race, both no doubt helped create the enormous popular success of an artistically flawed work.

After fifty-five years, *To Kill a Mocking Bird* now has its sequel, *Go Set a Watchman*, published in summer 2015. The novel takes place twenty years after the events of *To Kill a Mockingbird*. Scout Finch returns home to find well-intentioned liberal whites facing the figurative brick wall of a racial divide. It is not a comfortable book for the latter-day civil rights community and their oversimplified dramatizations of the struggle. *Go Set a Watchman* depicts the legacy of integration as it was forced on the South too quickly—in essence, with the too much, too fast approach in the usual hysterical way of American progressive movements. This reform agenda came complete with vilification for the opponents and sainthood for the promoters.

Faulkner's own advice to civil rights leaders was that you have right on your side, but "Go slow." The American answer was "Freedom *now!*" even to the point of what many political analysts have considered unconstitutional oversteps by the United States Supreme Court to implement sweeping social change overnight. Harper Lee's sequel, with hindsight, implies the wisdom of Faulkner's philosophy of "Go slow" by showing how "too much, too fast" created as many racial problems as it solved and left an era of strained relations. For those who say that racial divisiveness continues as a major problem, that era of strife which was ushered in by too much, too fast civil rights legislation that is with us today, may be seen as a direct result.

Lee's *Go Set a Watchman* is seldom mentioned now in the seven years after its publication. *To Kill a Mocking Bird* however was named the favorite American novel of all time in 2019 in a voting sponsored by PBS in a weeks-long series of considerations of the genre. The very biased liberal host of the series was visibly relieved to be able to announce that Lee's novel beat out second-place winner *Gone with the Wind.* After the suspect presidential election of 2020 and the Left-leaning political and cultural biases of PBS which this election made even more apparent than ever, one may rightly question the "Favorite American Novel" polling result. The point made here still stands however. *To Kill a Mocking Bird* is still very well-known indeed, being taught in so many American high schools, while *Go Set a Watchman* was not so much as mentioned in the series. Cancel Culture most certainly applies to the consideration of novels on PBS and elsewhere.

Faulkner's *Intruder in the Dust* (1948) follows Lucas Beauchamp, the Edmonds and McCaslin families, and the Gavin Stevens of *Go Down, Moses* in a tale of murder, racial prejudice, and the narrator's coming of age through his successful attempt at proving the innocence of the wrongfully accused. The plot has many similarities to *To Kill a Mocking Bird* without its more blatant sermonizings on race. Artistically, and thematically, it is superior in all respects to Lee's novel, yet has not achieved its popularity.

Perhaps its best portrayal is the friendship between the young white narrator and the African American tenant farmer's son and hunting companion, Aleck Sander. Their relationship is very similar to the early friendship of Bayard and Ringo before they grow up in *The Unvanquished.* It is another example of Faulkner's depiction of human ties transcending abstracts, law, custom, caste, and color. Effective ties are once again successfully forged between individuals when the abstract becomes destructive and detrimental and on the verge of causing tragedy.

Racial tolerance, in one form or another and to one degree or another, has been a hallmark of Southern writing. Writers as diverse as James Lane Allen, Francis Hopkinson Smith, Thomas Nelson Page, Grace King, Kate Chopin, George

Washington Cable, Joel Chandler Harris, Ellen Glasgow, Allen Tate (see "The Swimmers"), Ernest Gaines, Eudora Welty (see "A Worn Path"), Zora Neale Hurston, Julia Peterkin, Lillian Smith, Harper Lee, Havilah Babcock Walker Percy, Shelby Foote (see especially *September, September*), and Robert Penn Warren of an older generation and scores in the new have this in common with Faulkner and the Southern literary tradition to which they belong.

It must be added that more of Faulkner's African American characters than Aunt Molly and Dilsey stand out for their good sense and admirable sound value systems. For instance, Faulkner must have admired the old gentleman in *The Reivers* who taught his young white charge that "De Thorybreds dey goes wid dee heads up till dee drap, you know." In fact, an interesting and revealing article might be written on African American wisdom in Faulkner's fiction.

Cleanth Brooks astutely remarked that in Faulkner it is not wealth, caste, or color that determines "aristocracy." Instead, an individual's values would make a character like house servant Elnora in "There Was a Queen" superior to her mistress Narcissa Benbow or to the other white "town trash" whom Elnora looks down upon for more or less the right reasons. She wisely defines quality as "It aint *is*, it's *does*" (*Collected Stories,* 729, 732). Elnora noted of Narcissa that "I nigger and she white. But my black children got more blood than she got. More behavior" (732). Shared values allow the white yeoman farmers the McCallums to be upon the same level as the patrician Sartorises in *Flags in the Dust*, Uncle Possum to be the equal of the Priest family in *The Reivers,* and Lucas Beauchamp to have similar virtues and shortcomings as the Edmondses and McCaslins in *Go Down, Moses.*

Brooks accurately concluded that in Faulkner's world "the yeoman white and black man can, in their own terms, qualify as 'aristocrats'" (*Toward Yoknapatawpha*, 335). In a decidedly un-Marxian way, race and class are thus far less important than a particular individual's character. In Faulkner's works, class struggle and racial strife give way to finding common ground and appreciation through shared values. Faulkner had certainly learned that lesson well—and, once again, in his own back yard.

Shelby Foote had an interesting view of the Southern origins of civil rights. In spring 1988, in conversation at a drop-in I gave for him at my home in Athens, Georgia, he commented that "Civil Rights grew out of Southern Protestantism." He continued, "What bothers me about civil rights is the way Southerners stood aside and let the battles be fought between the undesirables—the Northerners who came down, and the Ku Klux Klan. That wasn't right. Racism is a national problem, not just a Southern one" (Transcription of interview with Foote by Dr. David Aiken, 10 March 1988, James Kibler,

Southern Literary Collection, SCL). Foote understood that Faulkner was not one of the Southerners who stood by and let the undesirables dominate, and he always praised him for his stand, to me and in other interviews. For Foote's own stand, the Ku Klux Klan threatened him with violence, an event he never failed to comment upon to me and others. An Alabama license plate, in fact, occasioned such a negative comment in my hearing in 1988. Mr. Foote had a vacation home there, where he apparently met harassment.

Foote's inclusion of "the Northerners who came down" with "the undesirables" may partly explain Faulkner's famous comment that if it became a choice between defending Mississippi with guns against outside coercion and militant blacks, he would choose to stand with his Mississippi kin. This comment has often been attributed to Faulkner's drinking. Meriwether himself told me that if you took this statement seriously from a man in his cups, then you weren't thinking clearly yourself. Today, despite my regard for Dr. Meriwether, I am not persuaded by his reasoning. In my opinion, a perception of an invasion of his people under any guise had seared itself in Faulkner's psyche so deeply that such a threat, quite understandably, provoked a reciprocated hostility. Burned in the brain of many today are still the images of heavily armed uniformed Federal troops escorting little children into a school in Little Rock, Arkansas, and the many billboards along highways reading "Impeach Earl Warren."

Faulkner biographers down to the most recent still do not quite get it. Rollyson, the most recent, is a perfect example. He does an admirable job of researching Faulkner's film scripts, an area which has not been adequately explored heretofore, but puts an expected twist on his findings. The scripts are used to show Faulkner's superiority in racial matters to his Southern people. In Rollyson's hands, Faulkner unfortunately becomes a tool for Rollyson to berate a fascist, racist South, and Faulkner gets lost in the process.

ELEVEN

FAULKNER THE CONSERVATIVE

F aulkner has left a clear record of his political philosophy in his essays. It can be summed up as primarily and centrally Jeffersonian. His 1955 essay "On Privacy" is probably the single most important work that best states his philosophy. Here he says that Old America stood for the primacy of individual man. That was the legacy of the Southern founders of the new nation. Today's New America places man-in-the-mass, in the abstract aggregate. The demarcation between old and new is thus between a Jeffersonian and a Lincolnian concept of government, that is, of local limited government where the government exists for the individual and a distant strongly-centralized government where the individual is seen to exist for the government.

In 1903, Grace King wrote that "the Southern man has begotten in the country a confidence in self as self.... He stands for self against theories" (King, Writings, 386). Faulkner declared that the dream of Old America was to insure and protect the sanctity of the individual. But that is gone now, Faulkner wrote, because we "dozed, slept, and it abandoned us, and with it our individual freedom and liberty." Instead of these, "now what we hear is a cacophony of terror and conciliation and compromise babbling only the [hollow] mouth sounds" of liberty and freedom, "the loud and empty words which we have emasculated of all meaning whatever—freedom, democracy, patriotism—with which, awakened at last, we try in desperation to hide from ourselves that loss" by saying the mouth sounds over and over again (*Essays,* 65-66).

Faulkner declared that the goal of the New America is to reduce the individual to "one more identityless integer in that identityless anonymous mass" while covering up the scam under the "empty mouthsound of freedom" (*Essays,* 72). The old "moral verities" are gone that produced and protected these words, and now we have an America which is "one vast down-crowding presence to abolish" freedom and liberty both, "by destroying man's individuality." (*Essays,* 71). In 2022, one can see the end results in "Identity Politics"—of people divided and then reassembled and massed by identities and used for political purposes. The Marxist struggle between the classes has been replaced by the abstractionist struggle between the races, sexes, and sexual "preference."

Faulkner predicted the rise of a totalitarianism in which the obfuscators of truth will use the "emasculated" words freedom and liberty "as tools, implements, for the further harassment of the private individual human spirit,"— "their furious and immunized high priests…bellowing the words *Security…Prosperity…Democracy…The American Way…The*

241

Flag!" (*Essays,* 73). It will be easy enough for them to have their way, he said, because the listeners desire to hear it. The new slavery, he declared, will be superior to the old in that Americans will be slaves and not know it (Faulkner-Cowley File, 70-80). "Let us beware," Faulkner warned, the obfuscators won't stop there (*Essays,* 73). Recent Fear instilled as a result of Covid-19 is a perfect example of a population's trading of freedom for security.

The essay "On Privacy" shows that Faulkner was deeply and passionately concerned about the American drift to totalitarianism. He was in touch with his time and actively involved in it. His Delta Council address of 1952 had set the stage for the 1955 essay and helps to provide context. Three years earlier, the chief focus was on the word *Security*, which had become to him the security to keep one's place on a "public relief roll" or "bureaucratic gravy-trough." (*Essays,* 130). Individual security had been replaced by Social Security and Welfare. Faulkner wrote, "We have made respectable and even elevated to a national system, that which the old tough fathers would have scorned and condemned: charity…. We no longer have responsibility" (*Essays,* 131). Again, Grace King had said the same a half century before about the traditional Southerner in contrast to the New American. Southerners, she declared "are wont to give, but not to ask charity" (King,

Writings, 387). That was the old way of Faulkner's childhood, but he had witnessed the shift and was very disturbed by it.

It took both great insight and courage for Faulkner to state in the midst of the Cold War, that now the enemies of our freedom are not foreign but reside "beneath the eagle-perched domes of our capitols and from behind the alphabetical splatter on the doors of welfare and other bureaus of economic or industrial regimentation" (*Essays,* 132). He said that the enemy does not wear a military uniform but is dressed in the promises of "peace and progress," and a prosperous economy. Faulkner continued that the enemy's artillery is a debased and respectless laughingstock currency "which has emasculated the initiative for independence." (*Essays,* 132). "What we need," he concluded, "is not fewer people, but more room between them, where those who would stand on their own feet, could, and those who won't, might have to. Then the welfare, the relief, the compensation, instead of being nationally sponsored cash prizes for idleness and ineptitude," could go to those who cannot stand—the sick and the aged (*Essays,* 133-124). He declared that this is the only charity the old tough fathers would have sanctioned. This is the only charity Grace King felt that Southerners would find proper and desirable.

Faulkner was no relativist in all this. In his "On Privacy" essay, he defined truth as immutable in this way: "Truth—that long clean clear simple undeviable unchallengeable straight and shining line." In New America, the obfuscators of truth have made it an "angle, a point of view having nothing to do with truth not even with fact but depending solely on where you are standing when you look at it. Or rather—better—where you can contrive to have him standing whom you are trying to fool...when he looks at it." (*Essays,* 72). In this absolutism, Faulkner was certainly out of step with the current academic progressive belief that all truth is relative. Given this fact, one must marvel that much of the criticism written on Faulkner has not been even more cock-eyed than it has always been and continues to be.

In 1955, Faulkner also wrote an essay for *Sports Illustrated* after witnessing his first hockey game. In the final paragraph he wrote that he just couldn't see what the hockey match had to do with the national anthem. "What are we afraid of?" he asked. Are we so doubtful of our national character "that we not only dare not open a professional athletic contest or a beauty-pageant or a real estate auction, but we must even use a Chamber of Commerce race for Miss Sewage Disposal...to remind us that that liberty gained without honor and sacrifice and held without constant vigilance...was not worth having to begin with? Or, by blaring it or chanting it at ourselves every time...young men engage formally for the possession of a puck or ball, or just one woman walks across a lighted platform in a bathing-suit, do we hope to so dull and eviscerate the words and tune with repetition, that when we do hear it[,] we will not be disturbed from that dreamlike state in which 'honor' is a break and 'truth' an angle" (*Essays,* 51). This paragraph is published from Faulkner's typescript in *Essays, Speeches & Public Letters.* Interestingly, it was omitted from the published *Sports Illustrated* article.[1] One may draw his or her own conclusions as to why. Whatever the reason, the reference to the lock-step adoration of the U.S. flag seems to be proved by the censoring of any questioning of that adoration. It is fortunate that Faulkner saved his typescript. He had become wise to such editorial games played on Southern writers by the Establishment.

In these essays and speeches, Faulkner revealed he was directly focused on what he considered the central scams of the new way. His powerful writing on the subject often has the authority of prophecy. This is an area the literary critic has for the most part ignored. The reasons are perhaps complicated, but it is a fact that the small 1,000 copy edition of the 1966 *Essays, Speeches and Public Letters* was never reprinted despite Faulkner's tremendous importance and the soaring sales of his novels. His New York publisher would not republish. When offered in the used book arena, the volume always brought four figures. Only with Meriwether's paperback edition of *Essays* published four decades later in 2004 have his words been readily available to students outside rare book rooms. It appears that critics have still chosen to ignore it.

In these pieces, Faulkner in no way conformed to Cold War "patriotism" or the American boosterism of the progressive-socialist image. Reading the essays will likely cause one to consider the fiction and biography in a new light. It did for me. Probably out of loyalty to my mentor, I was lucky enough to have purchased one of the thousand copies while a graduate student.

The sum total of criticism upon an author cannot help but have an effect on how the public sees that author. The critics have often made Faulkner something he was not, more created instead in their own popularly accepted liberal-progressive secular humanistic academic image than in an image faithful to Faulkner. To cite only one example—the early criticism of *Go Down, Moses* made the lawyer Gavin Stevens the novel's hero.[2] He has Harvard and Heidelberg University degrees, after all, among the rubes of Mississippi. In Mississippi, reasons the academic, such a man must be a hero to Faulkner. Critics do not quite get it once again. As shown in the previous chapter, Stevens is well-intentioned but totally out of touch with the world around him, lost in sentimental do-goodism and abstraction. They fail to get Faulkner's clue that most Southern readers outside the pale of the ivory academic tower pick up on—that his lifetime activity there in his law office is translating the Holy Scriptures back from the English into the original Greek.

Other than conservative critic M. E. Bradford, most academic critics have usually identified with the intellectual hyper-educated Stevens, not remembering that Faulkner called himself "an old veteran sixth grader" (*Essays,* 219). Faulkner never received a high school diploma. Faulkner made it very clear: "I have no degrees nor diplomas from any school." (*Essays,* 219). So indeed, here the critic creates Faulkner in the critic's own image. But wishing will not make it so. That is often the way of the literary critic, but not the good one. Good critics and seekers after the truth of Faulkner need to start here with his own statements and test their conceptions and misconceptions against what Faulkner actually said in his essays. He valued fidelity to words. He did not scam or twist meaning. He did not speak idly, and thus his words can often go reliably far in giving us the world view behind his fiction.

What is clear is that Faulkner's world view was not urban progressive-socialist man-in-the-mass, and abstractionist, but instead generally conservative (in the old root sense of "conserve"), rural, traditional, individual, personal, and concrete. In summing up, one might say that his philosophy was more or less the antithesis of the philosophy that dominates public discourse today—and coherently and cohesively traditionally Southern in sensibility.

Brooks once again went to the heart of the matter. In 1978, he explained why neither Faulkner nor the South was "fascist," and why those who have tried to label them so are gravely mistaken. Brooks said, "The modern progressive American, who subscribes to the usual stereotypes and slogans," would regard any traditional society or traditionalist as fascistic, but "what these people don't realize is ...fascism is a mass phenomenon, it's a phenomenon of mass man, not the aristocracy." He continued, "fascism is clearly a lower middle class phenomenon," and city-born, not rural and not a product of the gentry. He concluded, "People on the land were too traditional, too old-fashioned, too conservative in their habits and attitudes...to push themselves in some great anonymous mass movement screaming for the leader, whoever the leader was" (Brooks, Interview, 157-158).

Professor Eugene Genovese, who before his death a decade ago, had become a recovering New York City born Marxist-Leninist, put it most succinctly and memorably in our day: "The principal tradition of the South—the mainstream of its cultural development—has been quintessentially conservative" (1). Genovese continued: "Southern conservatives have condemned...the cult of scientism, atheistic and pantheistic rationalism, and a material progress that has resulted in the alienation of the individual from self and society" (12). Faulkner is a faithful register for that view and can be seen to be at the

248

heart of a traditional Southern way of seeing as expressed in the distinguished body of the majority of its literature.

TWELVE

WHAT FAULKNER THOUGHT

Mississippi Senator John Sharp Williams, an ancestor of Faulkner, upon leaving Washington, D. C. for the last time to go home, asserted, "I'd rather be a hound dog and bay at the moon from my Mississippi plantation than remain in the United States Senate."

In 1964, when the University Press of Virginia published a catalogue of Faulkner's library, it was missing a volume that has since been deposited in 1998 at the university library's special collections. It is among the most significant books for gauging the inner man—a copy of young Faulkner's King James version of the Bible autographed by his mother, Maud Butler Falkner (1871-1960) with her note: *"Just after his 7th birthday, William & Muddie were studying the Sunday School lesson. In reply to Muddie's.... 'William, what would you rather have than anything else?' he answered, after a moment's thought, 'I'd rather have honor and do what's right.' Saturday—Oct. 1—1904."*

To be specific, Faulkner's mother penned this inscription six days after William's seventh birthday. "Muddie" was Maud Butler's mother and William's maternal grandmother, Lelia Dean Swift Butler (1840-1907), who was living with them in 1904 and taking him to Sunday School. William called Lelia Butler "Damuddy" (grandmother) as Mrs. Falkner called

250

her "Muddie" (mother.) She died of uterine cancer three years after the inscription was made. Her quiet and uncomplaining suffering impressed the lad at age nine. Faulkner remembered Mrs. Butler as a gentle, kind presence in his childhood. There have been many biographies of Faulkner, but none has given a single better insight into the man than his mother's few lines.

One has only to telescope ahead half a century to Faulkner's address upon receiving the Nobel Prize in 1950. Here, he said that an author must write of "the old verities and truths of the heart, the old universal truths lacking which any story is ephemeral and doomed—love and honor and pity and pride and compassion and sacrifice." If the writer does not, "he labors under a curse. He writes not of love but of lust…not of the heart but of the glands." The writer's duty is to remind man of "the courage and honor and hope and pride and compassion and pity and sacrifice which have been the glory of his past." In so doing, he becomes one of the "pillars and props to help man endure and prevail." When Faulkner composed these lines at age fifty-three, he had lived up to the child's desire to be responsible and "do what's right." Throughout his life, "honor" had been a key word.

A history professor friend recently noted that no one speaks of honor anymore, that it is a forgotten word today, or, if used, is not taken seriously. It is seen as some strange antique notion with no real meaning to moderns. But honor in the South has been and remains a central ideal for traditional Southerners, a concept around which to conduct lives, or at least to attempt to. It is the chief attribute of chivalry. No matter the fashionable academic attempts to deconstruct honor, honor remains a pillar of Southern culture.

Brooks correctly treated Faulkner's last novel, *The Reivers,* as a "courtesy book," that is, a kind of handbook of behavior, as Baldassare Castiglione had done for Renaissance Italy in *The Book of the Courtier.* Since the grandfather Boss Priest tells the novel to his grandson Lucius, the work becomes a story defining what it is to be a gentleman. In the process, Mr. Priest tells his grandson that the gentleman takes responsibility for his actions and bears the burden of their consequences (Brooks, 353). The gentleman is generous with his inferiors, chivalrous to women, and refuses to exercise power over the weak and defenseless. He is honest. He tells and values the truth. Honor is his guide. Priest tells Lucius that a gentleman cries but dries his eyes before meeting the world. The word "gentleman" thus defines a culture's code of behavior, and its value system—unwritten, but all the more meaningful *because* unwritten.

Ben Wasson, who knew Faulkner from Wasson's college years onward, wrote that Faulkner "was chivalrous to all women, regardless of age. With them, from the youngest to the oldest, there was a suggestion in his manner that he wore a plume in his hat." Wasson described many examples of what he called "Bill Faulkner's gentlemanly code"—a code that "extended to men as well as women" (Wasson, 64-65). Wasson saw the code in action, in his treatment of Wasson's family members and their friends. Faulkner took the word gentleman very seriously. His doing so was no "pose," as a trendy Faulkner biography of the 1990s has suggested (Gray, 2). I consider this biographer's suggestion an insult to Faulkner.

Honor and trying to do what is right are concepts that stand very near a traditional Southerner's heart and color his thoughts and actions. Faulkner biographer Gray wrote, however, "The South, before and after the Civil War, wanted desperately to see itself as aristocratic, and, to this extent, many white Southerners were ready to turn themselves into actors: to adopt the aristocratic pose and so reinvent themselves as gentlemen and ladies" (2-3). Nowhere in Gray's biography does he mention Maud Falkner's inscription in William's King James. Pity. It follows from Gray's comments at his biography's beginning, that since he does not take Faulkner's concept of chivalry seriously, he must not be able to take Faulkner seriously. Double pity. In my opinion, such a reader of Faulkner is the real loser. Triple pity that the influence of his biography might have the effect of robbing others as well.

Directly contradictory to Gray, Montserrat Ginès in *The Southern Inheritors of Don Quixote* (2000) relegates two chapters to showing how seriously Faulkner took honor through his comments on *Don Quixote*. Faulkner said it was one of his favorite works and read it "every year, as some do the Bible" (72). Ginés considered it an essential work for Faulkner and shows why. Faulkner said of Quixote: "he is a man trying to do the best he can in this ramshackle universe he's compelled to live in. He has ideals that by the pharisaical standards are nonsensical. But by my standards, they are not nonsensical…. I can see myself in Don Quixote." Ginés' first chapter on Faulkner is appropriately entitled "Honor for the Sake of Honor." A citizen of Barcelona, Ginés understands Faulkner and his Southern culture of honor in ways no American critic has been able to do. Ginés' excellent treatment of Lucius Priest in *The Reivers* is much to the point. Ginés feels that Lucius' defense of Everbe is Faulkner's "final tribute to the chivalric virtues so pervasively present in his fiction" (103). It was not a matter of Faulkner's imitation of Cervantes but a moral and cultural compatibility.

As the case of Faulkner proves, the Southern sense of honor and "doing what is right" are centrally Christian in origin. That should be obvious, but for the academic, the obvious is often overlooked in attempts to be ingenious. At Rowan Oak, in his writing table drawer beneath his typewriter at the time of his death in 1962, Faulkner kept a well-worn pocket New Testament, the only book present in the drawer. It was still there undisturbed as he had left it when I saw it at Rowan Oak in May 1970. Mr. Beverley Smith, curator of Rowan Oak at the time, assured me the book had not been touched, that it was just as it had been at his death. This is another title that did not make it into Joseph Blotner's library catalogue. But again, its presence gives a most crucial insight into the man.

As we have seen in chapter four, William Gilmore Simms's very last review of 1870 spoke of how the North was ridiculing the term "chivalry." He wrote that the words "gentleman" and "chivalry," because associated with a defeated South, "had now become a sort of scoff among them, especially as they perpetually heard of these virtues from European tongues, as especially belonging to the South." For example, see Lord Acton, who deeply regretted the South's loss in 1865. Mark Twain may be cited as an excellent example of one of the scoffers. By this time, he had moved to New England to be near his friend William Dean Howells, who also shared the Northern distaste for Southern chivalry. A decade after Simms's death, Mark Twain wrote in *Life on the Mississippi* (1883) that the South suffered from what he called "the Sir Walter disease" of honor and chivalry. By that, he was referring to Sir Walter Scott's novels which dramatized and popularized these virtues. He said of Scott, "his enchantments...set the world in love with dreams and phantoms, with decayed and swinish forms of religion; with decayed and degraded systems of government…and the sham chivalries of a brainless and worthless long-vanished society."

In the wake of Mark Twain, William Peterfield Trent, Simms's very progressive, very unsympathetic first biographer in 1888, thought he was having the final word on the subject of gentlemen and chivalry when he wrote that Simms was not a barbarian because he was not a Southern aristocrat--and chivalry might have been a good thing in its day, "but modern civilization is a much higher thing."

Little did Trent know the power of the perduring curse of the poet that Simms was hurling in his last words at an empire that had made war on his people and their *mores*. Simms predicted that without the virtues of honor and chivalry, the alien culture will die a slow death by suicide. He concluded, "usurpation becomes tyranny, and tyranny always commits suicide" (Simms, *Selected Essays*, 192-193). Empires fall, most especially those forced by the sword and by victors who scoff at principles greater than lust for power and wealth.

It is pertinent to know that Trent was hand-picked by William Dean Howells to write the Simms biography for his American Man of Letters series. Howells' act was typical of the post-war intellectual imperialism that Simms had inveighed against before the war. One could not imagine a more hateful act than for a biographer to write a story of a person's life that undermined and contradicted the heart of everything the subject stood for. That of course did not matter to those who had jettisoned honor, respect, and fair play for the zealotry of a secular progressivist crusade. It may be rightly considered their early brand of cancel culture. Ralph Waldo Emerson spoke for many Northerners when he wrote in his journal that now that the South was defeated, the South would be fertile ground for young New England minds who could spread New England from Canada to the Gulf of Mexico and the Atlantic to the Pacific. He might have added the Hawaiian Islands, already being occupied by New England missionaries. Faulkner was born into this period of zealous and aggressive Northern imperialism.

With a prostrate South, Emerson had not counted on the strength of the Southern culture, families like the Falkners, and men like Faulkner. The resistance and continuity of Southern ways remained into the new century. I think G. K. Chesterton gauged the situation correctly. After his tour of America, a half century following Simms's death, he commented, "Old England can still be traced in Old Dixie. It contains some of the best things England herself ... has lost or is trying to lose" (*America What I Saw There*, 208). He had witnessed the triumph of "the heresy of materialism" and wrote in a tone as vociferous as Simms's that "An egotistical heresy, produced in the modern heathenry, has taught [Americans] against all their Christian instincts that boasting is better than courtesy and pride better than humility" (523-524). Chesterton declared that the North was full of "tangled things." Irish author Padraig Colum noted the similarities between Charleston and Dublin—that although broken and bent, they both still stood unrepentant, survivors shunned by progress, with memory "showing itself through landscape and character" a trait "better for poetry than anything else." The Irish writer, "A. E." (George Russell) also commented on the ways that the South reminded him of old Britain (Bellows, 63-64, 90, 138-139).

It should be noted that Mark Twain himself, after his celebration and monetary success for books that laughed at the South's ways, and then his later commercial failure in the rawly material rat-race of the business-industrial North, was having second thoughts, and maybe even third ones. His *A Connecticut Yankee in King Arthur's Court* (1889) is worth considering. Honor, courtesy, and honesty are not scoffed at here. The opposite Connecticut Yankee traits are instead held up for the condemnation and ridicule they deserve. *A Connecticut Yankee in King Arthur's Court* is hardly ever mentioned by critics and Clemens biographers. A notable example is the Ken Burns PBS series on Clemens. Perhaps this debunking of the Yankee way and the Northern myth of righteousness is one of the reasons it does not often get treated in a study of his works. It certainly should be but is ignored because it simply does not fit the usual accepted narrative. All the treatments never fail to cite Clemens' damning comments on "the Sir Walter disease" and Old South chivalry but never mention *A Connecticut Yankee in King Arthur's Court.*

Grace King (1852-1932) wrote in 1903, "Would it sound too aphoristic to say that if it were not for the South—the terms gentleman and lady would fall out of our vocabulary, which would contain only man and woman—or that the South has prevented us from being a nation of Yankees, that the South stands out for the heroic against the successful?" King cited the Southern ideals of generosity, hospitality, and chivalry as "the flowers of a past life that have borne fruit in individuals" (King, 388). As we noted in an earlier chapter, when Faulkner was in New Orleans in 1925, Grace King had a popular literary salon at her home in the city. There the writers of the area met and shared ideas in a social setting. Again, one wonders if Faulkner did not at least meet Miss King. She was one of the South's most famous authors nationwide at the time and Faulkner was publishing stories and sketches locally from January to September of that year.

Like his mother's inscription respecting honor, Faulkner's *Essays, Speeches & Public Letters* allows a look within the mind of the man, this time through the author's own words. This collection first appeared in 1966 and contained sixty-three Faulkner pieces. The new edition of 2004 increased the number of entries to 102. Both old and new editions contain many passing references to an author's role similar to the passages quoted here from the Nobel address. As one reviewer has written, they show that Faulkner's concept of the writer's duty "reflects a Christian sense of vocation."[1] Faulkner saw authorship as "calling" and service and thus deserving the care and anguish of hard labor—or, as Faulkner's fellow Mississippian, friend, and admirer Shelby Foote put it, an endeavor "worth a grown man's time."

As we have said, Faulkner's Nobel address declared that the writer who does not have faith in ideals like honor and courage is a writer merely of "the glands." The distinction may be a good way of differentiating Faulkner from Ernest Hemingway and his imitators. A case in point is that Hemingway's main character in *A Farewell to Arms* finds words like "honor," "bravery," and "love" meaningless, even sickening, and finally comes to believe only in the names on road signs, the only words that are real to him and deserving his respect. *A Farewell to Arms* portrays an empirically conceived world "of the glands" (to use Faulkner's phrase), a philosophy which finally can and does lead only to hollowness, cynicism, and ultimately to a culture of death, if not suicide itself.

The culture of death is an apt description of the world of *A Farewell to Arms*—a world impoverished of honor, faith, chivalry, and belief, and peopled by what T.S. Eliot called "hollow men." For all its material wealth, the dwellers in this man-made hell live well below the poverty line. They may know art and visit great galleries and museums, but they are essentially culturally deprived. Their existence is radically diminished to the biological, and severely circumscribed by having no true spiritual side. It is clear from both his fiction and his essays that Faulkner did not fall into that modernist trap.

In his important 1954 introduction to *The Faulkner Reader,* Faulkner summed up his aim in writing as the attempt "to uplift man's heart" and thus "say No to death" (*Essays,* 181). Hemingway's suicide may be pertinent here. Faulkner declared that through the "deathless excitement" engendered by the writer's creation, man is strengthened to endure. Here once again he reveals that same sense of vocation foreign to a culture of death, the death to which Faulkner said an emphatic No.

Although it is filled with many significant literary insights, *Essays, Speeches & Public Letters* is not primarily a collection about literature. In treating such a wide array of non-literary subjects, Faulkner has revealed himself to be a good and close observer of the current scene and a man actively involved with keeping up with what is happening around him in the world. He did not write in isolation from his time but was keenly aware of the issues of his day. It is clear that he was out of step with "progressive," socialist, boosterist, hedonistic,

261

"glandular" America. His was as far from a cash-register evaluation of things as was possible. He could not understand the blind patriotism of flag waving, national anthem singing, pledge-of-allegiance reciting, self-righteous citizens of a technocratic empire whose mantra was eventually to become "Follow the Science." Instead, he was a man of quiet faith, modest, thoughtful, private, reticent, independent, individualistic, and self-reliant and saw these as bed-rock traits of decent Old America not respected or even understood by the coarse, vulgar, conformist, dishonest, selfish, mindless, pushing-and-shoving New.

The two essays, "On Privacy" and "On Fear," discussed in the previous chapter, were planned as two chapters of a projected book which Faulkner was going to entitle *The American Dream: What Happened to It?*[2] Unfortunately, he never completed the volume. The essays of this collection, however, answer the question posed by the title quite satisfactorily. For Faulkner the American Dream had degenerated into a thoroughly materialistic, glandular "vision of ease and plenty" and a "universal will to regimentation" in which individuality was "cursed by one universal American voice as [being] subversive to the American way of life and the American flag" (*Essays*, 162).

In comments pertinent to the current American scene, he feared for a future in which Americans would only want comfort, security, and ease and would give up all individual rights and freedoms in order to insure them. In their blindness, he could envision Americans lock-stepping over a cliff without a thought, like lemmings to the sea. Even now, he wrote, the words "Freedom," "Security," and "Democracy" have only become "tools and implements for the further harassment of the private individual human spirit." The "furious and immunized high priests" of this tyranny go by the names of "Security," "The American Way," and "The Flag." Faulkner declared that the American sky that had once been the living breath of liberty and freedom was, "now become one vast down-crowding pressure to abolish them both." (*Essays,* 70-74).

Such debasement suggests a possible legacy of Puritan conformist and self-righteous materialism when wealth was deemed a sign of God's favor. The early Southern founding fathers who bequeathed the documents of Old America feared and rejected this influence. As Faulkner showed in his address before the Delta Council, and elsewhere in the collection, he clearly sided with the Jeffersonian rural ideal of life on the land and Jefferson's view that the best government is that which governs least.

It is clear from his essays and speeches that New America and its urban society had no attraction for Faulkner. Again, there are no real surprises here; his is a Southern attitude. His is no glib and superficial cocktail culture, no Manhattan city malaise, no deracinated abstract geography of nowhere, no sterile world city out of nature, no giving up freedom for security, no culture of death, no sickness unto death, no coming universal wish not to live. Instead, his belief in basic Christian charity and fellowship was central to his vision of the world.

That vision entailed a reaffirmation of rooted community, of hope and "honor and pity and pride and compassion and sacrifice"—in other words, the culture of life—in the teeth of the Cold War and the very real threat of nuclear annihilation brought on by the ruthless powers of great clashing empires. Again, we have only to remember that Faulkner, unlike Hemingway, said No to death. I suspect that Faulkner would have agreed with Wendell Berry's assertion that he is not optimistic about the future, but hopeful, because optimism is too much like a program and hope is a Christian virtue.[3] Southern writers have often shown that there is a big difference between optimism and hope.

Faulkner's Bible had declared that he who loves God loves life. His mother had seen the makings of this Christian vision in her son at age seven; and the collection of his essays and speeches quietly demonstrate it at every turn. *As the twig is bent, so grows the tree* is an old saying that once again proves true in Faulkner's case. More appropriately in this context, Proverbs 22 teaches *Train up a child in the way he should go, and when he is old he will not depart from it.* Mrs. Butler without doubt had often read these words and acted upon them. Both Faulkner's fiction and essays show that he is no secular humanist striving to place man upon God's throne or believing man can shape himself from his own clay. Faulkner obviously saw man as flawed and unperfectible, but also possessing an indomitable spirit and will to endure, capable of courage and bravery, of "love and honor and pity and pride and compassion and sacrifice"— "the old verities and truths of the heart," as he called them.

Faulkner was a product of "Reconstructed" Mississippi, that is, as he saw it, an invaded Mississippi robbed of what wealth the recent war had left. For him "Reconstructed" was a cruel official government "mouth-sound" too. The struggle for survival beneath the long shadow of war, military occupation and its aftermath was very real in Faulkner's world. As we have seen in chapter three, Faulkner's own family plantation was burned and its fields laid waste. His own great-grandmother had met soldiers at the plantation door. The home community of the Falkners was pilfered and never really recovered. Its agrarian base was irreparably damaged. As we have also seen, the author had a great wealth of family stories of loss, struggle, and the unvanquished spirit on which to rely, tales in which the memory of old times and values and strengths were tangibly present. This aspect of Faulkner's background factored strongly in what he was to become and is reflected in his fiction and essays. No critic or biographer has emphasized this truth sufficiently. Perhaps Cleanth Brooks has come the closest.

Faulkner's essays and speeches allow satisfying entrance into the mind of a responsible and dedicated man of honor—a thoughtful, common-sensical consciousness stamped by the Southern culture at its chivalric best. Faulkner's life, when it is known sufficiently well, can only be described as heroic. His was a life of sacrifice, duty, courage, conscientious hard work, responsibility, and commitment. Faulkner deserves to be honored with the greatest of Southerners—in literature and out.

It is also time that he is placed in the proper context of the chivalric culture that nurtured him. His essays and speeches, as a compilation of primary sources, will assist the student of his fiction in doing so. Here Faulkner spoke for himself without the distortion of interpretation, which so often in its obsessive small focus on this pet faddish issue or that, is blind to the greater truth of the man and his work. It is this myopic method that has contributed to the creation of what is perhaps the largest mass of uninspired criticism on a major literary figure the last century has known. Sadly, with many of these interpreters, Faulkner has been secondary and merely a pretext to voice topical causes, fashions, angles, and fads, fads that may be here today, and tomorrow, gone with the wind.

Proper consideration reveals a Faulkner much bigger and broader than the usual one of fads. He is an author who is not limited to the moment. It is clear that he takes an uncommonly long view, one that no doubt will ensure that his works will endure, and his vision prevail against the haters of mankind and their culture of death to which he has said an emphatic *No*. Thus his works are neither bound to time nor subject to its whims. It is hoped that his essays may yield a sounder approach to his fiction and its central assumptions about both man's limitations and redemptive possibilities. In too much of Faulkner scholarship, other than Brooks's masterful works and M.E. Bradford's *Generations of the Faithful Heart*, Faulkner criticism has yet to rise to the level of Faulkner's work itself—an inspired and exalted height indeed, but a noble ideal toward which the honorable critic might aspire.

One final note on the tradition of Southern letters is in order. Southern writing continues in the old honorable ways. Much of the best of it, as in the case of the late Larry Brown and Cormac McCarthy, exists outside the university. The academic scholar-gypsies who make a living from validating the hangers-on authors to English departments in the role of "creative writers," put forth an array of lesser lights in the forms of adherents to the vapid schools of "Southern Cute" or

"Progressive Urban or Suburban Shopping Mall Chic." No matter the hype, their stars are lesser lights indeed and most of them will be old news in a few decades (at most), along with their scholar-gypsy promoters.

The subject of the future of Southern letters has been treated by editors Jefferson Humphries and John Lowe in *The Future of Southern Letters* (Oxford University Press, 1994). Sadly, the volume is a rather feeble attempt owing too much to the short-sighted and pier-conscious world of the university and its creative writing apparatus. It does, however, make the valid point that there is more than "one South." The problem is that there has been no attempt at showing how with all the vast regional and racial differences, there are points of agreement and traits held in common. The volume's judgments are colored largely by scholar-gypsying, and the smug insider mentality—even when an author like Jim Wayne Miller appears to be criticizing it with a dialogue between himself and Sut Lovingood. The university itself has become a place of lesser lights who have to rely on elitist managerial arrogance and the accepted clichés to prove its worth and justify exorbitant sums of tax money, student fees, and alumni support.

Still, even in this benighted recent volume, the essay by Kate Daniels ("Porch Sitting and Southern Poetry") makes valid points about the continuum of oral narrative and storytelling in the recent writers of the South, and thus lending credence to our chapter four on Faulkner the raconteur. The essay by Professor Fred Hobson ("Of Canons and Cultural Wars: Southern Literature and Literary Scholarship after Midcentury") is an honest and forthright consideration of the scene at the end of the twentieth century. Dr. Hobson's account of a certain scholar-gypsying Vanderbilt professor's personal attack on *The History of Southern Literature* in accusing its editors of "literary secession" and of taking a "Fugitive-Agrarian view of Southern literature and a misguided partiality to the Vanderbilt University authors."

Professor Hobson is very clear about why, even if true, this Fugitive-Agrarian bias might not be altogether a bad thing, for as he said, in this skirmish between the conservative, traditionalist Agrarians versus liberal reform thinkers like Howard Odum and his Chapel Hill progressive sociologists, "Certainly not as social philosophers but as writers, the conservatives simply won the day" (Humphries, 79). Hobson writes that he has made this statement "as one whose natural sympathies lie with southern liberalism." Still Hobson, even as a self-proclaimed "southern liberal," says that he agrees with Donald Davidson that "a 'social program' never leads to the making of a great southern literature."

Hobson continues, along the lines of the venerable tradition of Southern writers eschewing *isms* and *ologies,* treated in chapter three,

The writer concerned more with reform than with story-telling—more with the plight of a region than with the individual drama at hand—with the story as an illustration of social ills to be exposed and corrected –is not likely to be, all other things being equal, as skillful a literary craftsman. He is not as likely to have his eye on the work of art. That alone hardly explains why William Faulkner was a better writer than T. S. Stribling or Paul Green, but it does, among other things, explain why the Agrarians won the literary battle (Humphries, 79-80).

As fair as always, the truly self-proclaimed "liberal" Hobson concludes,

And to the winners of the literary battle went the right to be the interpreters, the arbiters of southern literature. Just as surely as the North, after the Civil War, seized the opportunity to write American history, so the Agrarians and other conservatives seemed to have won the right not only to interpret but to define southern literature (Humphries, 80).

In 2011, Francis Beckwith and J. P. Moreland noted in their preface to *Christianity and Literature* that in the study of literature in universities today during this era of scientific naturalism and postmodernism, "there is no non-empirical knowledge, especially no …theological or ethical knowledge, no reliable or believable truth, goodness or beauty to be found in literature. This restricted view makes literature irrelevant except as ideology, and its study virtually meaningless" (i-ii). Writing degenerates into sociological treatise or propaganda of various sorts to persuade the reader to a particular cause or program. As a result, literature, made thoroughly material, thus loses its worth as providing the long view. Simms and other traditional Southern authors like Davidson, Weaver, Lytle, and Ransom, showed they were aware of the ever-increasing movement in this direction and deemed it a severe and dangerous setback to civilization.

One aim of the traditional Southern man of letters was thus to protect the vision of the traditional role of the writer as friend to man who says, like Keats's Grecian Urn, that truth is beauty and beauty truth. Simms shows that the essential tool of the writer—language—stands at the heart of that vision. Its validity as truth must be protected at all cost. Without belief in truth and the ability of language to convey truth, literature becomes pointless. To echo Wendell Berry in his essay collection, *Standing by Words,* the writer must stand by his words, say what he means, and mean what he says. As man of letters, Simms felt his duty to be the Word's faithful advocate, for as he concluded in a memorable declaration: "The virtues of a people depend very much upon the incorruptible integrity of language" (Charleston *Mercury,* 20 August 1859). Most Southern writers of the twentieth century have shared Simms's view without knowing it or him. It appears to be a belief preserved in the culture and understanding of the South and is in no small way a reason for the success of her literature.

But to return to Hobson's reference to the scholar-gypsy Vanderbilt professor. His attack on the editors of *The History of Southern Literature* for favoring the Vanderbilt Agrarians who taught at his university is a fable of current Southern academic deconstruction (and destruction.) This same professor has tried lamely and unsuccessfully to deconstruct the worth of Faulkner himself and, unfortunately, many things traditionally Southern, including the Southern code of heroism. The late Vanderbilt professor, Walter Sullivan, a true gentleman and a scholar, told me some of the details of how this same scholar-gypsy got hired at Vanderbilt in the first place. In delivering a sample talk "to try him out before hiring" (as universities do), the candidate gave a lecture extolling the virtues of Robert E. Lee (Conversation 12 May 1999; and letter, Walter Sullivan to James Kibler, 31 May 1999, Kibler Southern Literary Collection, South Caroliniana Library). Professor Sullivan felt that this was the foot in the door to go on and "trash" all that he felt Vanderbilt had stood for.

Unfortunately, this story may be told often in the colleges and universities of the South, and, indeed, in the culture at large. It represents a step in Italian Marxist philosopher Antonio Gramsci's "long march through the institutions."

But Faulkner and Southern literature will survive the unprincipled and sometimes downright dishonest scholar-gypsies on the make who go where the most lucrative job offers turn up. Honesty as an "old-fashioned traditional virtue" will also survive. And so too will survive the attributes of Southern letters exhibited in Faulkner and outlined herein in this work. They will survive as sound touchstones, inspiration, and an encouraging continuum to provide a seasoned richness, maturity, and venerableness to Southern literature. Even if diminished for a time, Southern values will reassert themselves because honest, valid, and humane in a world that is sorely in need of them.

THIRTEEN

A GENTLEMAN'S PREROGATIVE:
THE TESTIMONY OF A LOST INTERVIEW

To the deniers of the existence of honor and the gentleman descried in the last chapter, Faulkner himself stood in stark contradiction. In fact, Faulkner was clearly the honorable gentleman of old in many ways—not the least of which was in not wanting his private life displayed in the public eye. Accordingly, he did not grant interviews unless pressured by his publishers who had a difficult time selling his books until after the Nobel Prize was awarded him in 1950.

One example of an early interview to which he grudgingly agreed at his publisher's urging ran thus: "I was born in 1826 of a negro slave and an alligator—both named Gladys Rock. I have two brothers, one Dr. Walter E. Traprock and the other Eaglerock—an airplane." Or in another version he said:

Born male and single at an early age in Mississippi. Quit school after five years in seventh grade. Got job in Grandfather's bank and learned medicinal value of his liquor. Grandfather thought the janitor did it. Hard on janitor. War came. Liked British uniform. Got commission R.F.C. pilot. Crashed. Cost British Government 2000 pounds ($10,000). Was still pilot. Crashed. Cost British Government 2,000 pounds. Quit. Cost British Government $84.30. King said "Well done" (*Memphis Press Scimitar*, 10 July 1931).

An interviewer in 1954 noted that Faulkner "had the cold confidence and elemental courtesy of an aristocrat." Faulkner grew increasingly private and blamed the vulgar American system of advertising which despised privacy and courted bad taste. In effect, Faulkner in many ways was an 18th century Southern gentleman, like William Byrd, caught (if not trapped) in the 20th century.

Dr. James B. Meriwether's excellent introduction to *Lion in the Garden* detailed Faulkner's "love of privacy and hatred of publicity" (ix). Meriwether, who knew Faulkner well in his last years, concluded that he was "a man of profound courtesy" and "reserved informality." His gentlemanly reserved easiness in greeting strangers, however, did not extend to interviewers who hounded him. As Meriwether noted, he could get downright hostile and say "in a tone of deadpan, hostile irony" what he knew would outrage the invader of his privacy. In Fall 1931, for example, he recommended to a New York newspaper's audience that one of the cures for America's troubles was "a return to slavery for the Negro" (New York

Herald Tribune, 14 November 1931; *Lion in the Garden*, 19-21).

The reviewer took him seriously and asked that if this was so, then would Southern white men need "softening," to which Faulkner replied with loaded double meaning "Most white men wouldn't need very much softening." He concluded that he had "never heard or read about a lynching in the slave days" (*Lion*, 20). This must have unsettled both interviewer and reader alike, likely convinced as they were of the superiority of their time and place.

No work of scholarship is perfect, and this must be said of the nearly perfect *Lion in the Garden.* As comprehensive as the collection is, it failed to include one of Faulkner's best and most telling interviews conducted by a Southern lady reporting for the AP from the Memphis office in 1950. In 1994 I learned of this interview from Andrew Gainey of Birmingham, Alabama. His sister Marguerite McMillin did the interview, and at our request she told the story in a letter to her brother dated 4 September 1994, and passed on to me by Andrew on 10 September. Her narrative follows:

> AP in New York had asked me to try to get the interview in Oxford, which at that time had never been granted. Fortunately, I finally was able to get Mrs. Faulkner, after *two weeks,* to persuade her husband that having a personality type

interview would be good for *him* nationally be-cause so little was known about Faulkner. There had been many rumors about him, all different, but nothing Authentic.... After telephoning Mrs. Faulkner every few days, I finally received a pos-itive invitation to their home after more than two weeks of trying. And just in time! New York AP wanted the interview in time to publish it before Faulkner and daughter Jill left for Stockholm.... We drove down to Oxford only a few days before the [interview] publication date of December 10.

Mr. Faulkner was immaculately groomed, princely looking, and polite to the extreme, but he quite obviously was *not happy to be inter-viewed*! It was a *painful* experience for him, and he couldn't hide that, in spite of being completely polite. One stipulation he insisted on was that he flatly refused to say anything about his work. I got the impression that he probably would not have gone to Stockholm at all, except that Jill wanted to go and he thought it would be a good experience for her....

New York AP was good about sending [me] copies of newspapers that printed the story all over the country. But Larry and I liked the way the *Louisville Courier Journal* handled it better than any other paper, so we are sending you copies of that paper.

Andrew Gainey forwarded me a copy of his sister's 10 December 1950 *Courier Journal* interview, which follows in its entirety:

William Faulkner's Tough Writing Belies A Gentle, Retiring Nature

THE PERSONALITY PARADE

By MARGUERITE McMILLIN
Associated Press Writer

OXFORD, Miss., Dec. 9.—William Faulkner, whose tales are known for their violence and terror, is a gentle Mississippian who says: "I believe in people."

And though he won the 1949 Nobel Prize for Literature, he calls himself "a farmer who just happens to like to write. I'm not a literary man."

Though his stories deal with the Southern scene, he says he is not concerned with regional problems, but with "human" problems. "Observations on man—that's my trade," he insists. "I'm not a sociologist."

"I wrote about Mississippi because it's all I know. I've lived here all my life; and any time I've been away, I've come back as soon as possible."

He's Embarrassed

Before he left here for Stockholm to receive the award, he gave his views on literature and mankind in a rare interview at his antebellum home.

The 53-year-old author, small of stature and slight of build, moves with the soft, sure step of a veteran woodsman. His heavy shock of iron-gray hair, black mustache and searching black eyes accentuate the aristocratic features of a usually expressionless face.

He spoke in a soft, patient voice, but with obvious embarrassment most keenly evidenced when his writings were praised.

Sitting stiffly in his high-ceilinged living room, Faulkner gazed at the floor and fingered his mustache as he told how he felt about winning the highest international honor for such works as "Intruder In The Dust," "Light In August," "The Bear" and "Sanctuary."

"The honor is to the work," he said. "It doesn't matter so much who does it, what his name is, what sort of bloke he is in private life—so long as the work uplifted, strengthened or did something to other hearts."

He decided to go to Stockholm largely because his 17-year-old daughter, Jill, wanted to accompany him.

But he hated to give up his cherished p r i v a c y. His face showed pain, and his eyes flashed as he said, "My soul is not my own until this whole mess is over. But the trip will be a success if Jill enjoys it."

Did he see any grounds for optimism in present trends in the South?

"We're in a bad time. There are no longer any problems. Man is faced with one question: whether he's going to get blown up. There used to be problems of courage, honor, chastity, virtue. They don't exist any more. There are only 'angles.'

"But man is immortal. He'll work out his predicament in time, not by his own efforts. He'll outlast his trouble. I'm inclined to believe it'll come of sheer necessity. Some day, we'll run out of angles, and have to get back to virtues."

What about the published

Continued on Page 14

Continued.

279

Faulkner To Give His Nobel-Prize Money Away

Continued from Page 13

statement of Albin Krebs, young editor of the University of Mississippi campus paper, who urged admittance of Negroes to the university's graduate school?

"I think that young man started something that sooner or later his papa will have to accept." Perhaps, he added, "papas" throughout the South "will have to die" before it is accepted.

But, he hedged, "I'm not an expert. I'm mainly writing stories."

Never Satisfied

And as for his literary work: "If I could write it again, I'd do it better. I've never been completely satisfied with what I've done."

He would not comment on any of his specific writings. "If anything has to be explained, the work itself has failed. The work is there."

Faulkner expects to continue to write, as he has done in the past, interspersing his literary work with the duties of running his 300-acre farm, hunting and sailing his boat on Sardis Lake, near Oxford.

"I will probably keep on writing for many years, until I scrape the bottom of the barrel. I believe I'll know it's trash as soon as anybody else will. I don't believe I'll be fooled."

He said his new novel, "Requiem for A Nun," is almost ready for publication. He would not discuss it, saying crisply: "I don't talk shop."

Faulkner ranks the Elizabethans above all other writers for their achievement in English literature. No others have reached a height comparable to Shakespeare, Ben Jonson and Robert Herrick, he said.

"I read Shakespeare and Jonson over and over. Other writers, I read once, and that is all."

He Hurried Home

The novelist plans to give away the $30,000 prize money which comes with the Nobel award.

"The award made to 30 years of hard work, sweat and dissatisfaction of an anguished spirit shouldn't be wasted on a bloke 50 years old just so he can have a new suit and a new car," he said.

In his early years, Faulkner worked for a brief and unhappy period in New York City. He returned soon to Mississippi, and has remained here ever since.

has won other honors. He has been named a member of the American Academy of Arts and Letters, and has been given the William Dean Howells Memorial Award.

But he appears indifferent to public acclaim. He has been known to snub celebrities. He once refused to autograph a book for some admirers at the request of a relative. "I can do that for my family," he said, "but I don't want my name in the books of strangers."

'A Fine Man'

However, he sometimes drops his cloak of public silence to write a "letter to the editor" when aroused.

His friends describe him "as gentle as a woman and loved by children, dogs and horses." And Faulkner's eyes glowed as he described a friendly Dalmatian, playing about the yard, as "the matriarch" of the family's aggregation of seven dogs.

Once Faulkner paid tribute to public print to a former slave, "Mammy Callie," who died in her home on the Faulkner place. Mrs. Faulkner at her side. Funeral rites were held in the Faulkner home.

The attitude of Faulkner's neighbors in this quiet town was expressed by a service-station operator.

He commented: "He's a fine man. I've known him a long time. Used to sell him machine parts for his farm.

"When I meet him on the street, he doesn't know me. Some folks think because he won't speak, he feels he's above 'em. I figure he's just thinking about something else."

He chuckled indulgently, and said:

"Saw him uptown awhile back. He had patches on both elbows. Looked like he'd gone for an awful long time without a shave. He doesn't talk much. Just listens. . . . He's a fine man."

William Faulkner
'I believe in people'

"New York is all right. I go there like a Negro goes to Memphis' Beale Street on Saturday night. I'm fortunate. I'd rather be here, where I can hunt and fish. I don't have any literary fame to nurse. I don't have to write another book next year."

Although Faulkner used to fly his own airplane—he was a flier with the Royal Air Force in World War I—modern communications hold little interest for him. "I have no radio," he said. "When I want to travel, I go to my library."

Linked With History

Once he wrote his home town Oxford Eagle a scathing indictment of "modern progress" when a red-brick chain store in town replaced a 100-year-old church.

Faulkner lives in quiet life in his white, columned home, centered at the end of a winding, double row of ancient cedars. With him are his wife, daughter Jill, a stepson and a stepgranddaughter.

His family is linked closely with Mississippi history and public life. His father was business manager of the University of Mississippi. A great-grandfather was a railroad builder, Civil War leader and author of "White Rose of Memphis."

It was the great-grandfather, Col. William Cuthbert Falkner, for whom the novelist is named. The name was spelled that way before the "U" was added through a printing error in the prize-winner's first book.

A brother of William, John Faulkner, has written several books: "Men Working, A Story of The W.P.A.," "Dollar Cotton" and his latest, "Chooky." He also lives here.

"Billy," as his wife calls him,

The remarkable seven sentences in answer to Mrs. McMillin's question about optimism were to appear several days later in his Nobel address. So too were his comments about the award going to his work and not the man. His declaration that a work succeeded if it lifted or strengthened the heart would become a primary theme of the address. As he answered Mrs. McMillin, he was in effect letting her hear his speech in Oxford before the world received it. It is clear that the speech was already written or at least formed in Faulkner's mind at the time of the interview. In the absence of this interview, Faulkner scholarship has not credited this fact heretofore.

Mr. Gainey was himself a notable Mississippi gentleman, born in Meridian in 1918. He has had a versatile career as a leading baritone in the New York Opera Company. He is remembered for his role in *The Barber of Seville* and performed on Broadway as Petruchio in *Kiss Me Kate* and other musicals. He is most widely recalled for television appearances with the NBC Opera, CBS Ominibus, Kraft Theatre, and Studio One. It is through Mr. Gainey's kindness and love of Faulkner that the story of his sister's interview is here preserved. At age 82, he died in Birmingham, Alabama in 2000.

Dr. Meriwether, fortunately for this volume's treatment of Faulkner the farmer, did collect a 1955 interview in which Faulkner also said, "I'm a countryman. My life is farmland and horses and the raising of grain and feed…. I look after my farm and my horses and then when there is time, I write." He concluded, "but just to be a writer is not my life; my life is a farmer, so in that sense, I'm not a writer because that doesn't come first" (*Lion*, 169).

In another interview that same year, this time in Japan, Faulkner commented again, "I am a farmer. I like horses—I breed and train horses. That is what I like to do more than writing." With his usual humor, Faulkner observed of the expense, "The writer that owns horses must be a pretty successful writer" (*Lion*, 192).

A month before his death, Faulkner granted his last interview in May 1962 with Vita Markovic of the University of Belgrade. Here he declared he did not like "the hustle and bustle of town." To the question of whether he often went to town "to theatres and cinemas," he replied, "No. If I could ride into a theatre on horseback, I would go. I like riding. I don't like buses and cars. Imagine if I rode straight into a theatre and asked the attendant, 'Will you park my horse please'" (*Lion*, 283). He commented that with the flight to towns "how neglected the fields are" and that "in my time all the land was tilled. Now everybody rushes into towns and the land is decaying" (283).

Of his publishers, he commented, "I don't pay no attention to publishers. They write me a letter—If it don't have a royalty check in it, I throw it away." He repeated, "I'm a farmer... I like silence, silence and horses. And trees. You see what that big freeze last winter did to the trees in Mississippi? Seems like it happens ever' year. I got these cedar trees growin' along the front walk to my house. That freeze broke a heap o' branches off them cedars" (*Lion*, 64).

It is clear Faulkner was super-conscious of and engaged in the natural world and was always focused on the smallest things. Eschewing obsession with abstracts, he imagined from the local outward to the universal, as do all good Southerners born, bred, and true who have a proper fixed commitment to the well-loved place.

Mrs. McMillin's remarkable interview and related similar ones summarize much that has been said of Faulkner's Southernness in the preceding chapters and underscores their validity. The "princely," consummately polite Faulkner she encountered in December 1950 proved that the traditional gentlemanly South was alive and well and on the verge of worldwide recognition in just a few days.

APPENDIX

ADDENDA TO LIST OF BOOKS IN FAULKNER'S

LIBRARY

The following list is compiled from notes taken on a visit to Rowan Oak 9 May 1970, seven years and ten months after Faulkner's death. I was particularly interested in what books were in the home. Mr. Beverley Smith, docent and guide there, gave me much valuable information, which I recorded on the spot. He said that the books in Faulkner's library and his study had undergone "some shuffling" in the past seven years, and "many listed in Joseph Blotner's *William Faulkner's Library. A Catalogue* (1964) "are no longer present in the house." He said, "Jill and Estelle have likely had a hand in this. Many may have found their way to Charlottesville, Virginia." Smith said that Blotner and Tommy Tullos of Memphis State University "took a weekend to compile the books" and "did not see all the books if they were in closets or upstairs. For example, signed books in a nook in the room between the Library and Study were overlooked." In 1970, three of these signed by Faulkner had not been recorded in Blotner's *Catalogue*. The three were:

> Buck, Pearl. *Sons.* Signed by Faulkner, Rowan Oak, 1932.
>
> Dalton, Henry. *Hill Born.* Signed by Faulkner.
>
> Lardner, Ring. *Round Up.* Signed by Faulkner.

Beverley Smith related that the following fourteen books were brought to Rowan Oak after Faulkner's death and may not be his. They occupied two bottom shelves in the first bookcase by the entrance to the library. The titles with an asterisk are not in Blotner's *Catalogue.* The others are listed there:

> Anderson, Sherwood. *Letters of Sherwood Anderson* (1953).
>
> Angle, Paul M., ed. *The Lincoln Reader* (1947). Signed Malcolm Franklin, Oxford, 27 April 1947.
>
> *Dickens, *Oliver Twist.*
>
> *Duvall, Mary Virginia. *Student's History of Mississippi* (1866).
>
> Freeman, Douglass Southall. *R. E. Lee: A Biography* (1944). Four volumes. Signed by Faulkner in all volumes, Rowan Oak, December 1944.
>
> Gogh, Vincent Van. *Lettres de Vincent Van Gogh a Son Frère Theo* (1953).
>
> *Miller, John C. *Origins of the American Revolution* (1945).
>
> Potter, Jack. *A Bibliography of John Don Passos* (1950).
>
> Nabokov, Vladimir. *Laughter in the Dark* (1938).
>
> Schulberg, Budd. *The Disenchanted* (1950).
>
> Stuart, Jesse. *Taps for Private Tussie* (1943).
>
> Toynbee, Arnold. *A Study of History* (1946).
>
> Warren, Robert Penn. *All the King's Men* (1946).
>
> Wheaton, Elizabeth. *Mr. George's Joint* (1941).

The following books were in Faulkner's library room on 9 May 1970 and were not cataloged in Blotner. No doubt many of these were brought there by Mrs. Faulkner between 1962 and 1970.

Smith recalled that upon noticing blank spaces on the bookshelves she often "brought in some books to fill them."

> Benet and Pearson, *Oxford Anthology of American Literature.*
>
> *The Best of the World's Classics.* 10 volumes. Greece, Rome, Great Britain, Ireland,
>
> Europe, and America (1909), ed. Henry Cabot Lodge..
>
> Blanton, Smiley. *Love or Perish.*
>
> Blythe, Samuel. *The Fakers.*
>
> Bristol, Claude M. *The Magic of Believing.*
>
> Caldwell, Taylor. *This Side of Innocence.*
>
> Clark, Walter V. *The Track of the Cat.*
>
> Connor, Ralph. *The Major.*
>
> Dos Passos, John. *42nd Parallel, 1919, and The Big Money.* Modern Library Giant. [My note in 1970 said the volume "Shows much wear."]
>
> Douglas, Ellen. *A Family's Affair.*
>
> Douglas, Lloyd. *The Robe.*
>
> Du Noüy. *Human Destiny.*
>
> Dutton, B. *Navigation and Nautical Astronomy.*
>
> *Encycopedia Britannica.* New Werner Edition, 24 volumes.
>
> Gavin, Marian. *Jailer, My Jailer.*
>
> Gibbs, George Fort. *The Flaming Sword.*
>
> Hemans, Felicia. *Poems.*
>
> *The Historian's History of the World.* 25 volumes.

Ingraham, Rev. J. J. *The Prince of the House of David* (1948).

Joyce, James. *Finnegan's Wake* (New York: Viking Press). My note says that the book was in a tall blue binding. Probably 1945.

Lewis, ed. *Winston Simplified Dictionary.*

Lyman and Hill. *Literature and Living.*

McAlpine, Frank. *Our Album of Authors. A Cyclopedia of Popular Literary People* (1885).

Mitchell, Margaret. *Gone with the Wind.*

Moore, Thomas. *Lallah Rookh.*

Nye, Bill. *Bill Nye's Comic History of the U. S.*

Oldham, Lemuel E. *Hughes on Evidence.*

Our Album of Authors.

Phillips, S. B. *The Gospels. Translated into Modern English.*

Republican National Convention, 1944.

Ridpath Library of Universal Literature.

Riemann, Dr. Hugo. *Dictionary of Music.*

Sabatini, Rafael. *Saint Martins Summer.*

Scott, Sir Walter. *Saint Roman's Well, Black Dwarf, Legend of Montrose, and Bride of Lammermoor.*

Stendahl. *The Charterhouse of Parma.*

Strong, Grace. *The Worst Foe: A Temperance Story.*

Travels in the Chinese Empire. Volume I.

Webster's Collegiate Dictionary. 4th edition. 1931.

In 1970, there were five books kept in a group in the Library (one dating from 1968). This block of religious works was possibly one of the groups of books Smith described as being added by Mrs. Faulkner in filling "blind spots" on the shelves:

> Peale, Norman Vincent. *Amazing Results of Positive Thinking.*
>
> _____. *Stay Alive.*
>
> Sherman, Harold. *The Power of Prayer.*
>
> Wilkinson. Winifred. *Focus on Living.* (1967).
>
> *Unity* (paper pamphlet, 1968).

In May 1970, four volumes not in Blotner were in Faulkner's study (room with his single bed, typewriter, and *A Fable* outline.):

> *Brandeis University General Catalogue 1961-1962.*
>
> *Cassell's French Dictionary.*
>
> Joseph Head and S. L. Cranston, *Reincarnation.* (1961).

In the drawer of Faulkner's writing table below his typewriter was a pocket New Testament.

In May 1970, Smith told me that the desk was left untouched, and as it was at Faulkner's death in July 1962. Smith also said there were "several New Testaments scattered through the house." These have not been mentioned in the Faulkner biographies. See Kibler, "As the Twig Is Bent."

NOTES

INTRODUCTION: RACCOON AND COLLARDS

[1]Professor James B. Meriwether frequently said that after *The Hamlet* and *Go Down, Moses,* Faulkner never opened his new works. Those his publisher sent him still had their wrappers when Meriwether did his Princeton University Library exhibit *The Literary Career of William Faulkner* in 1957. Faulkner felt it a waste of energy to do battle with insensitive editors or proofreaders. Instead, Meriwether said Faulkner meticulously kept and arranged his manuscripts and typescripts and deposited them at the Alderman Library of the University of Virginia. He would leave to scholars the task of de-editing and establishing good texts. To Meriwether, I think rightly, this was another indication of Faulkner's professionalism and the careful craftsmanship he shared with Cash Bundren in *As I Lay Dying* who says he builds "on the bevel" so that his work will last.

[2] Professor Meriwether published a significant essay, "What Happens When You Eat Magnolias" in a difficult to find paperback, *Faces of South Carolina*, ed. Franklin Ashley (Columbia: South Carolina Committee for the Humanities, 1974), 24-35. Here Meriwether used Columbia and her past as the basis for a discussion of the various destructive effects of a refusal to face facts. He concluded, "We are not likely to change our ways in the future if we cannot face what we did in the past" [as in admitting that Sherman's men burned Columbia]. What he called "the ostrich approach—it can't happen here—involves another kind of

blindness—it didn't happen here"—and will again if we "assume that only other people engage in mindless destruction" (35). In June 1974, I recollect telling Dr. Meriwether that I thought this was one of his best essays, at which he looked surprised, and signed my copy "For Jim Kibler, fellow scholar, fellow South Carolinian." In light of today's cancel culture, his comments are all the more appropriate.

[3]John B. Cullen, *Old Times in the Faulkner Country* (Chapel Hill, Univ of North Carolina Press, 1961), 19.

[4]Louis D. Rubin, Jr., "Changing, Enduring, Forever Still the South," in *The Prevailing South*, ed. Dudley Clendinen (Atlanta, Georgia: Longstreet, 1988).

CHAPTER ONE: OUTSIDE THE PALE

[1]Fred Chappell, "Not as a Leaf: Tradition and Innovation in Southern Poetry," an address delivered in Athens, Georgia, 14 May 1997, quoted from a transcription by James E. Kibler, Jr.

[2]James B. Meriwether, unpublished lecture, Southern League Institute, Lexington, South Carolina, 5 July 1996, quoted from a transcription by James E. Kibler, Jr.

[3]John Crowe Ransom, Introduction, *I'll Take My Stand* (New York, Harper, 1930), 21.

[4]In his 1834 essay "The Philosophy of the Omnibus," *American Monthly* (May 1834), 158-9, William Gilmore Simms wrote that Northern "levelism" yields a regimentation that endangers the individual. This important essay is one of the most penetrating critiques of the era and an excellent source for the differing

cultures North and South. Reprinted in *Simms Review*, 6 (1998), 13-23.

[5]William Faulkner, address to the English Club of the Univ of Virginia, 24 April 1958, in *Essays, Speeches & Public Letters,* ed. James B. Meriwether (New York: Modern Library, 2004), 162. I have used the text of the 2004 edition of *Essays* throughout. This is Meriwether's corrected and expanded republication of the original 1966 edition.

[6]Faulkner, letter to the president of the League of American Writers, Winter 1938, *Essays*, 198.

[7]Meriwether, unpublished lecture, 5 July 1996, transcribed by James E. Kibler, Jr..

[8]Donald Davidson, "On a Replica of the Parthenon," *Poems 1922-1961* (Minneapolis: Univ of Minnesota Press, 1966), 64.

[9]M. E. Bradford, "Donald Davidson and the Great-House Tradition, a Reading of 'Woodlands, 1956-1960" in Mark Winchell, ed. *The Vanderbilt Tradition* (Baton Rouge: L.S.U. Press, 1991), 87.

[10]Eugene Genovese, *The Southern Tradition: The Achievements and Limitations of an American Conservatism* (Cambridge: Harvard Univ Press, 1994; Paperback Edition 1996), 14.

[11]Faulkner's response to the title was passed down to me in conversation with James B. Meriwether in October 1967. Meriwether also included the information in lectures on the novel in his Faulkner graduate seminars at the Univ of South Carolina, 1967-1969.

[12]Jay Parini, *One Matchless Time*, 156. Parini also notes that Faulkner was reading *The Golden Bough* when he was restoring the house. The legend of the Rowan Tree may be found there.

[13]Faulkner referred to Curran in his address to the Delta Council, 15 May 1952, in *Essays*, 132. Simms refers to Curran, Irish Nationalist, in his 1828 poem, "Song of the Irish Patriot," published in *Selected Poems of William Gilmore Simms,* ed. James E. Kibler (Columbia: Univ of South Carolina Press, 2010), 311. He reviewed *The Life of Curran* in Charleston *Mercury* (20 November 1855). For Margaret Mitchell, see James P. Cantrell, *How Celtic Culture Invented Southern Literature* (Gretna, LA: Pelican, 2006), 193-208. For a discussion of Simms's Celtic traits, see Cantrell, pp. 83-98, and James E. Kibler, "Simms's Celtic Harp," *Studies in the Literary Imagination*, 42 (Spring 2009), 163-80.

[14]Edgar Allan Poe, *Broadway Journal* (22 November 1845), 309.

[15]For a treatment of Simms and Poe's opposition to the Boston Frogpondians, see James E. Kibler, Jr., "Simms Defends Poe and Poe Replies," *Simms Review*, 15 (Winter 2007), 27-33. In his 22 November 1845 *Broadway Journal* article cited above, Poe wrote that Simms was a "tried" and "true" friend of writers from the South. He concluded that America has a "sectional" New England literature because their writers have appropriated it exclusively to themselves. See also, Arlen Turner, "Poe and Simms," *Papers on Poe* (Springfield, Ohio: Chantry Press, 1972), 140-60.

[16]Florence King, "South Mouth: Why Liberals Hate Dixie," 21 April 1997, *Deja Reviews: Florence King All Over Again,* 171-2.

CHAPTER TWO: FAULKNER THE FARMER

[1]Faulkner, "To the Youth of Japan," 1955, in *Essays*, 82-85.

[2]Meriwether, conversation with Kibler and unpublished lecture, 5 July 1996.

[3]Meriwether, conversation with Kibler, 1968.

[4]Wendell Berry, *Imagination in Place* (Berkeley: Counterpoint Press, 2010), 10.

[5]Margaret Mitchell, *Gone with the Wind* (New York: Macmillan, 1936) 36, 435.

[6]William Faulkner, "There Was a Queen," in *Collected Stories* (New York: Random House, 1953), 729, 734.

[7]Ben Robertson, *Red Hills and Cotton* (New York: Knopf, 1942), 85.

[8]Chappell, address, 14 May 1997.

CHAPTER THREE: ABSTRACTION AS NEMESIS

[1]Louis D. Rubin, Jr., "The South's Writers," *Southern World* (May-June 1979), 26-7.

[2]Julia Peterkin, *Plantation Christmas* (Boston: Houghton Mifflin, 1934), 4. This title was first published in *Country Gentleman* in December 1929.

[3]Chappell, address, 14 May 1997. Also compare Yeats as quoted by George Moore: "There are no ideas in ancient literature, only things." Samuel Chew, ed., *Fruit Among the Leaves* (New York: Appleton, 1950), 202.

[4]William Gilmore Simms, "The Lions of Mycenae," *Selected Poems of William Gilmore Simms* (Columbia: Univ of South Carolina Press, 2010), 297-300.

[5]O. B. Mayer, "Little Dassie," in *Fireside Tales*, ed. James E. Kibler (Athens, GA: Dutch Fork Press, 1984), 150.

CHAPTER FOUR: THE BEST OF ALL TELLING: FAULKNER THE RACONTEUR

[1]Meriwether interview with Kibler, January 1972.

[2]George Moore reported Yeats' words in his *Hail and Farewell* (serialized 1911-14) and published in two volumes (New York: Appleton, 1925). Quoted here from *Fruit Among the Leaves* (New York: Appleton, 1950), 202.

[3]William Butler Yeats, *Essays and Introductions* (London; Macmillan, 1961), 524.

CHAPTER FIVE: BLOOD TIES: THE CENTRALITY OF FAMILY & COMMUNITY & THE IMPORTANCE OF PLACE

[1] James B. Meriwether, interview with Kibler, August 1995. In fact, Meriwether and Ann Simms Pincus organized the successful Simms-Faulkner Conference in New Orleans around this theme.

[2]Thomas Fleming, "Home for Political Animals," *Chronicles* (July 2011), 12. Gildersleeve, "The Creed of the Old South," in Briggs, ed. *Selected Essays of Basil Gildersleeve*

[3]For Simms's Celtic *duchas*, see Kibler, "Simms's Celtic Harp," 163-80.

[4]Meriwether, interview with Kibler, September 1967.

⁵Thomas L. McHaney, *"The Wild Palms,"* Ph. D. dissertation, Univ of South Carolina, 1969.

⁶William Gilmore Simms, "The Ages of Gold and Iron," was delivered as an oration on 2 November 1840 and was first published in *The Ladies Companion* (May 1841), 12-4; reprinted in *Simms Review*, 10 (Summer 2002), 1-11.

⁷Professor Clyde Wilson has often persuasively made this claim in conversation and his lectures.

⁸Henry Timrod, "Sonnet," *Collected Poems of Henry Timrod* (Athens, GA: Univ of GA Press, 1965), 18.

CHAPTER SIX: HUMOR

¹Faulkner in *Writers at Work: The "Paris Review" Interviews,* reprinted in *The Lovingood Papers* (Knoxville: Univ of Tennessee Press, 1963), 7, as "In Memoriam. Sut's Friend William Faulkner."

²"Letter from 'Mark Twain,'" No. 21, 23 May 1867, in San Francisco *Daily Alta California*, 14 July 1867. Here, he writes: "The book abounds in humor.... It will sell well in the West, but the Eastern people will call it coarse and possibly taboo it." As evidence of his continued regard for Sut, he collected "Sicily Burns's Wedding" in *Mark Twain's Library of Humor* (1888). For a ground-breaking article on Mark Twain's debt to Sut, see Hennig Cohen, "Mark Twain's Sut Lovingood," *The Lovingood Papers* (1962), 19-24. Cohen writes, "The fundamental bond between Harris and Twain was their sense of man's predisposition to dehumanize himself" (21). For specific borrowings in *Huckleberry Finn* and *Tom Sawyer,* see 21-3

Other critics who have explored *Huckleberry Finn*'s indebtedness to Sut are Jeannette Tandy, Bernard DeVoto, and Walter Blair.

[3]For a detailed treatment of Simms's defense of frontier humor, see his *Selected Reviews*, 28-33.

[4]Flannery O'Connor, *Collected Works,* 860.

[5] George Washington Harris, "Sut Lovingood, on the Puritan Yankee" (1866), in Harris, *High Times and Hard Times*, ed M. Thomas Inge (Nashville: Vanderbilt Univ Press, 1967), 284-7.

CHAPTER SEVEN: THE CREED OF MEMORY & ENDURANCE

[1] George Garrett's *New York Times* obituary, 30 May 2008.

[2]Donald Davidson, "The Center That Holds," *Southern Partisan*, 4 (Fall 1984), 18.

[3]Lee Anne Fennell, "Unquiet Ghosts: Memory and Determinism in Faulkner," *Southern Literary Journal*, 31 (Spring 1999), 35-49. Quotations are on p. 35.

[4]See for example, Simms's "Flowers and Trees," (1844) in *Selected Poems of William Gilmore Simms,* 128-9. The poem's last lines treating an ancient live oak are: "Decay is at his roots, —the storm has been/ Among his limbs, —but the old top is green."

[5]Simms, *Sack and Destruction of the City of Columbia* (Columbia, SC: Daily Phoenix Press, 1865). The text used here is of the earlier newspaper version edited by David Aiken as *A City Laid Waste* (Columbia: Univ of South Carolina Press, 2005), 85.

CHAPTER EIGHT: PRESERVATIONIST

[1]Interview of Dr. David Aiken by Kibler, 19 July 2010.

[2]Simms, "The Philosophy of the Omnibus,"

[3]Simms, "Veneration," *Southern Passages and Pictures* (New York: Adlard, 1839), 58-9.

[4]Anne Pamela Cunningham of Rosemont Plantation. Quoted in *South Carolina Encyclopedia,* ed. Walter Edgar (Columbia: Univ of South Carolina Press, 2006), 238.

[5]Davidson's poem "Woodlands" clearly outlines this significance.

[6]The phrase is from Mary Boykin Chesnut, *A Diary from Dixie*

[7]Yeats, *Collected Poems* (New York: 1955), 236, as quoted in Brooks, 343-344.

[8]James E. Kibler, "As the Twig Is Bent," *Southern Partisan,* 24 (July-August 2004), 24.

CHAPTER NINE: FINITUDE & THE MACHINE CULTURE

[1]Thomas Bangs Thorpe, "The Big Bear of Arkansas," *The Hive of "The Bee-Hunter,"* (New York: Appleton, 1854), 92-3.

[2]C. Vann Woodward, *The Burden of Southern History* (Baton Rouge: L. S. U. Press, 1960), 21.

[3]William Gilmore Simms, *The Social Principle* (Tuscaloosa, Alabama: Erosophic Society, 1843), 53. The address was delivered in 1842. See also Simms, *Poetry and the Practical,* 24: "Exhibit the longest stretch of railways and electric wires—show the most splendid cities—still, you have done little, in all this, to meet the wants of the true life of man."

CHAPTER TEN: RACE

[1]Zora Neale Hurston, *Dust Tracks on a Road* (1942).

CHAPTER ELEVEN: THE CONSERVATIVE

[1]*Sports Illustrated* (24 June 1955), 15.

[2]One notable exception was Southern critic M. E. Bradford. In his classes Professor Meriwether also always treated both Stevens and Ike McCaslin as ineffective failures. The preponderance of negatives in the diction of their language points to their essential negativity and denial of life.

CHAPTER TWELVE: WHAT FAULKNER THOUGHT

An early version of parts of this chapter appeared as "As the Twig Is Bent" in *Southern Partisan*, 24 (July-August 2004) and "What Faulkner Thought"—an address before the Euphradian Society at the University of South Carolina, in Columbia, SC, 6 December 2013.

[1]Clyde Wilson, Review of *Essays, Speeches & Public Letters*, in *Chronicles,* 2004.

[2]Meriwether, in conversation with Kibler and lectures.

[3]Wendell Berry, in conversation with Kibler, September 2000. Jill Faulkner Summers also returned two Faulkner family Bibles to Rowan Oak in 2005 (*Southern Register*, Spring/Summer 2005, 5).

WORKS CITED AND CONSULTED

Agar, Herbert and Allen Tate, eds. *Who Owns America? A New Declaration of Independence* (Boston: Houghton Mifflin, 1936). A new edition was published in 1999 by ISI Books, but page numbers cited in the text are from the original edition.

Babcock, Havilah. *My Health Is Better in November* (Columbia, SC: Univ of South Carolina Press, 1948).

_____. *The Best of Babcock,* ed. Hugh Grey (New York: Holt Rhinehart, 1974).

Bellows, Barbara. *A Talent for Living. Josephine Pinckney and the Charleston Literary Tradition* (Baton Rouge: L.S.U. Press, 2006).

Berry, Wendell. *The Memory of Old Jack* (New York: Harcourt Brace, 1974).

_____. *The Unsettling of America: Culture and Agriculture* (San Francisco: Sierra Club Books, 1977).

_____. *Standing by Words* (San Francisco: North Point, 1983).

_____. *Remembering* (San Francisco: North Point, 1988).

_____. *What Are People For?* (San Francisco: North Point, 1990).

_____. Conversation with James E. Kibler, September 2000.

_____. *Life Is a Miracle* (Washington, D. C.: Counterpoint, 2000).

_____. *The Art of the Common Place* (Washington, D.

C.: Counterpoint, 2002).

_____. *Imagination in Place* (Berkeley: Counterpoint, 2010).

_____. *This Day. Sabbath Poems, Collected and New, 1979-2013* (Berkeley: Counterpoint 2013).

_____. *The Need to Be Whole* (Berkeley: Shoemaker, 2022).

Blotner, Joseph. *William Faulkner's Library: A Catalogue* (Charlottesville, VA: Univ. Press of Virginia, 1964).

_____. *Faulkner: A Biography*, 2 vols (New York: Random House, 1974.)

Bradford, M. E. "Donald Davidson and the Great-House Tradition, a Reading of 'Woodlands, 1956-1960,'"

in Mark Winchell, ed. *The Vanderbilt Tradition* (Baton Rouge: L.S.U. Press, 1991), 87.

_____. *Generations of the Faithful Heart* (LaSalle, IL: Sherwood Sugden, 1983).

Brooks, Cleanth. *William Faulkner: The Yoknapatawpha Country* (New Haven: Yale Univ. Press, 1962).

_____. *William Faulkner: Toward Yoknapatawpha and Beyond* (New Haven: Yale Univ Press, 1978).

_____. Interview, 1978, with William Ferris, *Southern Reader,* Vol. 1, Number 1 (Summer 1989), 139-166.

Brown, Larry. *Joe* (Chapel Hill, NC: Algonquin Press, 1991). The setting of the novel is in Oxford, Lafayette County, and the surrounding countryside.

Carlton, Clark. "Our Altars and Our Fireside. Religion in the South-
    ern Way of Life," Lecture at the 13th Annual Abbeville
    Summer School. "The Southern Tradition" (13 July 2015).

Cantrell, James P. *How Celtic Culture Invented Southern Literature*
    (Gretna, LA: Pelican, 2006).

Chappell, Fred. "Not as a Leaf: Tradition and Innovation in South-
    ern Poetry," an address delivered in
    Athens, Georgia, 14 May 1997, quoted from a transcription
    by James E. Kibler.

Chesterton, G. K. *The Collected Works of G. K. Chesterton* (San
    Francisco: Ignatius, 1990).

Chinard, Gilbert. *Thomas Jefferson* (Boston: Little, 1929).

Clemens, Samuel Langhorne. "Letter from Mark Twain, No. 21, 23
May 1867," San Francisco *Daily Alta*
    California, 14 July 1867.

_____. *Life on the Mississippi* (Boston: Osgood, 1883).
_____. *A Connecticut Yankee in King Arthur's Court*
    (New York: Charles L. Webster, 1889).

Cohen, Hennig. "Mark Twain's Sut Lovingood," *The Lovingood*
    Papers (1962), 19-24.

Cullen, John B. *Old Times in the Faulkner Country* (Chapel Hill
    NC: Univ of North Carolina Press,
    1961).

Davidson, Donald. "A Mirror for Artists," in *I'll Take My Stand*
    (1930).

_____. "On a Replica of the Parthenon," in *Poems*

1922-1961 (Minneapolis: Univ of Minnesota Press, 1966), 64.

_____. *Southern Writers in the Modern World* (Athens, GA: Univ of Georgia Press, 1958).

_____. "The Center That Holds," *Southern Partisan*, 4 (Fall 1984), 18.

_____. "Woodlands, 1956-1960" in *Poems 1922-1961* (Minneapolis, MN: Univ of Minnesota Press, 1966), 19-22.

Doyle, Don H. *Faulkner's County. The Historical Roots of Yoknapatawpha* (Chapel Hill, NC: Univ of North Carolina Press, 2001).

Falkner, Murrry C. *The Falkners of Mississippi. A Memoir* (Baton Rouge: L.S.U. Press, 1967).

Faulkner, John. *My Brother Bill. An Affectionate Reminiscence* (New York: Trident, 1963).

Faulkner, William. *The Marble Faun* (Boston: Four Seas, 1924).

_____. Introduction in William Spratling, *Sherwood Anderson & Other Famous Creoles* (1926). Also in *Essays, Speeches & Public Letters*.

_____. *Father Abraham* [1926], ed. James B. Meriwether. (New York: Random House, 1983).

_____. *Flags in the Dust*, ed. Douglas Day (New York: Random House, 1973).

_____. *Sartoris* (New York: Harcourt, Brace, 1929).

_____. *The Sound and the Fury* (New York: Jonathan Cape, 1929).

_____. *As I Lay Dying,* (New York: Cape and Smith,

1930).

_____. *Sanctuary* New York: Cape and Smith, 1931).

_____. *Light in August* (New York: Harrison Smith, 1932).

_____. *A Green Bough* (New York: Harrison Smith, 1933).

_____. *Absalom, Absalom!* (New York: Random House, 1936).

_____. *The Unvanquished* (New York: Random House, 1938).

_____. *The Wild Palms* (New York: Random House, 1939).

_____. *The Hamlet* (New York: Random House, 1940).

_____. *Go Down, Moses* (New York: Random House, 1942).

_____. *Intruder in the Dust* (New York: Random House, 1948).

_____. *Collected Stories* (New York: Random House, 1953).

_____. *A Fable* (New York: Random House, 1954).

_____. *The Town* (New York: Random House, 1957).

_____. The *Mansion* (New York: Random House, 1959).

_____. The *Reivers* (New York: Random House, 1962).

_____. The *Faulkner-Cowley File. Letters & Memories, 1944-1962* (New York: Viking, 1966).

_____. *Essays, Speeches & Public Letters*, ed. James B. Meriwether (New York: Random House, 1966). Revised, corrected, and enlarged edition, Modern Library Paperback, 2004).

_____. *Lion in the Garden: Interviews with William Faulkner, 1926-1962*, eds. James B. Meriwether and Michael Milligate (New York: Random House, 1968).

_____. *Selected Letters of William Faulkner* (New York: Random House, 1977).

_____. "There Was a Queen," and "Barn Burning" in *Collected Stories* (New York: Random House, 1953).

_____. Faulkner in *Writers at Work: The "Paris Review" Interviews,* reprinted in *The Lovingood Papers* (Knoxville, TN: Univ of Tennessee Press, 1963), 7.

Foote, Shelby. "The Literature of Fury," *Carolina Magazine,* 46 (November 1936), 29-30.

_____. Kibler-Foote Correspondence, Kibler Literary Collection, South Caroliniana Library, Univ of South Carolina.

Fennell, Lee Anne. "Unquiet Ghosts: Memory and Determinism in Faulkner," *Southern Literary Journal*, 31 (Spring 1999), 35-49.

Fleming, Thomas. "Home for Political Animals," *Chronicles* (July 2011).

Fowler, Doreen and Ann Abadie. *Faulkner and Humor* (Jackson, MS: Univ Press of Mississippi, 1984).

_____. "Beyond Oedipus: Lucas Beauchamp, Ned Barnett, and *Intruder in the Dust*," *Modern Fiction Studies*, 53 (Winter 2007, 788-818).

Gallagher, Tim. *The Grail Bird* (Boston: Houghton Mifflin, 2005).

Garrett, George. *New York Times* obituary (30 May 2008), singled out what reviewers of Garrett's works all agreed upon: his "rapt attention to the sound of the voice."

Genovese, Eugene. *The Southern Tradition: The Achievements and Limitations of an American Conservatism* (Cambridge: Harvard Univ Press, 1994; Paperback Edition 1996).

Gildersleeve, Basil. "The Creed of the Old South," in Ward W. Briggs, Jr., ed. *Soldier and Scholar. Basil Lanneau Gildersleeve and the Civil War* (Charlottesville: Univ of VA Press, 1998), 361-385.

Gill, Richard. *Happy Rural Seat: The English Country House and the Literary Imagination* (New Haven: Yale Univ Press, 1972), 7, 227.

Ginés, Montserrat. *The Southern Inheritors of Don Quixote* (Baton Rouge: L.S.U. Press, 2000).

Girouard, Mark. *A Country House Companion* (New Haven: Yale Univ Press, 1987).

Gray, Richard. *The Literature of Memory: Modern Writers of the American South* (Baltimore: Johns Hopkins Univ Press, 1977), 231.

_____. *The Life of William Faulkner* (Oxford, UK: Blackwell, 1994).

Hamblin, Robert, "Lucas Beauchamp, Ned Barnett, and Faulkner's Will," *Studies in Bibliography*, 1979. 281-3.

305

Harris, George Washington. "Sut Lovingood, on the Puritan Yankee" (1866), in Harris, *High Times and Hard Times*, ed M. Thomas Inge (Nashville: Vanderbilt Univ Press, 1967), 284-7.

Harris, Joel Chandler. *Uncle Remus. His Songs and His Sayings* (New York: Appleton, 1880); New Expanded Edition, (New York: Appleton, 1896); and (New York: Viking, 1982).

Haynes, Jane Isbell. *William Faulkner's Lafayette County Heritage.* (Ripley, MS: Seajay Society, 1992).

Hemingway, Ernest. *A Farewell to Arms* (New York: Scribner, 1929).

Henry, Robert Self. *'First With the Most' Forrest* (Indianapolis: Bobbs-Merrill, 1944), 297, quoting from *Official Records of the Rebellion,* Serial No. 77, p. 171.

Humanist Manifestos I and II (New York: Prometheus Books, 1973).

Humphries, Jefferson, and John Lowe, editors. *The Future of Southern Letters* (New York: Oxford Univ Press, 1996).

Hurston, Zora Neale. *Dust Tracks on a Road* (Philadelphia: Lippincott, 1942).

_____. *Moses, Man of the Mountain* (Philadelphia: Lippincott, 1939)

Justus, James H. *Fetching the Old Southwest: Humorous Writing from Longstreet to Twain* (Columbia, MO: Univ of Missouri Press, 2004).

Karl, Frederick. *William Faulkner: American Writer* (New York: Weidenfeld, 1989).

Kasson, John F. *Civilizing the Machine. Technology and Republican Values in America, 1776-1900* (New York: Penguin, 1976).

Kazin, Alfred. *New York Herald Tribune* (20 February 1938), IX, 5.

Kibler, James E., Jr. "Simms's Prophetic Muse," *Mississippi Quarterly*, 49, 1 (1995-1996), 109-113.

_____. "As the Twig Is Bent," *Southern Partisan*, 24 (July-August 2004), 24-27.

_____. "Simms's Celtic Harp," *Studies in the Literary Imagination*, 42 (Spring 2009), 163-80.

_____. "Simms Defends Poe and Poe Replies," *Simms Review*, 15 (Winter 2007), 27-33.

King, Florence. "South Mouth: Why Liberals Hate Dixie," 21 April 1997, *Deja Reviews: Florence King All Over Again,* 171-2.

King, Grace. *Balcony Stories* (New York: Century, 1893).

_____. *Memories of a Southern Woman of Letters* (New York: Macmillan, 1932).

_____. *Grace King of New Orleans: A Selection of Her Writings*, edited by Robert Bush (Baton Rouge: L.S.U. Press, 1973).

Lee, Harper. *To Kill a Mockingbird* (New York: Harper Collins, 1960).

_____. *Go Set a Watchman* (New York: Harper Collins, 2015).

Legaré, Hugh Swinton. "On Classical Training" (*Southern Review*, 1 February 1828, 1-49).

Lytle, Andrew. *From Eden to Babylon. The Social and Political Essays* (Washington: Regnery Gateway, 1990).

Mayer, O. B. "Little Dassie," in *Fireside Tales*, ed. James E. Kibler (Athens, GA: Dutch Fork Press, 1984), 150.

McCarthy, Cormac. *The Road* (New York: Knopf, 2006).

McHaney, Thomas L. *"The Wild Palms,"* Ph. D. dissertation, Univ of South Carolina, 1969.

Marx, Leo. *The Machine in the Garden. Technology and the Pastoral Ideal in America* (London: Oxford Univ Press, 1964; paperback reprints 1967 and 1973). Text quoted herein is 1973.

Meriwether, James B. *William Faulkner: A Check List* (Princeton, New Jersey: Princeton Univ Library, 1957.)

_____. *The Literary Career of William Faulkner* (Princeton, New Jersey: Princeton Univ Library, 1961).

_____. Interview by James E. Kibler, Jr., September 1967. Kibler Literary Collection, South Caroliniana Library, Univ of South Carolina.

_____. Conversation with Kibler, 1968. Kibler Literary Collection, South Caroliniana Library, Univ of South Carolina.

_____. Interview by Kibler, January 1972. Kibler Literary Collection, South Caroliniana Library, Univ of South Carolina.

_____. "What Happens When You Eat Magnolias" in a

difficult to find paperback *Faces of South Carolina*, ed. Franklin Ashley (Columbia: South Carolina Committee for the Humanities, 1974), 24-35.

_____. Interview by James E. Kibler, August 1995. Kibler Literary Collection, South Caroliniana Library, Univ of South Carolina.

_____. Unpublished lecture, Southern League Institute, Lexington, South Carolina, 5 July 1996, quoted from a transcription by James E. Kibler, Jr. Kibler Literary Collection, South Caroliniana Library, Univ of South Carolina.

Millgate, Michael. *Faulkner* (Edinburgh: Oliver and Boyd, 1961; Reprinted, Writers & Critics Series, New York: Capricorn Books, 1971.)

_____. *The Achievement of William Faulkner* (New York: Random House, 1966).

_____. ed. *The Life and Work of Thomas Hardy* (Athens, GA: Univ of Georgia Press, 1985).

_____. *Faulkner's Place* (Athens, GA: Univ of Georgia Press, 1997).

Minter, David. *William Faulkner: His Life and Work* (Baltimore: Johns Hopkins Univ Press, 1980).

Mitchell, Margaret. *Gone With the Wind* (New York: Macmillan, 1936) 36, 435.

Montgomery, Marion. *Possum and Other Receits for the Recovery of 'Southern' Being* (Athens, GA: Univ of Georgia Press, 1987).

_____. "The Sense of Violation: Notes toward a Definition of Southern Fiction," *Georgia Review*, 19 (Fall 1965), 278-287.

Moore, George. *Hail and Farewell* (serialized 1911-14) and published in two volumes (New York: Appleton, 1925).

Morton, Clay. *The Oral Character of Southern Literature* (Lewiston, New York: Mellon, 2008).

Nicolson, Adam. *Gentry* (London: Harper, 2011).

Oates, Stephen. *William Faulkner: The Man and the Artist* (New York: Harper, 1987).

O'Brien, Michael. *A Character of Hugh Legaré* (Knoxville: Univ of Tennessee Press, 1985).

O'Connor, Flannery. *Mystery and Manners*, eds. Robert and Sally Fitzgerald (New York: Farrar, Strauss, 1969).

_____. *Collected Works* (New York: Library of America, 1988).

_____. "The Catholic Novelist in the Protestant South," in *Mystery and Manners*, eds. Robert and Sally Fitzgerald (New York: Farrar, Straus, 1969), and in *Collected Works* (New York: Library of America, 1988). Page numbers cited in the text are from the latter.

_____. Preface to the second edition of *Wise Blood* in *Collected Works* (New York: Library of America, 1988).

Parini, Jay. *One Matchless Time: A Life of William Faulkner* (New York: Harper, 2004).

Peterkin, Julia. *Plantation Christmas* (Boston: Houghton Mifflin, 1934).

Poe, Edgar Allan. *Broadway Journal* (22 November 1845), 309.

Powell, Frank B., III. *To Live and Die in Dixie* (Columbia, TN: SCV, 2014).

Ransom, John Crowe. Introduction, *I'll Take My Stand* (New York, Harper, 1930).

Robertson, Ben. *Red Hills and Cotton* (New York: Knopf, 1942).

Rollyson, Carl. *The Life of William Faulkner: Volume 1, The Past Is Never Dead, 1897-1934* and *Volume 2, This Alarming Paradox, 1935-1962* (Charlottesville: Univ of Virginia Press, 2020).

Rubin, Louis D., Jr. "Changing, Enduring, Forever Still the South," in *The Prevailing South*, ed. Dudley Clendinen (Atlanta: Longstreet, 1988).

_____. "The South's Writers," *Southern World* (May-June 1979), 26-7.

Rutledge, Archibald. *Life's Extras* (New York: Revell, 1928).

_____. *My Colonel and His Lady* (Indianapolis: Bobbs-Merrill, 1937).

_____. *God's Children* (Indianapolis: Bobbs-Merrill, 1947).

Schaeffer, Francis A. *A Christian Manifesto* (Wheaton, Illinois: Crossway Books, 1982).

Simkins, Francis Butler. *A History of the South,* Third Edition (New York: Knopf, 1963).

Simms, William Gilmore. *The Letters of William Gilmore Simms,* 6 vols. (Columbia, SC: Univ of South Carolina Press, 1952-2012).

_____. "The Ages of Gold and Iron," 2 November 1840, *The Ladies Companion* (May 1841),

12-4; reprinted in *Simms Review*, 10 (Summer 2002), 1-11.

_____. "The Philosophy of the Omnibus," *American Monthly* (May 1834), 158-9, William Gilmore Simms. Reprinted in *Simms Review*, 6 (1998), 13-23.

_____. *Castle Dismal: or, the Bachelor's Christmas* (New York: Burgess, Stringer, 1844).

_____. *Sack and Destruction of the City of Columbia* (Columbia: Daily Phoenix Press, 1865). The text used here is of the earlier newspaper version edited by David Aiken as *A City Laid Waste* (Columbia: Univ of South Carolina Press, 2005), 85.

_____. *Selected Poems of William Gilmore Simms,* ed. James E. Kibler (Columbia: Univ of South Carolina Press, 2010).

_____. *William Gilmore Simms's Selected Reviews on Literature and Criticism*, ed. James E. Kibler, Jr., and David Moltke-Hansen Columbia, SC: Univ of South Carolina Press, 2014).

_____. *The Social Principle* (Tuscaloosa, Alabama: Erosophic Society, 1843).

_____. *Poetry and the Practical*, ed. James E. Kibler (Fayetteville: Univ of Arkansas Press, 1996).

_____. Review of *The Life of Curran*, Charleston *Mercury* (20 November 1855).

_____. "Veneration," Simms's *Southern Passages and Pictures* (1839), 58-59.

_____. *Woodcraft* (New York: Redfield, 1854).

Stewart, George. *A Photographic Study of Faulkner's County* (Columbia: Univ of South Carolina Press, 2009).

Tate, Allen. *Collected Essays* (Denver, CO: Swallow, 1959).

_____. *Essays of Four Decades* (Wilmington, Delaware: ISI Books, 1999). The original edition was published in 1969.

Timrod, Henry. *Collected Poems of Henry Timrod* (Athens, GA: Univ of GA Press, 1965).

Torchiana, Donald. *Yeats and Georgian England* (Evanston, Illinois: Univ of Illinois Press, 1966).

Thorpe, Thomas Bangs. "The Big Bear of Arkansas," in *The Hive of "The Bee-Hunter,"* (New York: Appleton, 1854), 92-3.

Turner, Arlen. "Poe and Simms," *Papers on Poe* (Springfield, Ohio: Chantry Press, 1972), 140-60.

Twelve Southerners. *I'll Take My Stand* (New York: Harper, 1930).

Wasson, Ben. *Count No'Count: Flashbacks to Faulkner* (Jackson, MS: Univ Press of Mississippi, 1983).

Weaver, Richard. *The Southern Essays of Richard Weaver* (Indianapolis: Liberty Press, 1987).

Welty, Eudora. "Must the Novelist Crusade?" *Atlantic Monthly*, 216 (October 1965), 104-108.

Wilson, Edmund. *Patriotic Gore* (New York: Oxford Univ Press, 1962).

Winterer, Caroline. *The Culture of Classicism: Ancient Greece and Rome in American Intellectual Life, 1780-1910,* (Baltimore: John Hopkin's Univ Press, 2002).

Woodward, C. Vann. *The Burden of Southern History* (Baton Rouge: L. S. U. Press, 1960).

_____. *The Strange Case of Jim Crow* (Oxford: Oxford Univ Press, 2002).

Wulf, Andrea. *Founding Gardeners* (New York: Knopf, 2011).

Yeats, William Butler. *Essays and Introductions* (London: Macmillan, 1961).

Young, Stark. *So Red the Rose* (New York: Scribner's, 1934).

INDEX

317

Beauchamp, Lucas, 228, 229, 235, 237

Belloc, Hillaire, 211

Bellows, Barbara, 32-33, 79, 94, 95, 196, 258; *A Talent for Living*, 79

Benbow, Narcissa, 58, 236

Berkeley, George, 33

Berry, Wendell, 55, 62, 76, 80, 90, 105, 107, 115-118, 122, 133, 135, 160, 167, 179, 197, 198, 210, 211, 230, 264, 271; *Imagination in Place*, 118, 293; *Life is a Miracle*, 197; *Remembering*, 135; *Standing by Words*, 90, 271; *The Art of the Common Place*, 118; *The Memory of Old Jack*, 135; *The Need to Be Whole*, 105, 117, 179, 210, 230; *The Unsettling of America*, 117, 118; *What Are People For?*, 118

Bible, *see* New Testament and King James Bible

Blair, Walter, 296

Blarney Stone, 99

Blease, Coleman, 230

Blotner, Joseph, 1, 21, 30, 31, 82, 124, 255, 284, 285, 288

Bogart, Humphrey, 112

Boston, 29, 33, 67, 88, 292, 293

Bradford, M. E., 23, 110, 136-137, 169, 247, 267, 291, 298; *Generations of the Faithful Heart*, 267

Brooks, Cleanth, 7, 25-26, 31-33, 53, 54, 83, 84, 86, 87, 91, 104, 106, 107, 134, 138, 158, 163, 172, 173, 174, 178, 199, 231, 236, 237, 248, 252, 266, 267, 297; *Toward Yoknapatawpha and Beyond*, 25, 32, 54, 83, 84, 87, 91, 106, 134, 172, 174, 175, 199, 200, 237; *The Yoknapatawpha Country*, 32, 104, 106, 107

Brown, Larry, 15, 74, 79, 99, 107, 167, 168, 169, 170-171, 196, 267

Buck, Pearl, 284

Bundren, Cash, 26, 145, 150, 289

Burden, Joanna, 138

Butler family, 29, 99; Lelia Dean Swift, 101, 174, 250, 251; Maude, 48, 174, 250, 265; Burlina, 48

Byrd, William, 275

267, 272, 273, 291, 292; Agrarian, 40, 58, 193; Cancel, 23, 81, 86, 92, 209, 235, 257, 290; Creole, 3; Death, 113, 260, 261, 264, 267; Folk, 32; Machine, 60, 94, 117, 192, 204, 208, 210, 217, 218; Plantation, 49, 58; Southern, 53, 55, 59, 141, 159, 172, 193, 196, 252, 254, 257, 266

Curran, John, Irish Nationalist, 31, 292

Cunningham, Pamela, 156

Dadaism, 65

Dalton, Henry, 284

Daniels, Kate, 268

Davidson, Donald, 21, 22, 23, 50, 73, 89, 110, 115, 116, 133, 136, 137, 138, 170, 195, 196, 205, 207, 269, 271; "A Mirror for Artists," 115; On a Replica of the Parthenon," 21; *Who Owns America?, 50*; "The Center that Holds," 137

Deracination, 57, 101, 118, 135, 210

Derieux, Samuel A., 100

Determinism, 65, 70, 88, 138

Dickens, Charles, 29, 166

Dickey, James, 89

Didacticism, 67

Dogs, 54, 213-214, 250

Dos Passos, John, 286

Dostoyevsky, Feodor, *Notes from Underground,* 105

Doyle, Don, 48, 49

Dupre, Jenny Sartoris, 101, 138

Duvall, Mary Virginia, *A Student's History of Mississippi,* 285

Edmonds, Cass, 192, 223

Edmonds, Roth, 161, 192

Einstein, Albert, 91, 92

Eliot, T. S., 105, 260; "The Hollow Men," 261; "The Love Song of J. Alfred Prufrock," 105

Elnora, 58, 59, 178, 216, 236

226, 228, 235; *Light in Au-gust*, 7, 8, 9, 102, 105, 120, 162, 163, 169; "Missis-sippi,"178, 228, 230; "Pan-taloon in Black," 138; *Py-lon*, 212; "Race at Morn-ing," 197; *Sanctuary,* 6, 7, 82, 105, 120; *Sartoris*, 7, 22, 30, 47, 48, 49, 56, 57, 101, 136 *(see* also*: Flags in the Dust*), 134; *Sher-wood Anderson and Other Famous Creoles*, 28, 94; Snopes Trilogy: *The Ham-let, The Town*, and *The Mansion*, 114, 177; *Sports Illustrated* article, 244-245; "Spotted Horses,"121, 122; *The American Dream: What Happened to It?*, 262; *The Hamlet*, 6, 7, 15, 16, 76, 91, 105, 120, 121, 122, 141, 161, 168, 169, 175, 177, 289; *The Reivers*, 7, 20, 30, 54, 101, 120, 134, 236, 237, 252, 254; *The Sound and the Fury*, 6, 7, 10, 30, 45, 91, 102, 106, 120, 215, 225; *The Unvan-quished,* 4, 7, 27, 28, 33, 47, 49, 56, 58, 101, 140, 235; *The Wild Palms*, 7,

113; "There Was a Queen," 58, 236

Feminism, 66

Fennell, Lee Anne, 138

Fielding, Henry, 10

Fitzgerald, F. Scott, 112

Fletcher, John Gould, 38

Foote, Shelby, 16, 73, 77, 78, 121, 122, 236, 237, 238, 260

Forest(s), *see* Trees

Forrest, Nathan Bedford, 46, 47

Fourieritism, 66

Fowler, Doreen, 122, 123, 228

France, 2, 132; Paris, 3, 67, 112, 113, 114

Franklin, Benjamin, 45, 129, 130

Franklin, Malcolm, 2, 285

Frederic, Harold, 88, 92

Frost, Robert, 115

Gaelic, 31, 33

Gaines, Ernest, 236

Hightower, Rev. Gail, 102, 138

Hobson, Fred, 269-270, 272

Hoffman, Frederick, 1

Hollow Men (T. S. Eliot), 261

Hollywood, 111-112

Homer, 37-38, 42, 76, 108

Honor, Honoring, 14, 16, 52, 54, 59, 77, 92, 93, 96, 98, 111, 141, 151, 156, 161, 174, 175, 202, 223, 244, 245, 250-267

Horace, 21, 37, 42, 76

Horses, 53, 54, 60, 121-122, 166, 211, 222, 281, 282

Hospitality, 54, 84, 129, 259

Howells, William Dean, 88, 92, 125, 255-256

Humanist Manifesto, 194

Humor, 15, 34, 55, 75, 79, 82, 120-132

Humphries, Jefferson, *The Future of Southern Letters*, 268, 269-270

Hurricane Hugo, 158

Hurston, Zora Neal, 79, 107, 221, 224, 227, 236; *Dust Tracks on a Road*, 221; *Moses, Man of the Mountain*, 221

I'll Take My Stand, 38, 108, 109, 115, 154, 168, 207-208, 209

Imperialism, 51, 256; Northern imperialism, 257

Individual, Individualism, 19, 23, 24, 31, 35, 63, 64, 76, 89, 105, 107, 109, 133, 135, 139, 142, 154, 221, 224, 227, 230, 235, 237, 240, 241, 247, 248, 259, 262, 263

Industrial, 44, 62, 65, 116, 117, 166, 168, 206, 207, 217, 243, 258

Industrialism, 26, 196

Ireland, 29, 31-32, 33, 84; County Down, 148; Dublin, 33, 258

From Eden to Babylon, 22, 65, 109

Machine, Machine Culture, 23, 59, 60, 94, 95, 117, 139, 164, 167, 168, 177, 192, 204-212, 217-219

Mechanization, 210

Madison, Reverend James, 61

Mammy Callie, *see* Mrs. Caroline Barr Clark

Mamonism, 66, 69

Markovic, Vita, 282

Marshall Plan, 11

Marvell, Andrew, 170

Marx, Karl, 56, 193

Marxist, 24, 29, 35, 65, 66, 69, 89, 103, 173, 237, 241, 248, 273

Marx, Leo, 205, 206, 209; *The Machine in the Garden*, 205, 207

Massachusetts, 66, 77

Materialism, 26, 160, 173, 175, 208, 217, 257, 263

Mather, Cotton, 36, 37

Matthiessen, F. O., 127-128

McAlpine family, 29, 51

McCarthy, Cormac, 15, 31, 73, 80, 85, 99, 107, 123, 124, 127, 167, 267; *Child of God*, 127; *Outer Dark*, 127; *Suttree*, 124, 127; *The Road*, 85

McCallum family, 30, 237

McCaslin family, 30, 235, 237; Ike, 165, 192, 226, 298; Isaac; 103, 138

McCord, Louisa S., 79

McHaney, Thomas L., 113, 123

McMillin, Marguerite, 276, 280-281, 283

Melville, Herman, 127

Memory, 32, 51, 85, 133-140, 147, 224, 258, 265

Mencken, H. L., 131

Meriwether, James Babcock,; 4, 11-14, 18, 24, 53, 54, 91, 107, 112, 142, 238, 245, 275, 281, 289-291; *The Literary Career of William Faulkner*, 11, 289; with Millgate, Michael,

National Book Award, 29

Naturalism, 88, 271

Naturalists, 65, 88, 92

Naturalist-Realists, 94

Nature, 36, 60, 76, 160-161, 163, 166, 167, 168, 169, 193, 197, 201, 213, 226, 264; Human, 63, 72, 76, 85, 196, 202, 203 Wilderness, 162, 164, 165

New Orleans, 3, 4, 18, 28, 98, 113, 114, 134, 155, 259, 294

New South, 154, 155, 161, 215, 218; Progressive, 215

New Testament, 97, 98, 254, 182, 288; (*see* also King James Bible)

New York, 24, 27, 31, 66, 81, 115, 153, 176, 245, 248, 275, 276, 277; Opera Company, 281; *Herald Tribune*, 27, 34, 275-276; *Times*, 26, 80, 95

Nicolson, Adam, *Gentry: Six Centuries of a Peculiarly English Class*, 177

Nobel Prize, 15, 29, 85, 114, 139, 140, 141, 145, 150, 192, 251, 260, 274, 280

Norris, Frank, 88

Oates, Stephen, 1

O'Connor, Flannery, 15, 18, 70-74, 79, 83, 87, 88, 99, 107, 120, 124, 126, 167, 196, 197, 202, 203, 204; "The Enduring Chill," 71, 88; *Everything That Rises Must Converge*, 70, 167; "Good Country People," 71, *Mystery and Manners*, 74, 204; "Revelation," 71; *Wise Blood*, 127, 197, 202

O'Brien, Michael, 39-40

Odum, Howard, 269

O'Hara, Gerald, 58

O'Hara, Scarlett, 58, 140; *Gone With the Wind*, 58, 234, 287

Old Joe Parks Place, *see* Greenfield Farm

Old Southwestern Humor, 15, 79, 182, 123-127, 131, 295

Oratory, 81-82

Gold and Iron," 116; *The Golden Christmas*, 107; *The Social Principle*, 210, 297; "Veneration," 154; *Woodcraft*, 73, 107, 128; "Woodlands," 205

Simms-Faulkner Conference, 294

Sinclair, Upton, 88

Singer Sewing Machine Company, 164, 168

Smith, Beverley, 255, 284

Smith, Francis Hopkinson, 235

Smith, Lillian, 236

Snopes, 124, 173, 175-176, 178, 230-231

Snopes, Ab, 122

Snopes, Flem, 105, 161-163, 175, 176, 178

Snopes, Lancelot, 175

Snopes, Sarty, 152, 173

Socinianism, 66

Soil, 36, 42, 55-59, 63, 112, 115, 142, 146, 160, 210

South Carolina, 6, 8, 9, 10, 11, 19, 54, 102, 156, 201, 220, 230, 289; Calhoun County, 64; Carolinians, 113; Charleston, 21, 33, 39, 41, 42, 44, 64, 66, 68, 95, 96, 109, 155-157, 195, 258, 272, 292; Columbia, 13, 14, 102, 198, 289, 292; Edgefield County, 13; Euphradian Society, 16, 298; South Carolina College, 38, 40, 42, 43; South Caroliniana Library, 16, 121, 272; University of, 6, 13, 16, 160;

Spain, 2; Barcelona, 14, 254

Spenser, Edmund; *The Faerie Queene*, 31

Stalin, Josef, 89

Staying (put), 53, 105, 112, 115, 118, 210; *see* also Place

Stein, Gertrude, 3, 112

Stendahl, 287

Stewardship, 54, 109, 166, 170

Stone, Phil, 21, 45, 62, 179

Tullos, Tommy, 284

Tully (Cicero), 37

Twain, Mark, 15, 79, 81, 86, 93, 121-123, 125, 126, 255, 256, 295; *Adventures of Huckleberry Finn*, 93, 104, 125, 295-296; *Life on the Mississippi*, 93, 255; *Tom Sawyer*, 125, 295

Uncle Possum, 20, 108, 237

Uncle Remus, 192, 202

Underground Man, *see* Dostoyevsky, Feodor

United Daughters of the Confederacy, 51

Utopia, 44, 127, 203, 206

Varner, Eula, 161-162

Varner, Will, 175

Vergil, 37, 38, 42, 76; *Eclogues*, 42; *Georgics*, 42

Virginia, 29, 54, 111, 155; Charlottesville, 284

Virginia, University of, 42, 122, 124, 250

Wade, John Donald, 218-219

Wall Street, 81

War, 158, 168, 169; Civil,10, 32, 42, 47, 49, 50-51, 102, 134, 140, 146, 155, 170, 181, 194, 196, 198, 208-209, 217, 222, 230, 253, 265, 270; Cold, 19, 141, 243, 246, 264; Peloponnesian, 109; Revolutionary, 157; World War I, 112; World War II, 10 98, 150, 151, 161, 195

Waring, U.S. Colonel, 46

Warren, Robert Penn, 69, 73, 89, 110, 138, 167, 195, 236

Washington, George, 155, 157

Wasson, Ben, 2, 252-253

Weaver, Richard, 22, 24, 64, 65, 72-75, 90, 138, 194-196, 202-203, 271

Webster, Noah, 39, 41, 44, 45

Welsh, 111

Welty, Eudora, 69, 71, 79, 107, 236; *Delta Wedding*, 100

www.ingramcontent.com/pod-product-compliance
Lightning Source LLC
Chambersburg PA
CBHW051850090426

42811CB00034B/2280/J